Reflections
on Regionalism

BROOKINGS METRO SERIES

The Center on Urban and Metropolitan Policy of the Brookings Institution is integrating research and practical experience into a policy agenda for cities and metropolitan areas. By bringing fresh analyses and policy ideas to the public debate, the center hopes to inform key decisionmakers and civic leaders in ways that will spur meaningful change in our nation's communities.

As part of this effort, the Center on Urban and Metropolitan Policy has established the Brookings Metro Series to introduce new perspectives and policy thinking on current issues and lay the foundation for longer-term policy reforms. The series will examine traditional urban issues, such as neighborhood assets and central city competitiveness, as well as larger metropolitan concerns, such as regional growth, development, and employment patterns. The Metro Series will consist of concise studies and collections of essays designed to appeal to a broad audience. While these studies are formally reviewed, some will not be verified like other research publications. As with all publications, the judgments, conclusions, and recommendations presented in the studies are solely those of the authors and should not be attributed to the trustees, officers, or other staff members of the institution.

BROOKINGS
METRO
SERIES

Also in the Brookings Metro Series

Laws of the Landscape:
How Policies Shape Cities in Europe and America
Pietro S. Nivola

Savings for the Poor:
The Hidden Benefits of Electronic Banking
Michael A. Stegman

Reflections on Regionalism

Bruce Katz
Editor

BROOKINGS INSTITUTION PRESS
Washington, D.C.

Copyright © 2000
THE BROOKINGS INSTITUTION
1775 Massachusetts Avenue, N.W., Washington, D.C. 20036
www.brookings.edu

Library of Congress Cataloging-in-Publication data

Reflections on regionalism / Bruce J. Katz, editor.
  p.   cm.
  Includes bibliographical references and index.
  ISBN 0-8157-4825-6 (alk. paper)
   1. Regional planning—United States. 2. Regionalism—
United States. I. Katz, Bruce J. II. Title.
  HT392.R38   1999   99-050582
  333.77'0973—dc21   CIP

Digital printing

The paper used in this publication meets minimum requirements of the American National Standard for Information
Sciences—Permanence of Paper for Printed Library Materials: ANSI Z39.48-1984.

Typeset in New Baskerville and Myriad

Composition by Betsy Kulamer
Washington, D.C.

₿ THE BROOKINGS INSTITUTION

The Brookings Institution is an independent organization devoted to nonpartisan research, education, and publication in economics, government, foreign policy, and the social sciences generally. Its principal purposes are to aid in the development of sound public policies and to promote public understanding of issues of national importance.

The Institution was founded on December 8, 1927, to merge the activities of the Institute for Government Research, founded in 1916, the Institute of Economics, founded in 1922, and the Robert Brookings Graduate School of Economics and Government, founded in 1924.

The general administration of the Institution is the responsibility of a Board of Trustees charged with safeguarding the independence of the staff and fostering the most favorable conditions for scientific research and publication. The immediate direction of the policies, program, and staff is vested in the president, assisted by an advisory committee of the officers and staff.

In publishing a study, the Institution presents it as a competent treatment of a subject worthy of public consideration. The interpretations or conclusions in such publications are those of the author or authors and do not necessarily reflect the views of the other staff members, officers, or trustees of the Brookings Institution.

Contents

Foreword

In September 1998 I was pleased to speak at the Brookings Institution about the importance of building more livable communities—places where young and old can walk, bike, and play together; places where we not only protect historic neighborhoods but where farms, green spaces, and forests add life and beauty to the newest of suburbs; places where a high quality of life attracts cutting-edge businesses and talented employees; places where we can spend less time in traffic and more time with our families.

At that time I noted that a national movement was developing in communities across the country on this issue. Over the last year, this movement has only increased in intensity. More and more states are adopting "smart growth" plans, and in last fall's elections alone, more than 200 communities debated—and more than 70 percent adopted—measures to support smart growth.

We are finding, moreover, that building more livable communities is often about encouraging greater regional cooperation, and that the places that are successful are those most willing to reach out to neighboring communities.

Many issues—such as transportation, air pollution, and economic development—transcend defined borders, and so should our solutions. And the federal government is working to help communities meet this challenge—not through a top-down role, but by providing tools and information to help communities grow cooperatively, according to their own local values and goals.

Reflections on Regionalism, the third book in the Brookings Metro Series, offers provocative insights on applying the lessons of past attempts at regional partnerships to today's efforts. In so doing, it builds on the first book in the series, which discussed how different policies have helped to shape growth in Europe and the United States, and it opens discussion on a variety of related topics. The book indeed makes clear that regionalism can be a powerful way of thinking and acting.

AL GORE

Reflections
on Regionalism

Editor's Overview

BRUCE KATZ

Regionalism is hardly a new idea in American government and politics. Arguably, it has been around for more than 100 years, ever since the union of Manhattan, Brooklyn, Queens, Staten Island, and the Bronx made New York City a regional metropolis. In the 1960s and 1970s, regionalism was the subject of much academic discussion, research, and on-the-ground policy innovation. But after a burst of city-county consolidations in those decades, interest in regionalism, especially as a practical political matter, waned.

Now, many people—from academics to corporate leaders to political activists—are arguing that regionalism is still relevant. They insist that regions are critical functional units in a worldwide economy. Perhaps as important, they say, regions are critical functional units in individual American lives. More and more of us travel across city, county, even state borders every morning on our way to work. Our broadcast and print media rely on a regional marketplace. Our businesses, large and small, depend on suppliers, workers, and customers who rarely reside in a single jurisdiction. The parks, riverfronts, stadiums, and museums we visit serve and provide an identity to an area much larger than a single city. The fumes, gases, chemicals, and runoff that pollute our air and water have no regard for municipal boundaries.

The essays in this monograph do not comprise a debate, pro and con, about regionalism. Rather, the authors give their own perspectives on this phenomenon, based on their own backgrounds and experience. Some contributors have written close academic studies of how regional action occurs, while others give a historical account of a particular region. Some of these authors are ardent supporters of regionalism and lay out detailed political plans for achieving regional governance. Each brings a particular analytical lens to his or her chapter and highlights what he or she thinks are some of the salient characteristics of regionalism, past or present.

Taken as a whole, these essays address a series of questions: If regionalism is, as regionalists believe, a compelling idea and an inescapable reality, why did past efforts at regional collaboration fall apart? Given that the United States has almost no examples of regional or metropolitan governments, at what level of government does regional action take place? What did regionalist efforts of decades ago leave undone, and what new goals should regionalists set? How can regionalism work now?

The Argument for Regionalism

Robert Fishman's contribution to this monograph begins with Jane Jacobs's comment, "A Region, someone has wryly observed, is an area safely larger than the last one to whose problems we found no solution." The term *region* is certainly ill-defined in popular usage. It is sometimes used to describe a large city, the surrounding suburbs, and perhaps the farms, forests, or open space just beyond the suburban fringe. According to this description, region and metropolitan area are synonymous, and regionalist and metropolitanist are also interchangeable labels.

But this has not always been the case, as Fishman points out in his chapter. In a discussion of urban and regional planners of the 1920s, he defines metropolitanists as those who were committed to central-city dominance, even as the metropolitan area gained millions in population and stretched dozens of miles from its old center. They foresaw the continued development of suburbs, but as places clearly subordinate to the mighty downtown. Regionalists, by contrast, disparaged the concentrated power of the central city and sought dispersed settlements that "could combine all the economic benefits of living in a technologically advanced society with the human scale, local identity, and community of small-town America." They envisioned a series of towns nestled in rings of greenery, linked by highways and technology.

But what these views had in common was the recognition that cities, suburbs, and green space cannot be considered in isolation. The fundamental premise of regionalism is that places have relationships and connections to other places that should not be ignored. Contemporary regionalists object to the fact that these connections have had precious little effect on the way in which domestic policies have been designed and implemented. America has a fragmented maze of local governments and special districts that prefer fierce competition or splendid isolation to regional cooperation. As several of the chapters in this monograph note, Americans like the idea of small, accessible, responsive local governments and have not been quick to embrace larger governing bodies.

Regionalists (or metropolitanists—the terms are interchangeable in current use) argue that many pressing environmental, social, and governance problems cannot be solved by independent jurisdictions acting alone. As an example, they point to problems that accompany our current growth and development patterns.

On the one hand, many cities and older suburbs are either not growing or are in decline. Cities, particularly those in the Northeast and Midwest, have lost millions of residents, along with businesses and tax dollars. They are now home to increasing concentrations of poor people and lack the resources to deal with the problems of concentrated poverty: joblessness, family fragmentation, failing schools, and decrepit commercial districts. Older suburbs have found that so-called urban problems easily cross urban borders, and these communities are often even less able to cope than cities. Meanwhile, newly developing suburbs find that they are growing too fast. Traffic congestion increases, schools become overcrowded, and the open space that residents prize disappears under an onslaught of new construction.

Regionalists see all of these problems as related: urban decline increases development pressure on the suburban fringe; and government policies that facilitate fringe development and keep poor people concentrated in urban neighborhoods make it more difficult for cities to maintain their social and economic health. Their conclusion is that cross-jurisdictional problems demand cross-jurisdictional solutions.

Regionalism and Coalitions

Cross-jurisdictional solutions, in turn, demand strong, cross-jurisdictional coalitions. As urban scholar Ethan Seltzer puts it: "In general, coalition building is critical to regionalism because of the nature of a region. In most cases, the region is nobody's community. This means that getting any action at the regional scale requires creating new collaborative alignments among interests who previously either didn't believe that they shared issues in common, or who knew it but felt no compelling reason to act on it. In the end, the story of effective metropolitan regionalism is always going to be the search for cross-cutting issues, a never-ending saga that is the meat and potatoes of those efforts."[1]

Sprawl currently appears to be such a cross-cutting issue. In many regions across the country it is the catalyst for coalitions that include elected officials from cities, inner suburbs, and new suburbs that are finding it difficult to provide infrastructure to accommodate rapid growth; downtown corporate, philanthropic, and civic interests; minority and low-income community representatives; environmentalists; smart-growth advocates in the new developing suburbs; farmers and rural activists; and religious leaders. National politicians, such as Vice President Al Gore, are developing policies against sprawl and for smarter growth under the heading of a "livability" agenda.

Some of the chapters in this monograph directly address regional coalitions. But all of the chapters, whether they talk explicitly about coalitions or not, can be read as part of a larger conversation about how coalitions do or do not work and how they shape decisions about economic and spatial growth. For example, Fishman, Robert Yaro, Henry Richmond, Rosabeth Moss Kanter, and Margaret Weir all address some aspects of coalitions and regional growth, whether to outline the possibilities for new groups or to evaluate the successes and failures of previous efforts. The essays by john a. powell and Kenneth Jackson show how race has shaped space, something that new coalitions cannot afford to ignore. Finally, David Rusk and Paul Dimond present two very different arguments about the policies that regional coalitions should pursue.

The Essays

Henry Richmond's opening essay is a thorough primer on this issue, its many permutations and guises, and the missed opportunities of the past. Richmond explains the political history of land-use reform, focusing especially—and quite usefully—on why many previous attempts to change development patterns have failed. He concludes that their focus was mainly the environment, and therefore their base of support was too narrow. He goes on to explain the connection between current land-use patterns and "systemic problems" and thereby shows how broad a coalition for change might be.

Next, a trio of essays gives an overview of regional growth and governance. Robert Yaro uses New York City as a case study, noting that many of the challenges of other regions are exemplified, and amplified, in New York. The city's metropolitan area, spreading across three states and thirty-one counties, has consistently presented some of the most extreme challenges to efforts to supersede local boundaries and create metropolitan solutions. Yaro argues that new regional governing entities will never come into being, so regionalists should focus on practical, achievable goals, such as service districts and regional amenities, while keeping in mind that even these can take decades to create.

David Rusk focuses on land-use and growth management laws as "the pivotal issue" for regionalism. This means that regionalists have to act at the state level, since states control land-use laws and regulations. Rusk discusses recent growth management legislation and new coalitions in Missouri, Pennsylvania, and Ohio that are determined to win new land-use laws in their states. Finally, he explains how transportation investments are a critical land-use question, despite decades in which transportation planners focused only on highways and not on the fields, suburbs, or cities that surround them. Rusk predicts that, as a result of action on land use and transportation, America will see more directly elected metropolitan governments.

Robert Fishman's chapter considers the history and possible future of regional planning. He begins by explaining the two different strands of urban and regional planning that have been present (and often at odds) since at least the 1920s. They can be summed up in this question: should a region have one center or many? Fishman then notes that whatever planners thought the answer should be, whether urban renewal or new towns, they did not succeed in implementing their vision. Part of the problem was that there was no way for separate governments to make binding regional decisions, whether on tax-base sharing or land-use decisions.

There is no question that cities have grown in a way that is more in line with what Fishman describes as the old regionalist idea than the old metropolitanist vision. Rather than a single central city serving as the commercial, industrial, political, and cultural center and dominating its surroundings, urban areas have many centers in many different jurisdictions: central business districts, "edge cities," industrial areas, services clusters, and high-tech or commercial corridors. So, is the purpose of modern regionalist (or metropolitanist) efforts to restore the dominance of the central city, to establish a balance of power and prosperity throughout a region, or to keep weakened cities from collapsing utterly? What is the role of each element of a region—old central city, inner-ring suburb, new developing suburb, secondary city or town? Fishman does not provide a direct answer but insists that regional plans—and the coalitions that will form to implement those plans—must take both urban and environmental concerns into account.

Two essays focus explicitly on regional coalitions—political and business oriented. In her chapter Margaret Weir breaks down the elements of the successful efforts to create regional governance in Minnesota and Oregon, two states that regionalists generally regard with reverence. She then describes the different experiences of Illinois and California. The key, she finds, is state-level coalition building, because states have the power to enact or block legislation that creates regional political authorities (rather than weaker regional collaborative agreements). Committed civic coalitions are needed to keep the regional authorities strong, even after state legislation has been enacted.

As Rosabeth Moss Kanter points out, business coalitions, too, create an impetus for regional action. Because the opinions of business leaders carry enormous weight in the political sphere, especially locally, corporate acknowledgment that regions matter can be a powerful spur toward policy coordination or at least recognition of common interests. However, business coalitions have limits, just like political coalitions do. So far, they have not taken on fiscal disparities issues, for example, and their interest in difficult problems that take years to solve (schools, for example) can wane because business leaders usually expect quick results.

Any discussion of regionalism must address racial politics, and the next pair of essays speaks to regionalism and race. Many regions developed the way that they did because white Americans did not want to live near African Americans. Kenneth Jackson's contribution to this monograph eloquently tells the story of how race shaped three communities: Newark, Darien–New Canaan, and White Plains. He concludes that the sharp divisions between affluent and struggling communities within regions have to be breached, but doing so will take extraordinary policies that can gain the consent of a majority of a region's residents. The division that Jackson describes in the New York–Connecticut–New Jersey region is, of course, not unique, a fact that he duly notes.

What commentators have generally not pointed out is that this separation has in some cases been politically beneficial to African Americans, who have risen to the top of city governments. Even though regional action was never intended to rob local governments of all of their power, regionalism can look like a threat to African American political power and cultural identity, says john a. powell. Therefore, metropolitan coalitions, whether they originate in the corporate or government arena, must take race into account. Powell suggests combining regional action with maintenance of some local control to address the concerns of minorities. Failure to do so renders coalitions ineffective, he argues. Both Jackson and powell agree: policy fixes that do not confront the complexities of racial politics will either operate on the margin or fail to win majority support.

Finally, Paul Dimond, in his contrarian contribution, argues against a regionalist approach to policies, preferring instead a free-market model in which diverse local governments compete, much like firms, for businesses and residents (i.e., customers). While acknowledging that labor, housing, and finance markets are regional—not local—he insists that too often regional approaches hinder people's ability to "vote with their feet" and to choose which local government best suits their needs. The role of state and federal policies is not to override localities in the name of regional collaboration, but to enable all of them to compete on a level playing field. One way to do this—and in this suggestion Dimond ironically echoes many of the regionalists whose views he otherwise opposes—is to stop subsidizing development in some areas and instead require that all new houses, malls, office buildings, and other development projects pay for the roads, sewers, and utilities that serve them.

Conclusion

The rebirth of interest in regionalism comes at a time of enormous change in American society. The aging of the population is changing the mix of products and services that the marketplace provides and the patterns of life people pursue. The revolution in information technology is altering business imperatives and consumer choices. Devolution in governance is changing how we organize public investments in transportation, work force, and housing and how we respond to challenges from environmental pollution to concentrated poverty to continued economic competitiveness. All of these changes—in demography, markets, and governance—will have major effects on where people choose to live and where businesses choose to locate in the coming decades. There will be a different mix of forces supporting—or countering—regionalist efforts.

These essays have been written in the hope that reflections on past experiences will provide some kind of road map through this period of fast, far-reaching changes. Without an understanding of previous regional efforts and key issues, policymakers may find themselves "reinventing the region." These chapters explain how regionalism has played out in the past, how policies shape places, and the possibilities and limits of regional action. We hope that they will be a useful contribution to this round of regional debates.

The editor would like to thank Anthony Downs, senior fellow of the Brookings Institution; Jennifer Bradley, Amy Liu, and Stephan Rodiger of the Brookings Center on Urban and Metropolitan Policy; Starr Belsky for editing, Inge Lockwood for proofreading, and Julia Petrakis for indexing the volume for the Brookings Institution Press; and the anonymous reviewers of these essays. The John D. and Catherine T. MacArthur Foundation, the Ford Foundation, the George Gund Foundation, and the Rockefeller Foundation provided financial support for this project. Without their efforts, this monograph would not have been possible.

Note

1. Memo from Ethan Seltzer, Portland State University, to Bruce Katz, September 21, 1998.

CHAPTER ONE

Metropolitan Land-Use Reform: The Promise and Challenge of Majority Consensus

HENRY R. RICHMOND

How do efforts to address metropolitan land use and governance in the 1990s compare with such efforts in the 1960s, 1970s, and 1980s? In brief, ignorance of the causes and effects of land-use patterns has been the most important factor determining the rationale, goals, and effectiveness of reform efforts. Until the mid-1990s, this ignorance produced a narrow and distorted formulation of the issue. The result has been political weakness, if not irrelevance, in the face of a problem that is fundamentally grounded in existing policy and in the need to change that policy. As a result, the movement has hardly been able to articulate, let alone achieve, policy change.

In the mid-1990s, this began to change. A stronger, more comprehensive understanding of the causes and effects of land-use patterns has begun to be articulated by a small but vocal and diverse group of community leaders. The new formulation of the issue has created the potential for a majority of Americans to conclude that they have a stake in metropolitan land-use patterns. Whether this potential will be realized is unpredictable. Even less predictable is whether this sense of a common stake can be translated into active support for mutually beneficial, politically achievable solutions. Given the social issues and political obstacles involved, the task of devising, adopting, and implementing such solutions at the state and local level over the next twenty or thirty years is the most important political challenge America faces at the dawn of the twenty-first century.

The Law of the Land

In America sprawl is the law of the land. Of the many laws that prescribe or induce sprawl, municipal zoning laws are the most direct, pervasive, and important. In the 1920s, most state legislatures delegated their power to regulate land to some 39,000 municipalities by authorizing them to use zoning. A zoning ordinance is simply a list of uses a municipality allows in a specific area or "district" and the conditions that apply to these uses. Cities divided their jurisdictions into zoning districts by type of use to avoid conflicts between residential, commercial, industrial, and other activities. Lands zoned residential—involving the vast majority of American landowners—were stripped of their "right" to be developed at more lucrative commercial or industrial densities. Suburban municipalities used zoning to attract many kinds of development; however, fast-growing, job-rich suburbs also used zoning to exclude affordable housing, pushing it to the fringes. Zoning in poor areas allowed any development that would increase the tax base, such as cheap apartments, despite potentially higher costs down the road for schools or police. Counties or townships at or just beyond the suburban fringe used zoning to allow landowners to partition open land and develop commercial or residential projects as they wished. The unstated premise of suburban fringe and rural zoning—and the clear effect of such ordinances—is that landowners there have a right to develop land as they wish, a right their far more numerous central-city and inner-suburb counterparts have not had for seventy years.

State laws that authorize municipalities to tax real property or the sale of products or services also have promoted sprawl. Municipalities naturally use zoning to build their tax base so that school, police, and road costs can be paid. However, this taxing authority combined with state laws that make it easy for landowners to form new communities have created unanticipated land-use and social consequences. The growth of small suburban municipalities around central cities over the course of the twentieth century has gradually fragmented metropolitan regions into tiny tax and zoning blocks. Chicago is surrounded by 262 cities; Philadelphia, 245; and New York, 765. Disparate tax bases and tax rates among these municipalities induce cost-averse investors to locate in high-tax-base/low-tax-rate municipalities, usually at the metropolitan edge.

Housing laws also encourage sprawl. Federal, state, and local laws have concentrated public housing in small areas of central cities. Such policies not only isolate the poor from opportunity, they also contribute to sprawl by creating conditions (poverty-dominated schools, crime) that repel investment. Limiting federal subsidies to single-family housing also distorts the market forces toward sprawl. Congress guarantees about $700 billion a year in mortgage insurance for single-family homes and provides a cost- and risk-reducing secondary market for these mortgages. But Congress has never provided similar financial support to other more compact or transit-oriented residential development, such as mixed-use, multifamily development, despite the demand for it in the marketplace.

A vast array of federal, state, and local laws ostensibly unrelated to land use affect metropolitan regions and supercharge the sprawl proclivity of municipal zoning, taxation, and housing laws. For decades these non-land-use laws have opened vast new areas for development by subsidizing real estate investment at the outer edge of metropolitan regions. Highway, sewer, and water system programs are prominent examples of such government influence. The "average cost" policies most states use to set gas, electric, and other utility rates are another example. Low-cost ratepayers in the city pay more than what it costs the utility to serve them. The excess revenue collected in the city subsidizes utility service in expensive-to-serve developments in far-flung suburbs.

The "supercharge" effect is a product of federal, state, and local laws, as illustrated by the following scenario. A congressional committee approves highway money for a state. A state legislative committee approves a gubernatorially proposed, project-specific budget for a state department of transportation. The department lets contracts to build a highway on the edge of a region where the county long ago zoned everything for development. Thus do rural areas that have been quiet backwaters for decades become real estate bonanzas overnight.

Local planning commissions make the initial policy choice of anything-goes zoning that state legislatures have authorized municipalities to make, unfettered by any limitation or guidance. That policy applies to land where the new highway will go. Planning commissions typically include local realtors, town boosters, old-line landowners, and the occasional out-gunned, financially disinterested, and well-intentioned but bewildered citizen or two, participating more or less on a casual basis. Meetings last late, which is often when important votes occur. Those with something at stake stay until the end. Decisions are little noted in local newspapers, which have small reportorial staff and low tolerance for criticism from downtown advertisers.

Occasionally, a citizen or official proposes something offbeat that would restrain development. Such proposals are met with stern talk of "property rights" and the prospect of litigation that the county or township cannot afford. The county would have to pay outside counsel by the hour or hire a special lawyer from one of the firms downtown. "Better just to give in. Joe won't build for a few years anyway. Besides, I went to grade school with Joe. He's just doin' what everyone else is doin', or wished they could."

Once an anything-goes zoning law is adopted, it reigns supreme. A zoning ordinance adopted within the scope of the authority delegated by the state legislature is a law with as much force and effect as a bill enacted by the legislature itself or by Congress. A landowner may demand that the local government approve his or her development if the proposed use is authorized by the zone and if it meets typically straightforward conditions, such as approvals for septic tanks or wells. An adjacent landowner cannot prevent or invalidate such an approval except by going to court. This is as costly as it is futile. A court cannot revoke the ordinance, or any approval pursuant to the ordinance, unless it finds the ordinance to be unconstitutional. This is highly improbable and extremely rare.

A local zoning ordinance in one of America's 39,004 municipalities can be changed only two ways. First, the governing body might vote to change it, an unlikely reversal, given local fiscal incentives and political pressures. Second, the state legislature could enact a law conditioning municipal exercise of the zoning power on compliance with certain minimum state standards and requiring that existing zoning be changed to meet the new state standards.

Such is the law of the land. This complicated, multilevel, highly dispersed, legally well armored, and politically well defended bramble of laws is the heart and soul of America's land-use problem. Unless and until this bramble of laws is altered, sprawl will continue.

Of all these laws, local zoning ordinances are far and away the most important and challenging. Local zoning that geographically contains deconcentration would render benign, if not positive, the sprawl-inducing effect of non-land-use laws that currently energize anything-goes zoning ordinances. Conversely, simply changing various non-land-use laws will do little. For example, greater local flexibility in the expenditure of federal highway dollars will not prevent more belt-ways at the urban fringe without a new metropolitan land use policy that discourages deconcentration and encourages reinvestment and redevelopment.

Four Decades Of Failure

The movement to reform land use in America has not put a dent in the law of the land as described above. By that or any other measure, the movement has been a failure. There has been much well-inten-tioned talk, and a great deal of well-intended money has been spent. But very little has happened in state legislatures that has endured or been implemented, and even less has happened on the ground. In almost every state, there is more suburban sprawl and urban disinvest-ment today than there was ten, twenty, or thirty years ago. The com-paratively tiny bits of progress scattered here and there have been overwhelmed by the pace of sprawl and disinvestment nationally. With a few notable exceptions, for nearly half a century, the movement has been characterized by political weakness, if not irrelevance. The reformers' diagnoses have been wrong. Their goals are variously off target, too modest, too narrow, or all three, and their strategies are fatally apolitical.

In the 1960s, the issue of land use gradually seeped from the domain of academics and planners into the edges of the political realm, roughly tracking the emergence of the environmental move-ment. Since the late 1960s, there have been countless conferences and symposia, newspaper and technical articles, task force reports, agency studies, nonprofit newsletters, gubernatorial commission pro-ceedings, think-tank workshop materials, new foundation initiatives, and innumerable ad hoc committees and working groups on subjects ranging from biodiversity to infrastructure to affordable housing. Dozens of useful books have been written. The issue has been periodi-cally repackaged in mildly appealing but vague terms: land use and "carrying capacity" in the 1970s, "growth management" in the 1980s, "sustainable development" in the early 1990s, and "smart growth" in the mid 1990s. Doubtless it will be repackaged again within a few years, as the old bromides are seen to be unproductive and passé as the need arises to spice up agency newsletters and new project funding proposals. Innumerable earnest individuals have arrived on the nonprofit scene, laboring energetically for a few years before moving on to "real" jobs. An occasional member of Congress has gotten the bug and weighed in with a symbolic bill or op-ed piece. Now and then a governor features land use or sprawl in a "state of the state" speech or blue-ribbon commission.

However, the bottom line is that few legislatures have been inspired by any of this bustle to make land use a priority, let alone to enact bills. As a result, with the exception of Oregon, America remains zoned for sprawl. The few legislatures that have been asked to reconsider and modify the decades-old delegation of zoning authority to municipal governments have refused to do so. Most legislatures have not seriously debated the matter. Because the complex of laws that authorizes and induces sprawl remains in place, the sprawl that burst on the scene in the 1950s and 1960s—and accelerated in the 1970s, 1980s, and 1990s—is predicted to continue into the foreseeable future.

The first phase of reform, the so-called "quiet revolution in land use," was launched in the early 1970s as the environmental movement burst on the scene. Reform focused on states protecting "critical areas" and establishing permit systems for development that had regional impact. A few special areas, like the California coast and the pinelands in New Jersey, did benefit. However, over the next twenty-five years, statewide reforms were tried in only thirteen of the fifty states. Some suffered almost immediate legislative reversal; others were budgeted out of business. With the exception of reforms in Oregon and Hawaii, all of the rest have had no significant impact.

In the mid-1980s and early 1990s, seven states (Vermont, Florida, New Jersey, Rhode Island, Georgia, Maine, and Washington) followed Hawaii (1960) and Oregon (1973) in adopting programs featuring state goals and local plans. There was much talk of a rebirth of land-use reform. However, the Vermont and Maine programs were gutted or defunded. The voluntary programs in Rhode Island, Georgia, and New Jersey have had little effect. The 1972 Florida program, revamped in 1985, has had only modest impact. Undermined by budget cuts and legislative modifications, the Florida program has been politically orphaned by an unsympathetic new governor. The jury is out on the Washington (1993), Maryland (1997), and Tennessee (1998) programs.

Political weakness characterizes the land-use reform movement throughout both its early and late periods, and the constancy of that

circumstance is more important than all the differences between the
two periods combined. However, two major differences are noteworthy: (1) sprawl and disinvestment rose to fantastic rates after World War II, and
(2) America's financial capacity to respond to the cost of sprawl gradually decreased.

In the earlier decades, America was richer. Annual growth in economic output, productivity, and household income created America's
rapidly expanding and rapidly prospering middle class. This increasing base of wealth generated vast sums of public revenue that met key
social needs while requiring a smaller share of GNP than today. In
contrast, a surging Dow Jones average and low inflation do not mask
and cannot compensate for the fact that since 1973 slow economic
growth and low productivity have shrunk working-class and middle-
class incomes, increased tax payments as a percentage of GNP, and
slowed investment in roads, schools, and other infrastructure. Until
the last few years, tax cutting and deficits have dominated politics.

As America's economic strength weakened, sprawl and disinvest-
ments accelerated. For example, as measured by census tracts with
poverty rates of 40 percent or more, urban disinvestment increased
nationally by 54 percent in the 1980s alone.[1] Similarly, while the geographic extent of development in metropolitan regions has expanded
five to ten times as fast as population growth from 1970 to 1990 (see
table 1-1), America's fifth generation of sprawl is expanding regions
ten to fifteen times as fast as population growth in the 1990s.[2] While a
booming post-war America could afford not to worry about relatively
small costs of sprawl, that is not true today.

Despite these differences and others, the prevailing political weakness of the land-reform movement is paramount because sprawl and
disinvestment are rooted in law and policy. The effort to limit sprawl
and disinvestment must rest on a political strategy: build majority support that can persuade state legislatures to change the zoning laws
that continue to authorize sprawl and disinvestment. Well-intentioned
strategies that do not seek to correct defective municipal zoning—
such as buying land zoned for sprawl—are not only inadequate, but
also misdirect public attention, forestalling the policy change that is
most needed.

From 1970 to 1990, as far as the media and elected officials were
concerned, the land-use reform movement was a barely noticeable
sideshow usually led by politically naive do-gooders and speechifiers.
The posture of the movement's spokespersons and publications was

Table 1-1. *Geographic versus Population Expansion*
Percent

| Region | Period | Rate of Expansion | |
		Geographic	Population
Chicago	1970–90	46/74[a]	4
Cleveland	1970–90	33	–11
Kansas City	1970–90	110	29
Los Angeles	1970–90	200	45
New York	1960–85	65	8
Philadelphia	1970–90	32	2.8
San Antonio	mid-1950s–1990	600	100[b]

Sources: Northeast Illinois Planning Commission, Chicago; Anita A. Summers, "A New Strategy for America's Large Cities," speech, Chicago, October 20, 1994, p. 6; Chris Lester and Jeffrey Spivak, "Divided We Sprawl" (six-part series), *Kansas City Star*, December 17, 1995, citing U.S. Census Bureau of Mid-America Regional Council; Christopher B. Leinberger, remarks, Hilton Hotel, Portland, Oregon, April 18, 1993; Regional Plan Association, *The Region Tomorrow* (New York, 1990), p. 3; Greenspace Alliance, *Toward a Green Space Legacy: A Call to Action in Southeastern Pennsylvania* (Pennsylvania Environmental Council, 1994); Henry G. Cisneros, *Regionalism:The New Geography of Opportunity* (Department of Housing and Urban Development, March 1995), pp. 1–2.

a. Area increased 46 percent for housing and 74 percent for commercial use.

b. Population doubled to 1.3 million.

one of blithe resignation to political incapacity, as if personal association with a virtuous cause was more important than actually leading the cause anywhere. In the inner circles of the movement, including the movement's various funders, the lack of political clout was regarded as an unstated premise, an almost immutable given. Talk of justifiably ambitious goals was met with, "Oh, *that* could never happen in *our* legislature." Political strategizing occurred almost exclusively for defensive purposes. Legislative nose-counting for offensive purposes was practically unheard of.

Ignorance Begets Political Weakness

The land-use reform movement has focused almost exclusively on only the most readily apparent environmental concerns. One obvious lesson of the past four decades is that environmental concerns are too slender a political reed on which to base reform efforts, whether state-level policy change or implementation at the local level.

However, the political insufficiency of environmentalism as the rationale for land-use reform is merely symptomatic of a second, more important lesson. The reason land use and regional reform movements have been politically marginal for so long is that they lack understanding of the causes and broader effects of land-use patterns.

Without knowledge about the *effects* of land-use patterns on people, households, businesses, and community functions such as education and public safety, it is hard to see how moral standards, like simple fairness, or economic values, like productivity, relate to land-use patterns. Without this knowledge the impetus for change cannot develop, proposals cannot be advanced, and public consensus will not form. Thus the debate is limited to thinly documented, usually abstract utilitarian complaints.

Similarly, lack of knowledge about the *causes* of land-use patterns is mainly why change has seemed politically impossible for so long. For nearly half a century various "false devils"—racial prejudice, free-market forces, population growth, "greedy developers," or the automobile—have been incorrectly blamed for sprawl and disinvestment. Focusing on these issues was not only substantively off target, it was also politically self-defeating. These forces were so big and insuperable that change seemed impossible. Therefore people resigned themselves to nibbling around the edges and symbolic efforts.

Race

Race is certainly a factor in development patterns. Racial groups sometimes self-select to live among themselves. Also, different races discriminate against or avoid members of other races. These phenomena are real. However, it is also true that development patterns in American metropolitan areas are much the same, region to region, despite major differences in racial composition. Moreover, many areas within a given region have changed from being all-white, sparsely settled backwaters to all-white suburban boom towns to all-white declining suburbs dominated by dying shopping malls and cheap frame housing—all without a trace of racial change. Something else important is at work here.

Free-Market Forces

Free-market forces are often blamed for promoting sprawl. It is a common belief that government should not control sprawl because to do so would impair the market's ability to allocate critical resources. Ironically, ignorance about the influence of policy in land-use patterns has denied reformers the argument that sprawl must be limited to *protect* market functions. Markets operate well to align supply and demand with respect to specific transactions, but policy pervasively shapes the underlying strength of that supply and demand. If policy allows financial values (like infrastructure) to be integrated into projects free of charge and allows projects to externalize costs, then policy also makes these projects artificially attractive to capital investment by reducing their price below their cost of production and operation. Then businesses and households respond to these policy-induced advantages for metropolitan-edge real estate investments and to disadvantages for urban and inner-suburb investments.

Population Growth

Regions (not just central cities) that *lost* population from 1970 to 1990 (Cleveland and Pittsburgh, for example) disinvested and sprawled in much the same way as regions with rapid population growth. Moreover, nations such as England and Germany are the same size as Oregon and Colorado but have fifteen to twenty times the population of those states. Yet large populations have not wrecked England and Germany; to the contrary, Americans spend large sums to travel to those countries to marvel at the beautiful countryside, compact cities, and thriving transit. Therefore, population growth also does not explain sprawl.

Development

The "stop development" misconceptions inherent in the old-style approach to reform needlessly positioned developers as opponents of land-use reform. As long as the premise was that developers simply responded to consumer preferences, it was not surprising that developers would vigorously oppose reforms that appeared, at their core, to be antidevelopment both in motivation and effect. Developers were particularly ready to oppose reform when they heard themselves called "greedy land-rapers" by opponents of development projects, who diverted attention from their own self-interest by appearing under a "good guy" banner of environmentalism.

Yet developers are no more self-interested than any other class of economic players. Moreover, developers dislike the land-use process for allowing too little development as much as neighborhood and environmental groups dislike it for allowing too much. Far from being the cause of development patterns, developers essentially play the policy hand they have been dealt. For all their campaign contributions, public profile, and presumed political influence, developers have not been able to shape the development process to their liking. Furthermore, new development is the ingredient needed to repair the automobile-dependent fabric of the suburbs and the disinvested centers of the region. The dysfunctional, environmentally harmful suburban development fabric is a physical problem. It cannot be regulated away any more than it can be wished away. Only transit-oriented, mixed-use, affordable redevelopment and new development can "fix" this situation. When properly directed, development is not the problem—it is the solution.

Technology

Doubtless, technology contributes to sprawl. Freight delivery has switched from trains to trucks. Messages now are delivered instantaneously by fax and modem instead of by mail or messenger. Businesses and people are more footloose and less dependent on proximity than they used to be. Yet technological change spans the globe. Refrigerated lorries have not ravaged the Gloucestershire countryside; back office data processing and fax modems have not pushed sprawl beyond the service area of Hamburg's light-rail system.

Wealth

American wealth also is said to cause sprawl. Yet sprawl moved outward more rapidly from 1970 to 1990, when the real income of most American households stagnated, than it did from 1950 to 1970, when economic growth and household incomes boomed.

New Understanding Heightens Prospects for Change

A fuller understanding of the causes and consequences of metropolitan land-use patterns emerged in the late 1990s, improving the prospects for change. A broader range of concerned interest groups and citizens now see their stake in the issue. People are questioning whether sprawl may be at the root of systemic national problems such as slow productivity growth, unsuccessful schools, costly and ineffective public safety programs, and environmental conflicts. The powerful effects of sprawl and disinvestment are leading others to scale back the optimistic expectations of the 1970s that nonprofit, private-sector responses to sprawl and disinvestment, such as land trusts and community development corporations, could deal with these problems.

Sprawl: A Concern to More Than Environmentalists

The heightened pace of sprawl and disinvestment in the 1980s and 1990s, coupled with greater awareness of their effects, is leading many interests not previously associated with land use and regionalism to speak out. Officials in older suburbs, corporate and religious leaders, and urban advocates are introducing important new insights, energy, and people into the debate. In many metropolitan areas these interests are providing the most important leadership for the movement.

Suburban Interests

Suburban sprawl and urban disinvestment advanced outward so far and so fast from 1970 to 1990 that a majority of Americans are now adversely affected. This lesson has been learned only recently and very slowly. Sprawl and disinvestment have greatly harmed central cities and older suburbs, increasing the extent of repair work that is one of the key tasks of land-use reform. However, because that harm has been pervasive, a change in land-use policy has finally become politically possible in America.

The brilliant analysis of Myron Orfield, a Minnesota state representative, explodes the myth that suburbs are monolithically prosperous and happy and therefore will be bulwarks against reform. As project director of the American Land Institute's Metropolitan Area Program, Orfield analyzed eighteen major U.S. metropolitan regions from 1995 to 1998 and found that the majority of metropolitan populations would benefit from policies that rein in sprawl and encourage reinvestment. Far from being contented and prosperous, many low-tax-base suburbs—older inner suburbs as well as outer "sheetrock" suburbs—are suffering the same kind of disinvestment, school performance declines, crime rate increases, and property value stagnation and decline that rocked central cities decades ago.

Residents of older inner suburbs did not respond to environmental complaints about sprawl in the 1970s and 1980s. Incomes in many households in the older suburbs were flat or falling, and environmental complaints about sprawl echoed the conflict between jobs and the environment being played out at the national level and in the media. However, as sprawl continued moving out, its "backside"—disinvestment—moved out, too: out of the central cities and into the older suburbs. When the emphasis of the land-use debate shifted from natural resource issues to the fact that the socioeconomic rug was slowly being pulled out from under middle America's neighborhoods, suburbanites started having second thoughts. With the cost of housing in the new suburbs rising faster than incomes in the older suburbs, and with the value of older housing in the inner suburbs flat or falling, people were trapped in neighborhoods with failing schools, rising poverty, and declining social services. Land use suddenly became interesting, especially if (1) the local mayor or a familiar preacher, not some jargon-talking environmentalist, was the messenger; and (2) government action, not the market, was the cause of the problem. Moreover, unlike poor urban blacks, working-class white people were not politically marginalized and stigmatized; they could politically obliterate anyone who tried to tell them socioeconomic decline in their neighborhoods was explained by some kind of morally objectionable "culture of poverty."

As disinvestment engulfed older suburbs, the political underpinnings of the land-use reform movement began to be recast in three ways, vastly increasing the prospect that majorities could be built around metropolitan land-use issues.

First, the populations of older inner suburbs, outer low-tax-capacity suburbs, and central cities add up to 60 to 75 percent of total population in every U.S. metropolitan region the American Land Institute has studied. Each of these sectors is being harmed by the same patterns of development.

Second, the inner-suburb perspective on the issue strips the land-use debate of politically fatal misconceptions that have marginalized and immobilized it for three decades. Inner-suburb officials are objecting that state government allocations of highway money, and other actions that induce private investment, are causing sprawl at the metropolitan edge, thereby undermining inner-suburb property values, municipal fiscal well-being, and local control. These suburban officials are asking state legislators to give older suburbs their share of public investments and programs that attract private investment, strengthen housing values and tax bases, and create jobs and income.

For example, America's inner suburbs have substantial quantities of usable housing stock. With repair and renovation to accommodate smaller, older households, this housing can (1) contribute greatly to the nation's home ownership and housing opportunity goals, (2) anchor established neighborhoods, (3) improve the climate for private investments in the center of metropolitan areas, and (4) slow sprawl at the edge. However, continued central-city and inner-suburb disinvestment discourages repair and renovation, and federal and state housing policies mainly boost new housing at the fringe or provide housing for the very poor in the central city. Why should national and state housing policies ignore the huge housing needs in the inner suburbs?

The First Suburban Consortium in Ohio is the leading proponent of such arguments nationally. Mayors representing 750,000 citizens in twenty-six suburbs across Ohio are asking the state legislature for a fair share of highway and other public investments and a halt to state subsidies of sprawl. This pro-investment and pro-local-control rallying cry for land-use reform is 180 degrees different from the essentially antidevelopment, anti-local-government rallying cry of environmentalists in the 1970s, which stated that

— development causes sprawl,

— local governments cave in to developers,

— states must limit local government authority in order to prevent excessive development.

The new rationale makes local control one of the *purposes* of state-level reforms, not part of the problem that has to be reined in. Furthermore, private investment and development are viewed as principal means to achieve land-use reform, not a problem to be regulated. Under these banners, city officials and real estate investors interested in redevelopment and asset appreciation are no longer opponents, nor are they merely neutralized. Rather, they are important players in a restructured, potentially far more powerful movement.

The new suburban formulation also dramatically turns the tables on "property rights" advocates. Now property rights can be a reason to *stop* sprawl, not let it continue. The new formulation also politically isolates property rights advocates from their more respectable former allies: local officials and developers. It also reveals the property rights cause for what it largely is: a handful of landowners insisting on continuation of subsidized sprawl at the metropolitan edge, even though sprawl at the edge will flatten or reduce the property values of a far greater number of property owners in the interior of the region. The reform movement insists that the rights of all property owners—not just a few—be considered in the land-use policy debate,

The third way the land-reform movement will be recast is when urban minority and environmental interests follow the inner suburbs' lead because their goals of regional *containment, stability,* and *repair* also advance urban and environmental interests. Moreover, partnering with suburban leaders is the best way that urban minority and environmental interests can break out of self-defeating patterns of isolation and marginalization.

A recent study in Michigan illustrates the kind of land-use circumstance that could draw this new coalition of interests together. The Michigan Society of Planning Officials (MSPO) projects that all of Michigan's urban areas will expand between 63 and 87 percent from 1990 to 2020, while population will grow a modest 11 percent.[3] The MSPO report also finds that Michigan faces a $65 *billion* price tag for infrastructure repair, deferred maintenance, and construction backlog, much of it in the vast suburban areas that grew from 1960 to 1990. If the state continues to ignore the investment backlog in its older suburbs and continues to foster the vast expansion of sprawl at the metropolitan edge, then two things will happen. First, substantial portions of suburban areas developed since World War II will deteriorate, experiencing much the same process of abandonment and disinvestment that hollowed out Detroit from 1950 to 1990. Second, developed areas of Michigan characterized by lack of critical mass, inadequate tax base, operating inefficiencies, and inadequate public investment will expand.

Religious Leaders

The kinds of religious and moral arguments that have underlain great domestic causes in American history are now beginning to bolster the utilitarian and public health arguments about land use that environmentalists have advanced for the past thirty years. Religious leaders long have expressed concerns about sprawl on environmental grounds, most notably the "Heartland Catholic Bishops" paper in 1976 about farmland loss. In the 1990s, the nation's clergy began to express concern about the impact of sprawl on metropolitan regions and their populations. Most notable was Bishop Anthony M. Pilla, immediate past president of the U.S. Conference of Catholic Bishops. In his report *Church in the City*, Bishop Pilla cites "investment imbalances" between central cities, teetering older suburbs, and newer outer suburbs. The abandonment of private investments and of people is not just environmentally damaging; it also violates the central tenet of Catholic social doctrine: the inherent dignity of every human being. In a region that sprawled 33 percent from 1970 to 1990 while losing 11 percent of its *regional* population (and half its *central-city* population since 1950), the Church cannot afford to see its huge investment in physically sound schools, hospitals, and social service programs in the central city go underutilized and then duplicate them in the suburbs. No other enterprise can afford to, either.

National coalitions of locally grounded, faith-based organizations, such as the Gamaliel Foundation, are far ahead of national minority groups (the Urban League, Mexican American Legal Defense and Educational Fund, and NAACP, for example) and community development corporations in recognizing and responding to the harmful impacts of metropolitan-wide land-use patterns on the urban poor. Moreover, churches have a higher standing and better communication with urban and inner suburban neighborhoods and with elected officials than either of the other types of organizations.

Corporate Groups

For different reasons corporate leaders are concerned about the same patterns of sprawl and disinvestment as bishops and suburban mayors. Corporate leaders see how sprawl and disinvestment affect economic productivity, both at the macroeconomic level (nationally) and the microeconomic level (the individual plant). They see sprawl making unfeasible the public investment in infrastructure on which private capital depends for efficiency and profitability. They see disinvestment undermining the quality of schools and the work force. Corporate leaders also are concerned that sprawl-spawned housing costs and traffic congestion make it hard to recruit and retain employees.

The most powerful force for land-use reform and regional governance in California is the Silicon Valley Manufacturers Group (SVMG). SVMG believes that sprawling development threatens worker productivity and the future economic vitality of Silicon Valley. SVMG's analysis found that zoning in Santa Clara County's fifteen municipalities was driving up housing costs by creating a shortage of sites for housing and a huge surplus of industrial land. Zoning policy also compelled people to use automobiles by requiring development in patterns that made rail and bus service impossible.

SVMG's conclusions were better documented but less well publicized than Bank of America's now famous *Beyond Sprawl,* in which the nation's (then) second-largest bank stated that California could no longer afford sprawl.[4] In addition, SVMG made specific recommendations; their successful proposals for housing-policy reform, transportation investment, and urban growth boundaries (see "Lessons from Adopted Policy Changes") are the greatest unsung land-use success story in America. It will take time for SVMG's strategy of sprawl containment, deregulation of housing markets, and transportation investments to gradually change, through "corrective development," the patterns of the past four decades. But the policies and investment structure to do so are in place in Santa Clara County as firmly as any place in America.

Other respected corporate voices warning about the adverse economic effects of sprawl development include the Civic Committee of the Commercial Club in Chicago, Providence Gas CEO Jim Dodge in Rhode Island, and business groups in Grand Rapids, Michigan, and in midsize industrial cities in Pennsylvania.

Traditional Urban Interests

More African Americans live in urban census tracts of 40 percent or more poverty in 1990 than were living in slavery (3,953,580) in 1860.[5] Thus experts on and advocates for poor urban minorities have begun to speak out about the connection between sprawl at the edge and disinvestment in the center—the investment imbalance Bishop Pilla emphasized.

In 1954, when the U.S. Supreme Court handed down *Brown* v. *Board of Education,* 11 percent of the U.S. population was "minority." The Census Bureau now projects Caucasians will no longer constitute a majority of the population by 2040. Hispanics will replace blacks as the second largest racial group by 2010. As the United States undergoes this unprecedented change in its racial composition, the nation is coming face to face with its third great challenge of racial justice: ensuring that people of color have equal access to jobs, schools, and housing throughout metropolitan regions. That challenge requires modernization of existing land-use and public finance systems.

Harvard's William Julius Wilson, in *When Work Disappears,* calls for metropolitan-wide land-use and regional governance reform, emphasizing that isolated, go-it-alone strategies of the past will not work for the urban poor any more than they have worked for environmentalists. John Powell, former ACLU staff attorney and director of the Center for Race and Poverty at the University of Minnesota Law School, echoes Wilson's conclusions and advocates the formation of new metropolitan-wide coalitions to make policy change possible in state legislatures.[6]

Connection to Systemic Problems

The broadened base of concerned interests and citizens is one result of increased understanding about the nature and effects of sprawl. Greater knowledge is also leading people to ask whether local development patterns have something to do with larger systemic problems.

Standard of Living

Economists have been perplexed at the slowdown in annual productivity growth in the U.S. economy since 1973. Land-use patterns are the physical matrix in which all economic and social activity must take place, for better or worse. Productivity-spurring private investment depends in part on the integrity and extent of the nation's infrastructure. Does sprawl partly explain the slowdown in core infrastructure investment that has mirrored the quarter-century slowdown in productivity?

Economists of all stripes agree that the nation's standard of living is not determined by job growth, low unemployment, low inflation, or a surging Dow Jones (as important as those factors are), but by annual growth in productivity. This is because productivity growth is the key to per capita income growth and to economic growth that generally does not trigger inflation.

The problem is that growth in productivity has decreased in the last twenty-five years and with it America's standard of living, a development that has baffled economists and other observers. From 1973 to 1995, productivity growth averaged only 1.1 percent, less than half the 2.3 percent annual average since the Civil War and less than the 1.9 percent annual growth since 1909.[7] From 1989 to 1995, annual productivity growth has been an even lower 0.9 percent. This results in lower household incomes and a smaller economic pie.

It is well recognized that private investment relies on core infrastructure—roads, transit, sewers, and utilities—for its efficient operations. For example, businesses depend on transportation systems for efficient movement of employees, supplies, and finished products. Moreover, there is a well-established connection between public investment in core infrastructure on the one hand, and productivity growth and high rates of return on private investment on the other.

However, core infrastructure, in turn, depends on factors of density and distance for its initial feasibility and efficient operation. Have the rapid spatial expansion of America's metropolitan regions and low densities of new development contributed to America's productivity slowdown? From 1948 to 1973, when metropolitan areas expanded more modestly, the nation's stock of core infrastructure annually increased in value an average 4.2 percent, peaking at 5.2 percent a year during the 1960s. In that twenty-five-year period, as noted earlier, productivity and incomes boomed. However, from 1973 to 1996, as sprawl intensified, growth in the value of core infrastructure averaged only 2.4 percent a year; from 1979 to 1987, it was only 2.2 percent, half the 1948–1973 annual rate. During that latter twenty-three-year period, productivity growth fell by more than half, and incomes fell or were stagnant for half the population.

Education and Equal Opportunities

Sprawl and disinvestment make the nation's massive spending on schools inefficient and ineffective. Although many forces are at play, is it coincidental that the nation's public schools commenced a three-decade slide in SAT scores as suburban sprawl and urban disinvestment intensified in the 1960s?

America depends on its K–12 education system to supply the largest component of "capital" in the nation's economy—its high-school-graduate work force. Only about 30 percent of the work force are college graduates, a proportion not expected to change.

Urban disinvestment has created concentrations of joblessness and poverty that render America's once-great city school systems incapable of creating a skilled, adaptable work force. In the Chicago system, 73 percent of schoolchildren are from low-income households; in Rochester, 80 percent; and in Atlanta, 85 percent. The poor performance of poverty-dominated central-city school systems is the "thousand pound gorilla" that pulls down metropolitan and national test score averages—and this occurs in the same school systems, often the same buildings, that earlier produced America's greatest scientists and business and community leaders.

Central-city high school graduates gain comparatively low levels of skill. In addition, about 45 percent of entering freshmen drop out of central-city systems. This phenomenon annually pours hundreds of thousands of essentially unemployable young people into the already oversupplied, economically sinking, low-skill end of the work force. In Chicago alone there have been 73,000 dropouts from 1995 to 1999. In addition, children locked into failing urban schools by the residential isolation of their parents and the poverty concentrations in their neighborhoods are deprived of equal opportunity.

Sprawl also hurts school systems regionwide. Sprawl and disinvestment can cause construction of excess school capacity. When school districts close physically functional schools in the center of the region and build new schools at the edge, especially in times of a flat or falling school-age population, taxes for education needlessly rise, fueling tax-cut sentiments. State financing of local public education means all taxpayers' dollars participate in the waste, even though they may not reside in the districts where schools are being built. For example, in the Twin Cities, sprawl caused education officials to close sixty schools in the center of the region and sixty in the inner suburbs while building fifty new schools in the outer suburbs—even though the school-age population regionwide was declining. A new high school costs about $40 million to build; a new elementary school costs $20 million. Because of sprawl, money that could have been spent for enhanced curricula, smaller class sizes, and building maintenance was spent to duplicate physically sound facilities.

Public Safety

Sprawl makes it difficult for police to respond to or deter crime. While America sprawled, police strategies shifted from the cop on the street to the cop in the squad car to 911 systems. Businesses and homeowners have learned that the average burglary takes three minutes and average police response takes fourteen minutes. Government's inability to deter crime in sprawling regions is partly the reason why, by 1993, (1) police costs had risen 50 percent faster than inflation during the two prior decades and (2) there were two and a half times more people employed in private security firms than in all the nation's municipal police departments combined.

Between 1996 and 2010, the population of crime-prone juveniles is estimated to increase from 27 million to 39 million. The arrest rate for people aged twelve to seventeen is 48 percent higher than for people aged eighteen and older. The juvenile arrest rate in 1995 was 61 percent higher than in 1986. Most of this crime occurs in urban areas with high poverty concentrations.

Environmental Quality

The same patterns of development that make infrastructure investment unfeasible, stretch school budgets, and deny equal opportunity for education also damage the environment. The power and extent of locally authorized sprawl are so great that within 15 years they threaten to undo congressionally achieved reductions in air and water pollution since the early 1970s while intensifying unabated damage to natural resources.

Sprawl needlessly destroys productive farmland, scenic countryside, wildlife habitat, and creeks and streams. Because sprawl separates nearly every suburban destination by a distance requiring the use of a car, it also generates pollution and congestion by increasing vehicle miles traveled, which have increased three times faster than the rate of population growth since 1960. Pollution prevention, not regulation, has been the goal of national environment protection since William K. Reilly led the EPA. Yet, unchecked sprawl remains the greatest potential destroyer of the gains produced by pollution prevention in the past twenty-five years—as well as the greatest potential opportunity to extend the principle of pollution prevention.

Outdated Rationales

Activists, academics, and officials have increasingly inclined to the views of Columbia University professors Kenneth Jackson and Elliot Sclar and others that a mass of unintended or outdated public-policy interventions in local real estate markets is a major, if not primary, cause of sprawl and disinvestment in region after region.

For example, the zoning of most municipalities is still based on the nineteenth-century rationale of strictly separating different classes of use. Hence automobile-dominated suburban landscapes are caused not only by low densities and rapid expansion of urbanized areas, but by development patterns in which nearly all suburban destinations are separated by driving-only distances. With the growth of the service and information sectors, only about 18 percent of all jobs today are in manufacturing. In addition, modern manufacturing is largely clean and getting cleaner. The strict separation of uses that continues to blanket metropolitan real estate markets is not only almost entirely unnecessary, it also is a major cause of pollution and congestion by generating vehicular travel at a rate that exceeded population growth by three times since 1950.

With greater understanding of how policy influences sprawl and disinvestment, alternative land-use patterns seem more achievable as a political matter. The substance of reform is seen less as new regulation of market activity and more as repealing or modifying outdated laws and regulations that cause sprawl. Similarly, reform does not mean more of the same regulations of the past, or having a big fight with the market, or changing the American Dream, as some claim. Through judicious modification of existing law, reform can reduce sprawl and disinvestment and leave real estate markets with less net regulation than before.

Limits of Private Sector Intervention

Building houses for the urban poor and buying suburban-fringe land to fend off bulldozers cannot substitute for policy change, regardless of how much money is spent. Post–World War II development patterns have generated so much unemployment and poverty in inner cities and destroyed so much rural land and open space, they have overwhelmed heroic private sector efforts to respond to disinvestment and sprawl. In addition, the maze of laws pulls and pushes private investment ever outward, stacking the deck against church, community development corporation, and land-trust programs. Therefore, land-use policy change is essential if the huge investments in these efforts are ever to realize their full potential of social returns.

Churches

Thousands of central-city churches, especially Roman Catholic parishes and African- American congregations, operate major educational, hospital, and social service programs. Sprawl and disinvestment strain the financial capacity of these institutions to operate such programs. As middle-class households and businesses leave the central city and the inner suburbs, the operating efficiencies and financial base of these programs decline. At the same time, churches are under pressure to duplicate facilities and programs in the suburbs.

Community Development Corporations

More than 2,000 community development corporations have aggressively used tax credits and private grants to build inner-city housing. But rates of poverty and racial isolation in the working areas of the nation's strongest community development corporations have increased, not decreased, since 1980.[8] As valuable as housing is, it is not a substitute for either private investment that creates jobs and household income or for residential (not school-bus or van-pool) access to areas with successful schools and job growth.

Land Trusts

More than 1,300 land trusts creatively pry money from public agencies, individuals, and foundations to buy land zoned for sprawl. They also persuade generous landowners to donate land or development rights. Yet sprawl, subdivisions, and partitions consume more land each year than all the acreage that all the land trusts put together have saved in five decades, at least in areas in the path of development. Absent policy reform, lands saved by purchase or gift are often likely to end up isolated in a sea of sprawl, ultimately benefiting adjacent property owners more than the public.

For example, the Packard Foundation recently committed $175 million to protect 250,000 acres in seven California counties. This is a valuable initiative: many critical land-conservation objectives at particular sites cannot be achieved by policy because their conservation requires such substantial limitations on development or on agricultural or forestry operations that the regulations needed to achieve the conservation purpose would not be constitutional.

On the other hand, conservation objectives for nearly all the 80-million-acre balance of private land in California *can* be achieved by land-use policy because restricting rural land to farm and forest use is constitutional. Policies to achieve such land-conservation objectives are not in place, not because of any constitutional impediment, but solely because local political support to continue anything-goes zoning at the county level is stronger than community support to change such county zoning policies.

The success of both policy and land-acquisition strategies depends on (1) recognition of what each of these strategies can and cannot do, (2) using the strategies in mutually reinforcing ways, and (3) not using one strategy to do what the other can and should. Strategies to conserve land by acquisition or donation should focus on critical lands that policy cannot treat. If the functional lines of responsibility are not clearly observed, and if acquisition money is used to save land that policy should save, money spent to buy land or development rights ultimately will make policy reform politically impossible. Use of the acquisition strategy for lands more appropriately protected by policy creates a reasonable expectation of payment in the minds of all similarly situated landowners. With each inappropriate purchase, more rural and urban-fringe landowners will expect to be paid. The more that happens, the more difficult it becomes politically for state legislatures ever to adopt and counties ever to apply new policy to the vast extent of rural land that can be saved only by policy.

The $76 million purchase of 300,000 acres of forest land in New York State, Vermont, and New Hampshire in December 1998 illustrates this point.[9] Nearly 60 percent of this acreage was resold to investors who will manage the land for timber growth and harvest. Given the reasonable economic return implied by that resale, there would have been no "taking" if the New York and New Hampshire legislatures had required counties to limit land use on *at least* the resold lands to activities compatible with forest management.

This transaction has been hailed as the largest single land transaction in U.S. history. But it amounts to less than 1 percent of the rural land in New England, which has 26 million acres of forest land alone. And it is less than 0.05 percent of the 235 million acres of cropland, 525 million acres of pasture and rangeland, and 358 million acres of forest land in America. At the rate of one of these huge transactions a year—a herculean effort—we are a century away from "saving" New England's open space, and well over a millennium away from saving rural America, assuming no one develops this land in the meantime.

Vice President Gore's recent $9.5 billion proposal for "Better America Bonds" must recognize the different roles purchase and policy play in the cause of land conservation. If those roles are confused, a new federal policy that citizens must pay to preserve commercially useful farmland could fatally undermine America's land-use reform movement. The vice president's initiative could end up promoting the antiregulatory shift in public policy the property rights movement has pushed for unsuccessfully ever since zoning was established in the 1920s and upheld by the U.S. Supreme Court, even though zoning significantly reduced potential sale values.

America's land-conservation future depends on the democratic principle that state constitutions authorize state legislatures to condition municipal exercise of the zoning power to limit the development of farm and forest land to farm and forest uses. Such limitations most certainly are not a taking of productive farm or forest land within the meaning of the U.S. Constitution.

Apart from the fact that such land-use policy is not a taking, the taxpayers should not have to pay to avoid the harms imposed by sprawl. For example, why should taxpayers and property owners in established portions of Michigan have to pay suburban-fringe or rural landowners not to develop land, when the sprawl that results would cause far more harm to far more people in the existing cities and towns than it would benefit? The unfairness of paying to avoid such harm is particularly striking given that taxpayers have already paid to build the roads and public services that make the new suburban-fringe development possible in the first place. A New Jersey study projected that from 1990 to 2010, sprawl would benefit suburban-fringe and rural landowners by $357 million, but the same sprawl would impose $8 billion more in costs on the public just for infrastructure investments alone.[10] Should a small group of New Jersey suburban-fringe landowners be heard to insist that the U.S. Constitution entitles them to land uses that will impose great financial harm on the rest of society unless they are paid not to impose that harm? Should leaders of the nation's smart-growth movement applaud new laws that authorize such payments?

Substantial sums of public and private money will be needed far into the future to buy parks, secure public access to special areas, and protect habitats that are intolerant of farm and forest practices. But the use of those funds must not undermine the policy reforms that are not only fair but feasible means of maintaining the working rural landscape on, say, ninety percent of the 1.2 billion acres of the magnificent American countryside.

Lessons from Adopted Policy Changes

Experience to date with legislative efforts to overcome fragmentation, modernize zoning, and simplify procedures and processes has yielded seven lessons.

Saving the Countryside Boosts the City

Each of Oregon's 241 cities has urban growth boundaries (UGBs), including the regional UGB around the twenty-one cities in the Portland metropolitan area. Oregon's land-use laws require that soils outside UGBs that are rated I–IV, according to the U.S. Soil Conservation Service, be zoned "exclusive farm use." Over 16 million acres in thirty-six counties have been zoned that way, plus 9 million acres of forest land. This rural land-conservation law has done more to make Portland a beautiful, economically thriving city than the UGB itself or any other law, state or local. Limiting lands outside the UGB to farm uses has channeled tax-base-boosting, job-creating, quality-of-life-enhancing private investment into a critical mass in which old and new investments enhance each others' value. Portland has never been as physically attractive and pleasant, never been more alive on a twenty-four-hour basis, and never had more construction occurring downtown than is happening today. The biggest reason for this urban vitality is a protected countryside outside the UGB, just miles from Pioneer Courthouse Square.

Multiple Benefits a Political Key

Policy changes that advance multiple goals have political benefits—as well as the kind of operational benefits described above. If any given policy—rural land conservation, for example—is justified on the basis of how well it advances *only a single purpose*—such as protection of species habitat—that justification likely will be politically insufficient to support limiting development to serve *urban* purposes or other legitimate rural land-conservation purposes, such as avoiding falling water tables or wildfires. The result of a single-purpose rural land-conservation strategy is that any rural land not proven to be needed for such a purpose is open for development.

Comprehensive Approach May Be Easier

People recognize that both the land-use problem *and* the regional governance issues are comprehensive, but some say that trying to limit development "outside" and boost development "inside" at one time may be too much to bite off. In fact, the experiences in both Oregon and Santa Clara County, California, suggest that doing both is politically essential. Developers agreed with ruling 25 million acres of farm and forest land outside UGBs off-limits to urban-scale development in Oregon, but only if development would be faster and more profitable *inside.* Environmentalists accepted the risk of policies that support development inside the UGB only if a large area (the size of Ohio) *outside* the UGB was protected. That was the heart of Oregon's "grand compromise." If both had not been done, neither could have been done.

State Policy Key to Regional Success

Metro, the elected regional planning entity in Portland, has been effective because it administers mandatory state land-use laws, including judicially enforceable criteria for the UGB, fair-share housing, transportation, and conservation of land outside the UGB. Without these state laws, Metro would have foundered.

The Met Council in the Twin Cities has a budget three times larger than Metro's and also authority to adopt a metropolitan urban services area line, the "MUSA line." However, because the Minnesota legislature has not established a process to determine how much land the MUSA line may contain, or what may be built on farmland outside, the MUSA line might as well not exist. Counties are free to approve subdivisions outside the MUSA line. Inside a huge MUSA line, the Twin Cities region is the lowest-density, most sprawling large region in America outside of Atlanta.

Deregulation is a Prominent Strategy

In both Portland and Santa Clara County, stripping away outdated zoning restrictions on markets for residential and industrial land improved prospects for housing affordability and made transit feasible.

Market Sensitivity

Public and official acceptance of changes in zoning policy in Portland and Santa Clara County was grounded in independent professional surveys of consumer preference for housing type and means of transportation, in addition to basics such as absorption rate and projections for work, income, and house sizes. Similarly, in Montgomery County, Maryland, the successful, twenty-six-year-old assisted housing program avoided a formulaic or community "grid" approach to housing location issues and instead let the process be incentive based and developer driven. ("Let's see, with the density bonus the county gives me, where will this project pencil out?")

Many Winners

Where the adoption of modernized zoning tools is urged on the basis that it will advance numerous consensus goals, including investment feasibility, equal opportunity, and environmental quality, these new applications of zoning have won broad community support, as in Portland and Santa Clara County.

The Historic Challenge

Building a constituency for changes in land-use policy and governance, wresting corrective policy from 50 state legislatures, and implementing that new policy in 270 metropolitan regions and 39,004 municipalities is the most important community-building challenge to face America since the adoption of the Constitution.[11]

The substantive dimensions of the problem are difficult enough by themselves:

— reversing the anything-goes policy formally locked into suburban-fringe and rural zoning ordinances all across the nation,

— removing zoning barriers so people of color have residential access to areas in regions with successful schools and job growth,

— removing zoning barriers to new development that is needed to enable cost-effective public transportation investments that extend over many municipalities within a region.

However, even if we assume that state legislatures will modernize zoning to achieve these substantive goals, modernized zoning cannot be adopted or implemented without also addressing the historical challenge of governance. More than two centuries ago, under the old Articles of Confederation, states individually printed money, taxed each others' commerce, declared war on Indian tribes, taxed imports and exports, and raised armies. Subsequently, citizens in the individual states voted to give up some of the sovereign political authority provided by their state constitutions to create workable governmental authority at the national level—defined by the then-proposed U.S. Constitution—to protect the national community.

Few would argue that America would have flourished without clear, unfragmented governmental capacity to act as a nation, on behalf of all its people, in the face of national need—whether creating vibrant national markets in the late nineteenth century or defending liberty and democracy globally in the twentieth century. Most would agree that the Articles of Confederation would have nipped American greatness in the bud, as well as changed the course of world history for the worse. Worldwide, the U.S. Constitution—the design of our federal system—is regarded as the most successful political document of all time.

Today America faces a challenge of fragmented governance similar to that of the 1780s. This time the question is not unworkable fragmentation with respect to common national concerns, but unworkable fragmentation with respect to metropolitan concerns—and metropolitan regions are where 80 percent of the American people now live.

The current structure of municipal government prevents the American people from democratically determining matters of metropolitan character and condition that directly and daily affect their lives. The actions of a mass of governmental entities—from federal and state governments to municipalities and special districts—affect community and individual welfare on a metropolitan basis, on issues such as housing, traffic congestion, tax-base disparity, quality of life, and conservation.

The Oregon, Minnesota, and most recently, Georgia legislatures have passed laws creating metropolitan mechanisms that enable people of the Portland, Twin Cities, and Atlanta regions to address key regional issues.[12] Elsewhere, American citizens living in a given metropolitan region have no political means to hold government accountable for its performance in these regards, just as American citizens two centuries ago had inadequate means to ensure that their stake in a national citizenship was being protected.

As before, at the heart of the matter is the centrality of state legislative authority in the scheme of American politics. The authority of the federal government to act exists entirely by virtue of delegations of authority—by means of the U.S. Constitution—from the *states* to the three branches of the federal government. By the same token, the regulatory and taxing authority of municipal governments is also the result of laws passed by *state* legislatures, which delegate these powers to municipalities. If the state legislature had not delegated such authority, the localities would not have it. Although the fact is frequently lost in the national media's news coverage, the fundamental policymaking institution in America remains the state legislature.

This is why the political challenge posed by sprawl and by the fragmentation of metropolitan life in America today—whether in Denver or Philadelphia or Atlanta—is fundamentally a matter of state law. The problem is not the sheer number or rapid growth of municipalities and special districts in America today. The problem is that *state laws* have allowed the creation of 262 cities around Chicago, 245 around Philadelphia, and 765 around New York.

The national challenge of land-use reform cannot be addressed effectively by Congress or the federal courts. The substantive policy challenges are embedded in issues of land use and land taxation that must be played out primarily at the state and local level. The metropolitan governance challenges involved are primarily issues of state law. Rapid change in America is placing new and increasingly heavy burdens on the highly fragmented zoning and property-tax systems that were adopted to deal with conditions of bygone centuries and that proved inadequate for the comparatively modest pressures of post–World War II American life. Congressional "devolution" of formerly national policies (welfare, immigration) and financial responsibilities onto states will intensify the pressures that rapid social change is placing on outmoded state and local systems.

The American people created a great nation in the eighteenth century and defended it in bloody wars in the nineteenth and twentieth centuries. Those have been some of America's greatest achievements. The greatest political challenge in the twenty-first century will be a reprise of the eighteenth century—once again defining and building community to meet current social needs. The challenge is to make America's constitutionally based system work at the metropolitan level.

Notes

1. Paul Jargowski, "Ghetto Poverty among Blacks in the 1980s," *Journal of Policy Analysis and Management*, vol. 13, no. 2 (1994), pp. 228–310.

2. Christopher B. Leinberger, remarks, Hilton Hotel, Portland, Oregon, April 18, 1993.

3. Michigan Office of State Planning, *Michigan Trend Futures* (1995).

4. Bank of America and others, *Beyond Sprawl: New Patterns of Growth to Fit the New California* (1995).

5. The 1860 census reported 3,953,580 slaves and 8,099,760 whites in the slave states. Harold Underwood Faulkner, *American Economic History*, 8th ed. (Harper and Row, 1960) p. 316.

6. Institute on Race and Poverty, *Concentrated Poverty: Causes, Effects, and Solutions* (University of Minnesota Law School, September 1999).

7. The nation's 1.1 percent rate of productivity growth since 1973 is even punier compared to the nation's 2.7 percent yearly growth from 1946 to 1973. However, some say this period was an anomaly. For the sake of argument, this paper uses the more modest historic performance of 2.3 percent as a standard. (Productivity was only 0.04 percent since the 1970s). Peter G. Peterson, "Will America Grow Up Before It Grows Old?" *Atlantic Monthly* (May 1996). See also Alicia H. Munnell, "Why Has Productivity Declined? New England Economic Review" *New England Economic Development* (January–February 1990), table 4, p. 15.

8. David Rusk, *Inside Game, Outside Game* (Brookings, 1999), pp. 21–36.

9. Wilderness Society, "300,000 Acres of Northern Forest Protected by Landmark Conservation Deal," press release, December 9, 1998.

10. New Jersey Office of State Planning, *Impact Assessment of the New Jersey Interim State Development and Redevelopment Plan* (February 28, 1992).

11. The number of municipalities is from Bureau of the Census, *Statistical Abstract of the United States, 1997* (Department of Commerce, 1997), table 496, p. 305.

12. The Georgia legislature created the Georgia Regional Transportation Authority in 1999.

PART ONE

REGIONAL GROWTH AND GOVERNANCE

CHAPTER TWO

Growing and Governing Smart: A Case Study of the New York Region

ROBERT D. YARO

At the end of the twentieth century, the question of how to govern and plan for the future of America's sprawling metropolitan regions has become the subject of urgent and contentious debate. It is now widely recognized that the nation's metropolitan regions are its basic economic units. The largest of these places are incubators of new technologies and industries and centers of American culture, communications, and media. They are the crucibles in which the new American society of the early twenty-first century will be formed from the swelling ranks of immigrants and native-born Americans who live in them.

But across the country, rapidly deconcentrating metropolitan regions have expanded beyond arbitrary and fixed political borders established decades or centuries ago. The results are racial, economic, and social divisions; increasing traffic congestion; inequities in infrastructure and school finance; adverse environmental effects; and other concerns that are causing citizens and business and political leaders to question how metropolitan regions are governed. Metropolitan governance systems established in the late nineteenth or early twentieth centuries clearly are not up to the challenges that will confront America's twenty-first-century metropolitan regions.

A number of regional governance experts have called for the creation of powerful new metropolitan governments or regional service or tax districts; others have called for sweeping new annexation powers for center cities or for city-county consolidations. Indeed, a handful of regions, including Portland, Minneapolis, Indianapolis, and Jacksonville, have demonstrated that these innovations are possible. But most other regions, including many of the nation's largest and fastest-growing metropolitan areas, have been unable to overcome the insurmountable political and practical obstacles that prevent the creation of similar regional institutions.

As desirable as it might be to promote such changes, in most large U.S. metropolitan regions (particularly those that span state or county boundaries), they will be difficult or impossible to carry out given the political, economic, and demographic realities. Instead, government and civic leaders would better use their time and political capital if they were to focus on initiatives that *can* happen and can make a difference in these places. Examples would include the establishment of (1) regional service and infrastructure finance and development districts and (2) commissions to plan and implement construction of transit, park, cultural, and tourism facilities and related downtown investments that benefit both cities and suburbs. Civic leaders also should focus on creating the civic groups and coalitions required to support these outcomes, many of which may take years or even decades to achieve.

The New York metropolitan region provides historic and recent examples that illustrate and support this argument. Of particular importance is the role that a not-for-profit advocacy group, the Regional Plan Association (RPA), and other civic groups have played in shaping the New York region.

For more than a century, this region, the nation's largest urban area, has confronted challenges similar to those facing U.S. metropolitan areas today. These include assimilation of millions of immigrants; rapid, unplanned development at the suburban fringe; and the pressing need to develop the transportation and environmental infrastructure required by a rapidly expanding metropolis.

In 1898 the region responded by consolidating Manhattan and five suburban counties into "Greater New York," the nation's first metropolitan government. Subsequently, however, comprehensive, region-wide solutions have not been instituted. Instead, a network of service districts, regional land-use regulatory agencies, and in one limited example, a regional tax district have been established, in most cases as a result of effective advocacy by civic groups. Other metropolitan areas have much to learn from this experience.

The terms *New York region* or *New York* as used in this chapter denote the thirty-one-county New York–New Jersey–Connecticut metropolitan region, or tri-state region, as currently defined by the Regional Plan Association and the region's metropolitan planning organizations. This area includes several primary metropolitan statistical areas (as defined by the Census Bureau) that stretch along a 100-mile radius from Manhattan. Its boundaries encompass New Haven, Connecticut, and Poughkeepsie, New York, to the north; Trenton, New Jersey, to the south; and all of Long Island to the east.

RPA's definition of the region is based on its transportation, economic, and environmental systems, such as commuter sheds, housing markets, and recreational and public water supplies. Fully 98 percent of the metropolitan area's commuter trips, for example, originate and end within this thirty-one-county tri-state region. RPA's definition of the region has been adopted by the metropolitan planning organizations and is increasingly used by the public and the media. (New York–based news media now purvey "tri-state news and weather," and businesses now promote themselves as tri-state enterprises: the metropolitan Honda dealers, for example, now advertise themselves as the "Tri-Honda dealers.")

A Century of Governance Innovation

The story of New York is the story of entrepreneurship, innovation, and tolerance of new groups and ideas. The upper reaches of its society have always been more welcoming to ambitious newcomers with foreign-sounding names and large bank accounts and not just to those with social pedigrees. Furthermore, New York never aspired to become "a City upon the Hill" or "the City of Brotherly Love"—a well-ordered, cohesive place like its northern and southern competitors.

New York's indifference to efforts by these and other places to create an ideal society has extended to the question of governance. Throughout this century there has been little political or public interest in comprehensive reforms to the region's governance system. This "system" has no metropolitan government, effective public region-wide planning, or institutionalized coordination between its 3 states, 31 counties, 800 municipalities, and more than 1,000 service districts. In spite of how inefficient and disorganized this system may appear to scholars, good-government advocates, and visiting public officials, most residents and their elected officials like the relative autonomy it affords to municipal governments.

New York is not alone in its failure to create a governance system that can adapt easily to metropolitan decentralization and growth. Most other great world centers also have failed to create metropolitan governments that increase geographically and functionally with their growing regions. The former Greater London Council and the new London Authority, for example, have had jurisdiction only within the inner urban ring of a metropolitan area that now spans all of south-eastern England. Tokyo Metropolitan Government also has failed to extend borders fixed in the 1930s in a region that now includes three suburban prefectures. In North America the greater Toronto region has expanded into three suburban jurisdictions beyond the borders of Metro Toronto, the consolidated city government established in the early 1950s (and recently restructured by the province in a controversial and still incomplete reform effort).

Political Geography and Governance

The New York region has never been a neat, tidy, well-organized place. Ironically, this now may be one of the region's unique advantages in a global economy that rewards creativity and innovation, since the region's chaotic look and feel provide a fertile setting for innovators and entrepreneurs. Moreover, the region's political fragmentation is not a recent thing. In the seventeenth century, when King Charles II divided the region between the provinces of New York, New Jersey, and Connecticut, he unwittingly established the current state boundaries for what in the twentieth century would become the world's economic capital. The British monarch also ensured that this region would always be politically fragmented. Later this political geography would create a unique set of challenges in governing the growing metropolis. Being located at the convergence of three states—the governance equivalent of plate tectonics—has meant that, like other multijurisdictional metropolitan areas, this region never has had a strong sense of common identity or destiny.

These obstacles to creating regional institutions have been compounded by the three states' very different political systems, the product of divergent values and traditions:

— Connecticut is the southwestern outpost of New England town meeting democracy; its 169 cities and towns operate like independent republics, unsupervised by county officials (counties having been abolished in the 1950s) and subject to only limited state controls.

— New York has a tradition of strong state government and of counties and large towns that function in many ways as regional governments. (Some Long Island towns, for example, have populations exceeding half a million residents.)

— New Jersey has the densest concentration of local government in the region. For example, Bergen County's 246 square miles (located across the Hudson River from Manhattan) are divided into seventy municipalities and dozens of school and service districts. By comparison, Virginia's Fairfax County, with a similar population, economy, and place in the metropolitan Washington region, has only one general-purpose government—the county—and only one school district. New Jersey is also unique in the metropolitan area in that it has a state growth management plan; Connecticut has an "advisory" plan, and New York State has no state planning process.

A feature common to all three states, however, is their citizens' deeply held reverence for home rule, whether by town selectmen in Connecticut, supervisors in New York, or freeholders in New Jersey. Home rule is so strongly valued, and development so extensive and decentralized, that there are no unincorporated areas in any of the three states. Moreover, municipalities remain heavily dependent on property taxes, with the result that they are suspicious of tax reform or tax-sharing proposals that might jeopardize their fiscal independence.

A number of other large U.S. metropolitan regions—Philadelphia, Washington-Baltimore, Chicago, St. Louis, and Kansas City—have also spread across state borders. A few of these places (Philadelphia and Washington, for example) now have weak advisory metropolitan planning organizations or regional transportation authorities; but as with New York, none have created effective regionwide general-purpose governance or growth management institutions.

Rapid Growth Requires Innovations

A series of adept innovations and investments by New York City (then only the island of Manhattan) and its entrepreneurs in the first quarter of the nineteenth century helped New York become the East Coast's principal shipping and financial center by 1840. These included the city's 1811 "commissioners" plan that established the city's street grid; the first scheduled trans-Atlantic steamship service; and the construction of the Erie Canal. Subsequent ambitious investments in public water supply systems, parks, and railroads ensured that the city had the infrastructure, amenities, and quality of life to attract a rapidly expanding population and to become by midcentury the nation's undisputed economic and cultural center.

However, as a result of these actions, by the end of the nineteenth century, the city was literally choking on success, with tenement districts, streets, and streetcar lines overwhelmed by vast numbers of immigrants from southern and eastern Europe. Immigration also threatened the political power of the city's native-born elite. Another challenge to the city's primacy in the national economy was posed by a rapidly growing Chicago, which threatened to surpass New York in population early in the twentieth century, unless the city took bold action to consolidate with its neighboring cities and counties.

In response to these challenges, a group of progressive political and business leaders called for the consolidation of New York and four suburban counties into "Greater New York," in effect a regional government encompassing the vast majority of the metropolitan area's residents and jobs. The group's goal was to ensure that the consolidated city had the economic resources to invest in the subways, bridges, parks, water supplies, and other facilities required by the growing metropolis. (In the late nineteenth, as in the late twentieth, century, the federal government could not be relied upon to finance these systems.) Suburban leaders sought the tax base in the Manhattan business district, then—and now—the nation's largest. And Manhattan's native-born Protestant business and political elite saw consolidation as a way of ensuring a growing economy while maintaining political control of a city with a growing population of immigrant Catholics and Jews, who were heavily concentrated in the ghettos of Manhattan's Lower East Side.

After a lengthy and contentious political debate, Greater New York was constituted in 1898. Early in the new century, the consolidated city initiated a vast infrastructure development program, including the construction by 1940 of the world's largest subway, water supply and wastewater treatment systems, and networks of bridges, highways, schools, parks, and other facilities required by the growing metropolis. (In 1965, ten years after the initiation of the interstate highway system, nearly two-thirds of the nation's limited-access high-way miles were located in the New York region.) As a result of consolidation, residents of communities in the outer boroughs clearly benefited from the city's expanded tax base and services, although they did lose political control over their own communities and municipal services. Residents of Manhattan's poorest minority and immigrant communities lost both political control and a share of Manhattan's commercial tax base.

A century later, the vast majority of large U.S. metropolitan areas now face problems similar to those of New York in 1898. These include growing isolation of immigrants and minorities in center cities and older suburbs, extreme congestion and the need for major new regional infrastructure investments in growing suburbs, and concerns about competition with other regions. But among the nation's largest metropolitan regions, none are considering the kind of multi-county consolidation that New York achieved a century ago. And in only a handful of places (Indianapolis, Nashville, Jacksonville) have city-county consolidations occurred. At the end of the twentieth century, three key factors impede further consolidation or annexations in most of the country:

— the extreme segregation of poor African Americans in center cities and older suburbs and the fear on the part of both inner-city and suburban elites that their political monopoly might be undercut by city-suburb consolidation;

— the shift of a rapidly growing share of regional employment, retail, and other activities (read: tax base) from center cities and older suburbs to outer-ring suburbs, with the resulting perception by outer suburbs that they have little to gain and a lot to lose from consolidation or annexation;

— the wall-to-wall incorporation of suburban areas surrounding most Northeastern, Midwestern, and West Coast cities, including Boston, Philadelphia, Chicago, Los Angeles, and San Francisco, creating a virtual political firewall guarded by suburb-dominated state legislatures.

Only in the South and Southwest have center cities continued to annex growth areas—places that David Rusk terms *elastic cities*. These places have the advantage of being surrounded by unincorporated, largely rural regions, and they continue to dominate regional and state politics.

Greater New York

Greater New York's role as a regional government was short lived since it failed to expand as the region grew well beyond its boundaries. Ironically, the political compromises that made Greater New York possible precluded its expansion in succeeding decades. The political "deal" cut with the suburbs over the creation of Greater New York guaranteed the independence of its suburban neighbors, Nassau County to the city's east and Westchester County to the north. State borders to the south, west, and northeast precluded expansion in other directions, making Greater New York's boundaries, for all intents and purposes, permanently fixed.

Consequently, less than two decades after the creation of the consolidated city, the metropolitan area had expanded beyond the city's limits into seventeen suburban counties in parts of New Jersey, Connecticut, Long Island, and the lower Hudson River valley. This resulted from the city's inelastic boundaries and the region's dramatic growth and decentralization.

Despite rapid deconcentration of population, the region continued to be dominated well into the 1960s by the city and its near monopoly on employment and retail, culture, higher education, and other specialized services. Today the region extends into twenty-six suburban counties in New York, New Jersey, and Connecticut. Northeastern Pennsylvania also is tied into the region's economy, commuter sheds, and transportation system, in effect making this a four-state region. Beginning in the 1970s, however, rapid decentralization of employment and other activities decreased the city's dominance over suburban districts.

Interestingly, today other metropolitan governments with boundaries fixed since the late 1960s face similar challenges. Indianapolis, for example, with its consolidated city-county government, is now growing new suburbs well beyond Marion County's permanent boundaries. As with New York, this growth beyond the metropolitan government's inelastic borders is occurring less than a quarter century after they were established.

Within two decades of the creation of Greater New York, growth and its impacts led the region's government, business, and civic leaders to the conclusion that new infrastructure was required to meet the needs of a growing city and metropolitan region. With no potential to expand metropolitan government beyond New York City's five boroughs, new public institutions would be required to build and manage the highways, bridges, tunnels, parks, and port facilities the region would require to continue to grow and prosper. A new strategy was chosen to finance, build, and manage these facilities: specialized regional authorities and service districts, many of which still shape the region and its infrastructure.

Special-Purpose Regional Authorities

Since 1922, when the Port of New York Authority was established, several special-purpose regional authorities have been created to deal with particular needs. This approach to regional problem solving—creating narrowly focused authorities rather than general-purpose regional government—has been a hallmark of regional governance in the New York metropolitan area in the twentieth century. The divisions between the three states, the strong tradition of local home rule, and the suburbs' suspicion of their powerful urban neighbor continue to preclude a more comprehensive approach.

This process occurred largely in an unplanned, ad hoc manner. Usually these institutions were established when governors or master builders worked in partnership with civic leaders. Although this approach doesn't make for a neat organization chart, these specialized authorities have largely met the needs they were intended to address. However, proposals have been made in recent years to reform these authorities and to improve coordination between them.

The Port Authority

The first, largest, and most influential of New York's regional authorities is the Port of New York Authority (now the Port Authority of New York and New Jersey), established in 1921 to improve seaport and trans-Hudson freight and passenger facilities. In the early post–World War II era, under the leadership of master builder Austin Tobin, the Port Authority assumed additional responsibilities for building and operating a broad range of infrastructure, including LaGuardia, Newark, and Kennedy Airports; several modern marine freight terminals; the Port Authority Trans-Hudson transit system; the World Trade Center; and various economic development and urban renewal programs.

In recent years the Port Authority's independence has been compromised by the direct participation of the two states' governors, who routinely exercise veto powers over its actions and investments. The setting of tolls and fares, for example, has become a highly politicized process. And in the early 1990s, the governors began to use the Port Authority's surpluses to fund each state's pet infrastructure and urban development projects (including waterfront redevelopment projects in Hoboken, New Jersey and Queens, New York; industrial parks in Yonkers, New York; an office building in Newark, New Jersey, and other distractions). In some years Port Authority funds have even been used to close annual state budget deficits. In addition to undermining the Port Authority's autonomy, these actions have ultimately compromised its ability to fulfill its core mission: building and managing world-class sea- and airports and trans-Hudson transportation facilities.

Bridge, Tunnel, and Highway Authorities

Several toll road and bridge authorities were established, beginning with the Triborough Bridge and Tunnel Authority in 1931 under the leadership of master builder Robert Moses. Four highway authorities were created in the early post–World War II era to build new toll roads: the New York Thruway, New Jersey Turnpike, New Jersey Highway (which builds and maintains the Garden State Parkway), and Connecticut Turnpike Authorities. All but the last survive.

Since the late 1960s, the states have tightened their control over these freewheeling public authorities. In 1968 Moses's Triborough Bridge and Tunnel Authority was brought under the control of the newly constituted Metropolitan Transportation Authority. Since the 1970s, succeeding New Jersey governors have taken steps to tighten their control over that state's toll road authorities. Toll road authorities in Connecticut were abolished when tolls were eliminated in the early 1980s.

Transportation Authorities

In 1968 Governor Nelson Rockefeller established the Metropolitan Transportation Authority (MTA) and Metro-North Commuter Railroad to revive the failing New York City subway and suburban commuter rail systems. The then-private Long Island Rail Road, the nation's largest commuter rail network, was acquired by the state and reconstituted as an operating unit of the MTA. New Jersey Transit was established to assume a similar role by acquiring and operating several bankrupt commuter rail companies.

The MTA consolidated these systems as well as the operations of the Triborough Bridge and Tunnel Authority into a single operating entity. This facilitated cross-subsidies from automobile tolls to the transit system and provided a financial base for a program of new rail services. Unfortunately, this ambitious capital investment program was stymied by the fiscal crisis that struck New York City and the state in the mid-1970s. A $25 billion capital program has restored these systems since 1980, contributing to the region's economic revival in the 1990s.

Environmental Management and Regional Park Commissions

Several agencies that were established in the 1920s to protect regional environmental systems continue to fulfill important roles. The Palisades Interstate Park Commission was established to manage the nation's first regional park, the lands atop the majestic Palisades escarpment on the Hudson River's west bank in New York and New Jersey. This commission remains active today and as recently as 1997 led the successful partnership between New York and New Jersey to protect Sterling Forest (a vast 21,000-acre open space that straddles the state line less than forty miles from Manhattan). Through Robert Moses's leadership, New York State established several other regional park authorities in the 1920s. Moses used them to build and operate his vast empire of parks and parkways over four decades, beginning in 1928. All of them were consolidated into New York State's parks department in the 1960s, as part of Governor Nelson Rockefeller's campaign to rein in Moses and the authorities.

In the area of water quality, the Interstate Sanitary Commission was established by interstate compact in the 1920s to set standards for cleanup of interstate waterways. Although it has had virtually no public visibility, for three-quarters of a century, the commission has played a critical role in setting mutually agreed upon targets for pollution reduction in New York Harbor, Long Island Sound, and the Hudson River.

The Regional Plan Association

In most cases these public authorities were established or had their responsibilities broadened by activist governors or master builder-bureaucrats. But their policies and investments have been guided and coordinated by a dense network of local and regional civic groups, many of them established to play this role. Foremost among these with regard to metropolitan planning and development issues is the Regional Plan Association (RPA), an independent, not-for-profit civic group established to prepare and promote adoption of a long-range, comprehensive plan for the region.

RPA had its origins in the Committee on the Regional Plan for New York and Environs, an ad hoc group convened in 1922 by visionary business leader Charles Dyer Norton, who was president of First National City Bank (now CitiGroup). More than a decade earlier, Norton, a native Chicagoan, had chaired the Civic Committee of the Commercial Club of Chicago, which sponsored Daniel Burnham's precedent-setting Chicago Plan. After arriving in New York in 1916, Norton quickly realized that metropolitan New York faced an even tougher set of planning challenges, given its rapid growth and expansion into three states.

Norton brought together a distinguished group of civic and business leaders to form the Committee on the Regional Plan. He convinced the Russell Sage Foundation to underwrite the preparation and publication of the *Regional Plan for New York and Its Environs,* the nation's first comprehensive, long-range metropolitan plan.[1] It was completed in 1929, and RPA was incorporated that same year as an independent not-for-profit organization to promote its implementation. Almost seventy years later, Norton's son, Charles McKim Norton, who served as RPA's president from 1940 until 1968, stated that he never envisioned RPA as a permanent group. "I never thought it would last," he said, thinking that at some point a public agency would step forward to take its responsibilities. This never happened, however, and sixty years after its incorporation, the association remains hard at work promoting implementation of its Third Regional Plan.

RPA is an independent, tax-exempt membership organization. Its 1,200 members range from concerned citizens to municipalities to small and large businesses. In recent years, contributions from its members have provided about half of the association's operating budget, with most of these funds coming from about one hundred major employers. (The other half of the association's funds comes from foundations and government grants and contracts.) More than half of RPA's sixty board members are business leaders. Other members include university presidents, civic leaders, and former mayors and governors. State committees in all three states consist of business, civic, and environmental leaders who provide policy guidance to the association on RPA projects and policies affecting each state.

Lacking any official responsibilities or legal powers, RPA has never had the ability to compel action on its recommendations. However, due to the clout of its powerful and well-connected board of directors, the credibility of its research, and the persistence of its staff, many, if not most, of its recommendations have been implemented over the years. It is difficult to measure precisely the association's power, since much of its advocacy is conducted behind the scenes through private discussions with opinion leaders and decision-makers.

Much of RPA's effectiveness results from its efforts to shape public opinion over time, to create a political environment in which difficult decisions or controversial investments can be made. Also, since much of RPA's advocacy occurs through coalitions of civic groups, separating the efficacy of the association's work from that of its coalition partners is sometimes difficult.

Coalition building has been the key to RPA's successful advocacy in recent years. In virtually all of its major advocacy efforts since 1968, the association has worked with coalitions of other like-minded civic, business, environmental, community, or other advocacy groups, drawing on the region's extensive network of not-for-profit civic organizations. Collectively, these groups have enormous power. In some cases RPA convenes and leads these groups; in others it provides limited staff support or performs a more narrowly defined task, such as media relations.

Patience and perseverance are the hallmarks of RPA's work and the keys to its success. In large metropolitan areas, public issues can take years and occasionally even decades to "ripen." A recent example is the 17,000-acre Sterling Forest, an exceptional natural area straddling the New York–New Jersey border only forty miles northwest of Manhattan; it was acquired for conservation purposes more than sixty-five years after RPA's First Regional Plan recommended its protection. In the intervening years, there was always someone on the association's staff responsible for promoting its protection and opposing any inappropriate development.

The acquisition finally proceeded when, at the urging of a broad coalition of civic and environmental groups (including RPA), New Jer-

sey governor Christine Todd Whitman committed her state's tax dollars to the acquisition of Sterling Forest lands in adjoining areas of
New York State. Whitman's commitment leveraged matching contributions from New York State, the federal government, and private
philanthropies. It should be noted that Whitman is a long-time member of the association and daughter of a prominent RPA board member and benefactor. In her address to RPA's 1998 annual regional
assembly, Whitman noted, "The preservation of Sterling Forest was
certainly also a great moment for New Jersey. I want to applaud RPA's
advocacy for this historic and critical purchase."

The 1929 Regional Plan

RPA's 1929 plan envisioned a New York that would be the hub of
national and global markets, a center of culture and civic beauty that
would provide all of its residents with the opportunity to live "the
good life." The plan suggested an extensive program of infrastructure
investments to enable the region to achieve this goal. It proposed construction of vast new regional networks of commuter railroads, parks
and parkways, bridges and tunnels, and other facilities to accommodate the projected more than doubling of the region's population to
20 million by the plan's 1965 target year.

Although not anticipated by the plan, the arrival of the Great
Depression and the New Deal actually expedited its implementation.
When Roosevelt's vast public works employment programs were
begun in 1933, New York was the only region in the country with a
detailed public works master plan and complete preliminary engineering for major projects. Also, RPA retained a direct connection
with the Roosevelt administration through its president, Frederick
Delano, Roosevelt's uncle. Master builders Robert Moses (creator of
the Triborough Bridge and Tunnel Authority and New York State's
park commissions) and Austin Tobin (head of the Port Authority)
expedited construction of most of the Regional Plan's highway, park,
and other investment projects during the 1930s and 1940s. As a result
of these projects, the region contained more than 60 percent of the
nation's limited-access highway lane miles as late as 1965.

A major exception to this successful record, however, was the failure of RPA's ambitious proposals to expand and integrate the subway
and commuter rail systems. This initiative was adamantly opposed by

executives of the private commuter rail companies and by New York City mayor Fiorello LaGuardia, who feared the loss of autonomy such a plan would entail. Ironically, by 1965 (the Regional Plan's target year) both the subways and commuter rail systems were on the verge of bankruptcy due to the loss of markets that would have been served by RPA's proposal and to the success of RPA's highway plan, which was largely implemented. With good highways and poor transit alternatives, most of the region's growth in the postwar era occurred in suburbs well served by the new highways and poorly served by rail.

The relationship between Robert Moses and the association was complex and changeable over the years. Moses used the Regional Plan to shape and build public support for his park, bridge, and highway proposals, and RPA became a vocal advocate for many of these projects. By the late 1930s, however, the association began to oppose several of Moses's highway and bridge projects that it felt were detrimental to the interests of inner-city communities, the environment, or the larger public interest. As a result of RPA's opposition, Moses suffered his first major defeat in 1940, when he lost federal funding for his Brooklyn Battery Bridge. Moses never again had a good word to say for the association and its policies.

Partly as a result of the vast new highway, bridge, and tunnel systems; extensive large-lot suburban zoning; and federal tax- and housing-incentive programs, the region's suburbs burgeoned during the early post–World War II period. The plan's advocacy for planned suburban centers was largely ignored as Levittown and its counterparts literally invented the American suburb. The suburban malls and office parks of the 1960s and 1970s succeeded the housing tracts of the 1940s and 1950s. As early as the 1950s, public officials, civic leaders, and scholars raised concerns about the changing shape of the region and the growing divisions between city and suburb.

The Second Regional Plan

In 1968 the Second Regional Plan was initiated to shape these trends.[2] Its research base included an in-depth study of the region's increasingly decentralized governance system, summarized in Robert Wood's 1959 landmark book *1400 Governments*.[3] Wood quantified the increased cost and complexity of this system, but he did not prescribe any solutions, and further fragmentation of local government went on largely unaffected by this research.

The association's Second Plan proposed strategies to control suburban sprawl, expand the regional open space system, and rebuild the regional rail network. The plan also supported the creation of new transportation agencies, including the previously mentioned MTA, Metro-North Commuter Railroad, and New Jersey Transit.

A major feature of the second plan was its proposal to create a network of "metropolitan centers" as a means of reining in low-density, "spread city" development that was then rapidly changing the face of the region. The plan proposed that these transit-oriented satellite employment centers be organized around a revitalized regional rail system that could capture development that would otherwise end up on "greenfield" sites in the suburbs.

Today, as a result of decades of advocacy and investment, more than a million jobs (approximately 10 percent of the region's total employment base) and most of the region's new cultural and educational institutions are located in these centers. Approximately half of the region's employment base remains in New York City and the metropolitan centers, a far higher proportion than virtually any other large U.S. metropolitan region. Despite these efforts, suburban sprawl has continued in the region throughout the 1990s: RPA estimated in 1996 that over the previous quarter-century, although the region had grown in population by only 13 percent, urbanized land had increased by more than 60 percent.

Although the Second Regional Plan did not recommend the creation of a regional government to carry out its development strategies, it did propose that counties or new regional planning agencies implement the plan through fair-share allocations of affordable housing and other facilities. It also proposed tax reforms that would remove the incentives for fiscal zoning. These steps were not adopted, however, until the New Jersey Supreme Court, in its landmark Mt. Laurel I and II decisions (in 1975 and 1983, respectively), required that fair-share housing programs be prepared as called for in the second plan.[4] These decisions led to the adoption of New Jersey's State Development and Redevelopment Plan in 1992 (discussed later). It is unclear to what extent RPA's advocacy for fair-share housing influenced or encouraged the New Jersey Supreme Court in its Mt. Laurel decisions, although the association did raise this issue to a place of prominence in public discussions and gave it legitimacy during the late 1960s and 1970s.

The Heyday of Regional Planning

From 1956 to 1981, the region experimented with several public regional planning bodies, some of which continue to operate, but two of which failed due to absence of public support. These were the Metropolitan Regional Council and the Tri-State Regional Planning Commission, initiated by activist elected leaders; New York City mayor Robert Wagner and New York governor Nelson Rockefeller. The two agencies that survived were both regional land-use regulatory commissions: the Hackensack Meadowlands Development Commission and the New Jersey Pinelands Commission.

Metropolitan Regional Council

In 1956 New York City mayor Robert Wagner invited city and county officials from the metropolitan region to join him in creating the Metropolitan Regional Council (MRC). This ad hoc association of chief elected municipal officials was established in response to growing concerns about suburban sprawl and the need to rescue a failing regional transit system. Wagner hoped that the MRC would promote cooperation on these and other regional issues.

When New York City later urged that the MRC gain legal status, most suburban counties and communities declined to support the proposal, and several withdrew from the group. The MRC never gained broad political support and expired in 1979, when public funding for its activities was withdrawn.

New York City mayor Rudolph Giuliani briefly revived a successor group (also called the Metropolitan Regional Council) in 1994 as a political alliance of the city and suburban counties to promote reform of New York State's social service finance system. Soon after these reforms were realized, this group disbanded. The MRC experience underscores the limitations of voluntary associations of city and suburban governments with fundamentally different interests, led by politicians who come and go every four years.

Tri-State Regional Planning Commission

The Tri-State Regional Planning Commission was established in 1961, and its responsibilities dramatically expanded in 1971 to coordinate planning and public investment strategies, principally in the transportation area. The impetus for its creation was pressure from the federal government to better coordinate plans between the states, but the commission never gained broad local or state support for its activities. State transportation officials, who set the agency's policy agenda, dominated the commission's board. In 1981, when federal support was withdrawn for metropolitan planning, the Tri-State Commission had virtually no public backing, and first Connecticut, then New Jersey withdrew from it. Its responsibilities were transferred to several metropolitan planning organizations (MPOs), each with jurisdiction in only a limited part of the region.

Metropolitan Planning Organizations

Every large U.S. metropolitan region now has an MPO with responsibility for transportation planning, as mandated by successive federal transportation grant programs. In the New York region, as in many others, the MPOs are financed and controlled by the state transportation departments, which dominate their agendas. In Connecticut, regional planning agencies were established to represent regional interests when county governments were abolished in the 1950s. These organizations serve as MPOs, governed by boards of directors dominated by their municipal participants but funded largely by grants from the Connecticut Department of Transportation. In most cases these groups mediate between conflicting municipal objectives, often to the disadvantage of the larger regional interest.

In its transportation planning, RPA takes a more comprehensive and activist role than the MPOs normally do. RPA's plans cut across MPO boundaries and look at the whole region's transportation system rather than the restricted political jurisdictions that the MPOs represent. (This limitation is now being addressed by the region's MPOs, which recently began coordinating their transportation plans.) Furthermore, RPA is unconstrained by current federal policies that limit MPO plans to current revenue streams. The association also provides public advocacy on transportation issues, unrestrained by short-term political considerations that limit the activities of MPOs in New York and elsewhere.

Land-Use Regulatory Commissions

The Second Regional Plan's ambitious open space program, the "Race for Open Space," helped raise public awareness of the threats to the region's natural areas and open spaces and built political support for their preservation. As a result of RPA's advocacy, several large new parks and reservations were established, including the Fire Island National Seashore, the Upper Delaware National Recreation Area, and the nation's first urban national park, Gateway National Recreation Area. At the same time, new regional land-use regulatory commissions were created for key resource areas in New Jersey: the Jersey Pinelands and the Hackensack Meadowlands. Both entities were established to manage growth in important natural areas adjoining the region's urban centers. (In addition, all three states administer coastal zone management programs and river corridor protection systems.)

The Hackensack Meadowlands Development Commission (originally proposed in RPA's 1929 plan) was established in 1969 to manage growth in a thirty-one-square-mile area of marshland, landfills, and uplands adjoining the Hackensack River in Hudson and Bergen Counties just west of New York City. The commission administers land-use plans and regulations in this centrally located area, which now contains major retail, commercial, and recreational facilities, including Giants Stadium and the Continental Arena. A major feature of the commission is its tax-base sharing system, which distributes tax receipts among fourteen participating municipalities. (This is the only such district of its kind in the New York region and one of only a handful in the country.)

In 1980 the New Jersey Pinelands Commission was established to regulate development in this vast natural area at the metropolitan area's southern edge. The political impetus for the commission's creation came from a severe drought in the early 1960s that left the northern urbanized portion of the state seriously short of drinking water. The Pinelands contained a vast reserve of pristine groundwater that could be used as a backup water supply for the state's growing northern and central areas. The area also had unique natural, scenic, agricultural, and historic resources that were threatened by an expanding Philadelphia metropolitan area and resort and second-home development.

Governor Brendan Byrne and a state legislature dominated by metropolitan interests forced the commission on local communities, despite their strenuous opposition. The commission adopted a stringent plan for growth management in the Pinelands and imposed it on the municipalities of the region. Virtually all new development and subdivision activity now requires permits from the Pinelands commission, which continues to be dominated by the governor's appointees.

The Third Regional Plan

In the late 1980s and early 1990s, a series of threats to the region's economic prospects, environment, and social order led civic, business, and community leaders to the conclusion that the region's quality of life and well-being were at risk. After the 1987 stock market crash, the economy of the New York region suffered its worst economic slow-down since the Great Depression, ultimately losing almost 10 percent of its employment base by 1993. Even the region's mainstay industries—financial and business services, media, and advanced technology clusters—lost national market share, convincing business and civic leaders that the region's economic health was at risk. Meanwhile, the region was attracting an influx of immigrants, most of them people of color from third world countries, causing concern about further racial and social polarization in the region. Finally, a series of environmental controversies emerged during this period over the impacts of sprawl on public watersheds, estuaries, and forests. As a result of these issues, RPA's board decided in 1989 to prepare its Third Regional Plan, *A Region at Risk*, which was completed in 1996.[5] The plan called for a twenty-five-year, $75 billion program to invest in infrastructure, the environment, education, and cities as a prerequisite for the region's continued competitiveness and quality of life. Key policy and investment recommendations included

— expansion of the regional rail network and integration of several subway and commuter rail lines into a regional express ("Rx") system to accommodate forecasted increases in travel demand in a region with little unused highway or transit capacity;

— creation of a vast new metropolitan "greensward" of protected natural resource systems that could preserve water supplies, ecological resources, and recreational opportunities while serving as a "green edge to growth" (in effect a regional growth boundary);

— economic development focused on New York City and an expanded network of "regional downtowns," including the former metropolitan centers designated in the Second Plan as well as new suburban centers.

The plan attempted to demonstrate these new approaches either by documenting their success in other world centers or through pilot projects. RPA has found that the successful application of a new policy or technique in one state can often be replicated in another.

A Region at Risk also proposed several improvements to the regional governance system.[6]

Reform of Existing Authorities

The plan proposed that existing authorities, in particular the Port Authority and MTA, be reformed and refocused. For example, it urged that the Port Authority refocus its attention and investments on building and managing world-class airports and seaports and a proposed new trans-Hudson freight tunnel. This recommendation has been largely implemented, primarily as a result of New York governor George Pataki's strong advocacy. The Port Authority is now pursuing the sale of the World Trade Center and disposal of industrial parks, urban renewal projects, and a number of other extraneous programs.

The Third Plan also recommended that if existing institutions were unwilling or unable to finance or build a regional express and other infrastructure systems (and the jury is still out), two new institutions should be established to complete them. A new "regional transportation authority" would be established to coordinate development and manage the tri-state rail, bridge, and tunnel system. This system and other infrastructure improvements would be financed by a proposed new "tri-state infrastructure bank," which would use the proceeds from dedicated transportation taxes, fares, and tolls to finance these systems. No action has been taken on these recommendations to date; however, the debate now beginning over the MTA's 2000–2005 capital program, the failure of Governor Whitman's proposed transportation program, and Connecticut's gas-tax reductions and disinvestment in its transportation systems may stimulate action.

State Planning and Smart Growth

The Third Regional Plan strongly supported implementation of New Jersey's incentive-based State Development and Redevelopment Plan, adopted in 1992 after an intensive process of "cross-acceptance" between state, county, and municipal governments. Unfortunately, the lengthy period required for its adoption meant that the plan was not executed by the same state officials who created it. Furthermore, a deep recession severely limited the state's discretionary spending. Without funding, it became an incentive-based plan that could provide few incentives for its implementation by municipalities. For example, Maryland's incentive-based smart-growth program makes an approved municipal plan a prerequisite for state school or transportation funds; under its state planning program, New Jersey offers only a vague promise of increased eligibility for these funds for communities with designated centers.

In 1998, at the urging of RPA and other civic groups, Governor Christine Todd Whitman strongly endorsed strengthening the 1992 state plan and increasing the incentives required to promote its implementation. Whitman also proposed other measures called for in the Third Plan to reclaim urban brownfields, improve transit, and preserve open space.

In New York State in the early 1990s, RPA promoted the establishment of a state growth management system. However, lack of political interest, coupled with the state's deep recession at the time, prevented action on this proposal. Recently, the New York State Council of Mayors endorsed legislation to create a "smart growth" or incentive-based state planning system. Although the resulting smart-growth legislation failed in the 1999 legislative session, Governor Pataki is expected to issue an executive order requiring that state agency actions be guided by smart-growth principles. In addition, discussions have begun in Long Island on the need for a regional growth management system there. These related movements could lead to some kind of improved state or regional planning system for New York.

In Connecticut a civic coalition convened by RPA in the early 1990s advocated improvements to put teeth into the state's advisory Conservation and Development Plan. Only a small portion of this agenda was put into effect, including new requirements that municipalities update their master plans every ten years and that state agency investments and permits be consistent with the plan.

Compact-Based Land-Use Commissions

RPA's Third Plan called for the creation of a vast, new greensward of protected natural systems encompassing the region's green infrastructure of estuaries, mountains, rivers, forests, and public water supplies, creating a permanent green edge to growth in the region. By the early

1990s, however, it was clear that the region's current elected leadership would not support "top-down" regional land-use regulatory systems such as those developed for the Adirondacks or the Jersey Pinelands in the 1970s and 1980s. Instead, a new "bottom-up" or compact-based planning model emerged in the region, first in the Hudson River Greenway and later in Long Island's Central Pine Barrens and New York City's vast upstate watershed system. These systems built on the experience in Cape Cod and other regions, where new bottom-up land-use regulatory systems were developed in the late 1980s and early 1990s.

The Long Island Central Pine Barrens Commission was established in 1993 to manage growth in 100,000 acres of Suffolk County in eastern Long Island. This area has the island's largest reserve of pure groundwater available as a drinking water supply; it also contains the state's largest concentration of rare species and plant communities. The commission was created through a bottom-up process of planning and advocacy by dozens of environmental, business, and civic groups, including RPA, after years of litigation by environmental groups over proposed development. Four of the five commission members are chief elected officials of the participating towns and Suffolk County. The commission's regulations went into effect only when all three affected municipalities adopted implementing laws called for in the Comprehensive Management Plan for the region. The management plan provides provisions for improved land-use regulation, land acquisition, and transfers of development rights required to preserve this important natural resource system.

A less structured system was established in 1996 to manage growth and preserve water quality in the one-million-acre New York City watershed, which provides drinking water to 9 million city and suburban customers. In return for city financing of local economic development and infrastructure, watershed communities have agreed to new land-use regulations and conservation land acquisition administered and financed by the city to protect water quality. As a result, the U.S. Environmental Protection Agency has waived the Safe Drinking Water Act requirement that the city filter its water supply; this has allowed the city to avoid investing an estimated $6 billion in a filtration plant.

Education Finance Reform

The Third Regional Plan proposed that the states assume the cost of public primary and secondary education, both to address inequities between urban and suburban schools and to reduce incentives for "fiscal zoning"—zoning regulations primarily designed to increase tax revenue by attracting new tax development. Since education expenses represent more than two-thirds of most municipal budgets, shifting education finance to broad-based, state-collected taxes achieves most of the objectives that might otherwise be achieved through regional tax-base sharing.

When the Third Regional Plan was released in 1996, New Jersey and New York faced legal challenges to their education finance systems, with plaintiffs arguing that these systems relied on inequitable real estate property taxes favoring well-to-do suburban schools over center-city schools. In Connecticut's *Sheff* v. *O'Neill* lawsuit, plaintiffs representing inner-city parents argued successfully that the state's balkanized school districts resulted in racial segregation of urban schools, in violation of the state constitution.[7] However, they did not claim that the state's education finance system—in which the state pays for most urban education expenses—violated the constitution.

In the spring of 1998, the New Jersey Supreme Court found in favor of Governor Whitman's school finance reform plan, whereby the state provides additional funds to urban schools and sets new statewide standards for educational achievement. No action has been taken in New York or Connecticut to reform their school finances, although Connecticut's limited response to the *Sheff* decision may still lead to further litigation over this issue.

Restructuring Municipal Government

By the early 1990s, the regional governance system had grown in size and complexity from the 1,400 governments described in Robert Wood's 1959 study to 2,000 governmental units, including more than 800 general-purpose municipal governments.[8] This growth was due to both the region's expansion from twenty-two to thirty-one counties and the proliferation of special-service districts and general-purpose municipal governments.

New York State, in particular, has seen a proliferation of very small incorporated villages, established in many cases to control growth and exclude low- or moderate-income housing through new village zoning ordinances. Extreme examples of this phenomenon are the incorporated resort villages of Dering Harbor and Westhampton Dunes, both located on islands off eastern Long Island. The towns are unique in that they have no year-round residents. Dering Harbor does, however, have an employee whose job it is to raise and lower the village's flag. And Wodmington Phipps, which was incorporated to promote new public shore erosion control projects required to protect its million-dollar-plus vacation homes, may have no permanent residents, but it does have lawyers and lobbyists.

RPA went into the planning process determined to find ways to limit the growth in local government and even to eliminate or consolidate some of the existing 800 municipalities. It soon became clear that this would be difficult or impossible to achieve. As a part of the process, RPA participated in several county planning projects where this issue was raised, but then dropped. In suburban Westchester County, RPA staffed a task force that investigated local government, school finance, and administrative reform, in partnership with an accounting firm that quantified with great authority the costs of the county's extremely decentralized system of schools and municipal government.

With a million residents, Westchester has dozens of school districts and incorporated villages, towns and cities, many of them with overlapping or inefficiently delivered services. The county's resulting high property taxes are a major concern to residents, particularly in those communities with the smallest school populations. But public forums on the issue and RPA's own public opinion surveys determined that suburban residents would fight attempts to consolidate or eliminate school districts or general-purpose local governments.

Most suburbanites, it turns out, were quite satisfied with the quality of schools and other services being delivered by their towns and villages; in most cases they moved to these places to gain access to these very services. Moreover, they viewed the accountability of local officials to their needs as a fundamental and inviolable right. Consequently, citizens made it clear that they would strenuously oppose any proposals to eliminate or reduce the autonomy or accountability of their own municipality or school system.

For this reason RPA did not propose the abolition or consolidation of general-purpose municipal governments. Instead, the Third Regional Plan proposed that the states provide new incentives for service sharing among political jurisdictions, particularly for less politically volatile services such as fire protection, composting, wastewater treatment, recycling, and solid waste disposal. Indeed, there have been a number of successful examples of service sharing in West-chester and other suburban counties in all of these functional areas.

Although the plan also supports consolidation of school districts and other more politically sensitive services, there have been few successful examples of service sharing involving communities of widely divergent ethnic, social, or economic characteristics. In September 1998 New Jersey governor Christine Whitman endorsed proposals by a special state commission to consolidate administrative, transportation, and other services among school districts. Even this modest proposal will undoubtedly face strenuous opposition from suburban town and school officials and their legislative representatives.

The Third Regional Plan did promote private initiatives to provide affordable housing, based on the successful experience of Fairfield 2000 Homes, an outgrowth of RPA's Fairfield 2000 plan in Connecticut.[9]

Reactions and Early Results

A number of critics have questioned the validity of a comprehensive plan today, in an era when the region's political leaders seem less interested than ever in taking a regional perspective. Others have questioned whether an elite organization like RPA and its relatively unrepresentative group of business and civic leaders have the right to propose policies for an increasingly diverse region.

Despite these reservations, the plan has produced important results, particularly as a catalyst for investments in transit infrastructure and open space protection and for creative thinking about the shape and function of urban and suburban centers. Several major cities and edge cities are now basing new master plans on its recommendations. In much of the region, transportation policies and investments are being guided by its principles.

In several cases new civic coalitions have formed to advocate implementation of the plan's major investment and policy recommendations. These include

— the Coastal Corridor Coalition: This group of eleven business, civic, and environmental groups, including RPA, has developed a strategy for managing transportation demands in Connecticut's I-95 corridor from New Haven to Greenwich. Governor Rowland and the state's department of transportation have adopted the coalition's major recommendations, including its goal of attaining a 5 percent reduction in peak-period traffic volumes by 2005.

the East End Initiative: This group of environmental organizations has successfully promoted creation of land banks in all five of Long Island's East End towns. It now is working on other proposals to preserve open space, agriculture, and rural character in this threatened resort area.

— the Empire State Transportation Alliance: This new coalition of business, labor, environmental, and civic groups is promoting long-term investment in New York State's transportation systems, with a special focus on financing the Third Regional Plan's transit recommendations.

The *New York Times,* other newspapers (including those serving the region's minorities, such as the *Amsterdam News*), and other media have editorialized in favor of the plan and its recommendations. In addition, all three governors have at least generally endorsed the plan's goals. New Jersey governor Christine Todd Whitman has strongly embraced the plan and incorporated its investment and policy recommendations into her second-term priorities—including proposals to strengthen the state's 1992 Development and Redevelopment Plan, preserve 1 million acres of open space, and reinvest in cities. Connecticut governor John Rowland has endorsed a new $100 million open space program called for in the plan and adopted the plan's transportation strategies as discussed above. Governor Pataki of New York has moved aggressively on the plan's open space recommendations and committed funds to build the first phase of the plan's transit development program.

Lessons Learned

The experience of the New York region over the past century, and particularly over the past decade, suggests several principles that should guide governance reform in large metropolitan areas.

Limits to Comprehensive Solutions

Reformers should not waste a lot of time or political capital on comprehensive governance solutions that look attractive on paper ("let's create a regional government") but are politically unattainable in very large multicounty or multistate regions. There may be some places where these reforms can succeed, in particular where there is bold political leadership from governors, mayors, or top business leaders. Comprehensive solutions are especially likely to succeed in smaller regions with very small minority populations, successful center cities, and long traditions of progressive civic and political leadership. Outside of these places, as Mario Cuomo used to say, "Fogetaboutit."

Metropolitan Governments, City-County Consolidation, and Annexation

Efforts to create metropolitan governments or city-county consolidations will be unrealizable in most large multicounty and multistate regions. The political obstacles to city-county consolidations were demonstrated recently in Miami, where city voters, mostly Latinos and African Americans, defeated a referendum on city-county consolidation because they feared domination by mostly white suburbs.

While annexations will continue in parts of the South and Southwest, this procedure will not be reintroduced in the other parts of the country because of the extensive incorporation of suburban areas.

Incremental Solutions

Reformers should focus on more modest initiatives that can succeed: creation of regional service districts, cost- and tax-sharing among municipalities and school districts, and area-wide land-use regulatory systems. Efforts to improve regional transit, park systems, water quality, or cultural institutions can produce tangible results and build support for broader regional initiatives. Reformers should bear in mind, however, that virtually no place has succeeded in creating regional authorities or districts that provide sensitive, "close-to-home" social services such as schools or affordable housing.

Tax-Base Sharing

Metropolitan or multijurisdictional tax sharing has succeeded in only a handful of places, notably Minneapolis–St. Paul and in New Jersey's Hackensack Meadowlands. Myron Orfield's experience in the Twin Cities and other places provides hope that coalitions of center cities and inner-ring suburbs can move such initiatives through reluctant state legislatures.[10] Similar coalitions are forming in metropolitan

Chicago and Cleveland.[11] But the political obstacles to regional tax-base sharing will remain formidable.

On the other hand, recent experiences in Michigan, Washington, Texas, Illinois, and Vermont demonstrate that state initiatives to reform school finances can succeed, achieving many of the same goals advanced for metropolitan tax-base sharing.[12] Most of these reform efforts have shifted school finances—the largest share of municipal budgets—from local property taxes to broad-based state taxes.

Consolidation of Multiple Communities

Consolidation of general-purpose municipal governments or school districts will be extremely difficult to achieve. Instead, the focus of reform efforts should be on service sharing between communities or school districts. Municipalities will join regional service districts if it is in their own interests, particularly if the services are not politically sensitive and if their neighbors share similar demographic and economic characteristics. They may, for example, share purchasing or fire-fighting equipment, but they will not share classrooms unless the communities are similar in ethnicity and income. States can and should provide incentives for service sharing, as Governor Whitman has recently proposed.

Living with Multiple States or Counties

Although having multiple states or counties within a single metropolitan area makes governance more difficult, it also creates opportunities for experimentation. In New York the bad news is that the metropolitan region consists of three states; but the good news also is that the region consists of three states. Each state functions as a laboratory for governance innovations of all kinds. New Jersey's brownfield reclamation program, for example, is a model for the other two states. New York's regional school districts and cooperative education system are a model for the others, and so on. Having a model in one state often makes replication possible in the others.

Public Authorities

Creation of regional service districts and authorities may be appropriate for some multijurisdictional metropolitan areas. In some places this is already occurring: Portland Metro emerged from the amalgamation of several single-purpose service districts. It does not always work this way, however. Boston's Metropolitan District Commission, an early twentieth-century amalgamation of regional park, sewer, and water districts, failed to sustain broad public support, and through the 1970s and 1980s, it was stripped of its independence and most of its authority.

Most metropolitan areas already have limited regional service districts—airport, seaport, highway, water, sewer, or solid waste districts—that could be expanded or redirected to better serve the needs of growing regions. In most cases these do not, however, span state borders. Even in metropolitan Portland, for example, separate port authorities compete with each other on opposite sides of the Columbia River. (A dialogue is now underway, however, that could improve coordination of their activities.) The experience of Chicago's regional toll road authority illustrates two of the shortcomings of many regional authorities: (1) it operates only in the Illinois portion of the metropolitan area, even though it serves commuters traveling to and from suburban areas in Indiana and Wisconsin; and (2) its ambitious highway-building program and the sprawl it generates run counter to the interests of transit and environmental advocates (and its decisions are not subject to direct political control by the voters).

Public Sector versus Civic Leadership

Through much of this century, powerful governors, mayors, and aggressive authority executives provided bold public sector leadership on metropolitan governance, infrastructure, and land-use issues. In taking courageous action on unpopular issues, governors such as Al Smith and Nelson Rockefeller, mayors such as Fiorello LaGuardia and Robert Wagner, and bureaucrats such as Robert Moses and Austin Tobin represented true "profiles in courage." Their actions frequently put them far out in front of public opinion, and when required they took controversial and unpopular actions that they felt were in the public interest. In this context, the role of civic groups was to provide legitimacy for bold public action and not infrequently, to attempt to rein in overreaching public officials. But rarely did civic leaders have to instigate public action.

Since the 1980s, in New York and across the country a different model of public leadership has emerged in which many elected and

appointed leaders take initiative only when it is politically safe to do
so. (It should be noted that the voters who elect these leaders are
apparently comfortable with this new mode of leadership or "follower-
ship.") The civic sector has filled the resulting leadership vacuum and
now serves as instigator and advocate for public action. Individual
civic leaders or coalitions of civic groups have been essential catalysts
for virtually all of the New York region's major governance initiatives
in recent years. In this context, one of New York's special advantages is
its "civic infrastructure": literally thousands of community, environmental, business, and other advocacy groups. Their job is to exhort
politicians and bureaucrats on to action, although not infrequently
they must also work to rein in overly ambitious public officials.

A valid criticism of the region's civic leadership is that in many
cases it represents elite groups and interests such as corporations. The
Regional Plan Association is now trying to include grassroots community and environmental groups in civic coalitions, both to broaden
their representation and to increase their political clout.

A growing number of other regions have groups similar to RPA.
Notable among these are Chicago's Metropolitan Planning Council
and a new group being established to promote implementation of the
Commercial Club's new regional plan for Chicago. The council's
membership, funding base, and outlook are similar to RPA's: its board
represents a cross-section of city and suburban business, civic, and academic leaders, and a majority of its budget comes from its members,
both corporate and noncorporate.

Eco-City Cleveland has become an effective voice for a metropolitan outlook in greater Cleveland and has helped convene a new
statewide coalition of older suburbs to promote a smart-growth plan
for Ohio. San Francisco's Greenbelt Alliance has moved beyond advocacy for open space acquisition to successful promotion of urban
growth boundaries and other growth management techniques.
Finally, the dozens of smart-growth advocacy groups now emerging
across the country have the potential to mature into permanent voices
for more effective metropolitan planning and governance.

Across the country a score of "thousand friends" groups have
been established at the state level to push for improved land-use, environmental, and transportation policies. The first of these, 1,000
Friends of Oregon, was established in 1975 by Governor Tom McCall
and Henry Richmond, then the director of Oregon's Public Interest
Research Group. The intent was to ensure a strong civic voice in the

implementation of Oregon's visionary growth management act.[13] In Oregon and elsewhere, these groups have played a critical role in providing a strong base of public support for adoption and implementation of similar programs.

The Role of Regional Plans

Every large metropolitan region in the country has a metropolitan planning organization, usually established to fulfill federal transportation-planning requirements. Most MPOs are creatures of state transportation departments, which provide the vast majority of their funds and control appointments to their boards and technical advisory committees. Others answer to municipal governments, which control their boards of directors. In both cases, these groups are reluctant to propose radical actions or investments that might threaten the status quo of their powerful (and usually cautious) state or local leadership.

In a handful of places such as Portland, MPOs are more progressive and representative of regional interests; these have adopted bold plans that represent the interests of the metropolitan region. More typical is New York's experience with its Tri-State Regional Planning Commission: this group rarely went beyond advocacy for the projects proposed by its member agencies. In fact, the commission's espousal of fair-share housing for the region helped lead to its demise when Connecticut dropped out, in part due to this contentious issue.

In large regions like New York that lack metropolitan government or public regional plans, civic planning groups such as RPA can provide long-range plans that catalyze and guide public action and investment. As noted earlier, several other regions now have civic groups that are developing similar plans.

The Three Ts: Things Take Time

In very large and complex metropolitan regions, bold enterprises, including construction of major infrastructure systems or creation of new institutions, can take decades to plan or execute. In New York some proposals of RPA's first and second regional plans, such as the protection of Sterling Forest, took several decades to implement. Luckily, the region and its economic and environmental systems are remarkably resilient and can tolerate these delays. Civic leaders must be in it for the long haul and must create civic groups with the staying power to act when political opportunities present themselves.

The Three Ps: Persistence, Patience, and Perseverance

This principle relates to the one just described: successful civic leaders must persist, sometimes over very long periods of time. They must wait patiently until the opportunities—the right combination of threat, leadership, funding, and vision—come along or can be created. And they must persevere despite occasional setbacks.

Conclusion

As noted at the beginning of this chapter, the New York metropolitan region has never had, and probably never will have, a neat, tidy organization chart or a highly structured, coherent system of regional and local governance. In this respect it is similar to other great world centers, including London and Tokyo, and to the largest U.S. metropolitan regions, including Los Angeles, San Francisco, Chicago, Washington, Boston, or Atlanta. None of these places have metropolitan governments that encompass their entire regions, although some, including Boston and Atlanta, do have effective regional planning agencies.

The New York region's continued deep political and social divisions and strong tradition of local home rule will likely prevent the creation of a general-purpose regional government or the consolidation of the region's decentralized municipal governments in the foreseeable future. Regional tax-base sharing almost certainly will not occur in the near term. And the area's growing racial and ethnic diversity will continue to impede regional solutions to pressing social needs such as school integration or construction of significant amounts of affordable housing in the suburbs. Similar circumstances are also present in virtually every other large U.S. metropolitan region.

But on a number of occasions in this century, and particularly over the past decade, the New York region has had effective regional leadership when major opportunities or threats to its well-being have arisen. Several times in this century, strong, visionary leaders have emerged to create new authorities or other institutions or to make major investments needed to safeguard the region's interest. In every generation public entrepreneurs like Robert Moses or governors like

Nelson Rockefeller have come forward to provide this leadership and have gained regional support for bold public action. In each case the region's civic leaders also have come forward to support and sustain these efforts (and as in the case of Moses, have subsequently worked to slow or reverse excesses).

Thus despite the New York region's lack of an efficient, well-coordinated regional governance system, it continues to be a very successful and livable place. It remains the center of U.S. and world business, finance, culture, and communications and has an economy of nearly three-quarters of a trillion dollars, making it perhaps the wealthiest metropolitan region in the world. Its public transportation system carries a growing share (more than a third) of total U.S. transit ridership, and it retains a wide diversity of communities, many with the highest property values and incomes in the country.

Much remains to be done to improve economic prospects and living conditions for the region's growing minority and immigrant populations, to increase the skills of its work force, to manage sprawl at its edges, and to create new capacity for growth in its communities and infrastructure. These are the goals of the Regional Plan Association's Third Regional Plan. The region's future vitality and livability will depend on its success in dealing with these concerns.

From this experience it is possible to conclude that it is not necessary to have a regional government or a well-ordered organization chart for very large, multijurisdictional, and multistate metropolitan regions. Furthermore, incrementalism may be the only way to proceed in these places. Finally, while bold *political* leadership is essential, of equal importance to the success of these places is patient, persistent, and effective *civic* leadership.

Notes

1. Committee on the Regional Plan for New York and Its Environs, *Regional Plan for New York and Its Environs* (New York, 1929).

2. Regional Plan Association, *The Second Regional Plan* (New York, 1968).

3. Robert Wood, *1400 Governments: The Political Economy of the New York Metropolitan Region* (Harvard University Press, 1961).

4. Mt. Laurel I: *Southern Burlington N.A.A.C.P.* v. *Township of Mt. Laurel,* 67 N.J. 151, 336 A.2d 713 (1975); Mt. Laurel II: *Southern Burlington N.A.A.C.P.* v. *Township of Mt. Laurel,* 92 N.J. 158, 456 A.2d 390 (1983).

5. Robert D. Yaro and Tony Hiss, *A Region at Risk: The Third Regional Plan* (Washington, D.C.: Island Press, 1996).

6. Ibid.

7. *Sheff* v. *O'Neill*, 238 Conn. 1, 678 A.2d 1267 (1996).

8. Wood, *1400 Governments.*

9. Regional Plan Association, *Task Force on Housing, Final Report, Fairfield 2000* (Stamford, Conn.: 1987).

10. Myron Orfield, *Metropolitics: A Regional Agenda for Community and Stability* (Cambridge, Mass. and Washington, D.C.: Lincoln Institute of Land Policy and Brookings, 1997).

11. From author's interviews with Mary Sue Barrett, president, Metropolitan Planning Council and Judy Rawson, city councilor, Shaker Heights, Ohio.

12. Joan Scheuer, *Options in School Finance Reform in New York State* (New York: Education Priorities Panel, 1995).

13. Oregon, *Land Use Act* (1973).

CHAPTER THREE

Growth Management: The Core Regional Issue

DAVID RUSK

Urban sprawl is consuming land at almost three times the rate of population growth. On the threshold of the twenty-first century, the rate of outward expansion of low-density development is outstripping the ability of even the most annexation-minded central cities to keep pace. The leadership of almost all central cities (whether locked in like Cleveland or expansionist like Charlotte) faces a common challenge: defending their city's viability by controlling sprawl through regional growth management.

Regional growth management must also be a key target of the social justice movement in America. While barriers based purely on race are slowly coming down, barriers based on income are steadily rising in most metropolitan areas. Sprawling regional development patterns are closing off avenues of advancement for low-income minorities. Sprawl is leading to (1) greater dispersion of jobs, placing low-skilled jobs beyond the reach of many low-skilled potential workers; (2) growing fiscal disparities, which impair the quality of services in inner cities and older suburbs; and (3) greater concentrations of poverty, which have devastating impacts on the education of inner-city children.

Strong regional growth management practices, by themselves, will not be instant solutions for all these problems. Growth management is the essential framework within which access to low-skilled jobs can improve, fiscal equity can be achieved, and greater economic integration can be promoted. The political coalitions necessary to secure, through state legislatures, effective regional growth management will also be the source of support for other policies (such as regional tax-base sharing or fair-share affordable housing) that can achieve greater social equity.

Highways and Sprawl

Suburbanization has been a constant phenomenon in America, beginning with the first national census in 1790 that reported on the "suburbs" of Philadelphia.[1] America's urban experience has been a history of changes in transportation modes that constantly extended urban development outward from the core settlement. However, though suburbanization as we know it began in earnest with mass automobile ownership in the 1920s, it accelerated from the mid-1950s onward. Indeed, America's most influential urban planner may well have been President Dwight David Eisenhower.

In 1956 the Republican president convinced a Democratic Congress to launch the federal interstate highway system. In the midst of the cold war, the new law was styled the National Interstate and Defense Highway Act. In political myth, it was born out of young Major Eisenhower's experience in leading an army convoy coast to coast shortly after World War I—a journey of fifty-nine days!

From a vantage point four decades later, the interstate highway system has been militarily insignificant in our overcoming the Soviet Union. However, the interstate highway system has had a fateful impact on America's cities.

In order to build new interstate highways, federal highway appropriations were ratcheted up dramatically. In one decade, total federal highway outlays rose fivefold from $729 million (fiscal year 1956) to $4 billion (fiscal year 1966). By fiscal year 1996, the federal highway program had expended $652 billion (in 1996 dollars), compared to just $85 billion in federal mass transit aid (which was initiated in 1965).[2]

The great bulk of the 43,000-mile interstate system may be interurban—connecting different urban regions—but its primary impact has been *intra*urban—promoting low-density, sprawling development around core cities. With federal highway grants typically covering 90 percent of project cost, building sprawl-supporting highways was virtually cost-free for state governments. Other inducements to highway construction and sprawl were cheap gasoline (based on low federal and state taxes); easy, interest-deductible automobile loans; other federal infrastructure grants (such as $130 billion in wastewater treatment grants); and housing finance and tax systems that greatly favored homeowners over apartment dwellers.[3]

What picture emerges from calculating the growth of America's "urbanized areas" (as contrasted with the growth of county-defined metropolitan areas)? The 1950 census reported that 69 million people resided in 157 urbanized areas covering almost 13,000 square miles. By 1990 the population of these same 157 areas had grown to over 130 million people occupying almost 46,000 square miles. While urbanized population grew 88 percent, urbanized land expanded 255 percent (almost three times the rate of population growth). By 1990 the average resident of these 157 communities was consuming 90 percent more land area than just 40 years before.[4]

Central Cities as Quasi-Regional Governments

Many political commentators and scholars may decry the absence of metropolitan government in America. However, at midcentury there was still an implicit system of quasi-regional governance in place in the great majority of America's metropolitan areas: the dominance of the central city that spread a de facto unity over its region. Almost 60 percent of the nation's metropolitan population lived in 193 central cities. Most area children attended the city school system. Most area residents used city parks and libraries. Most area workers rode city buses, streetcars, and subways to blue- and white-collar jobs within the city or occasionally, to nearby factories just outside the city limits. Most of the region's voters cast their ballots for the same set of local offices. Although there were often fierce rivalries among ethnic and racial groups, city-based public institutions were unifying forces (except in the legally segregated South with its sets of parallel institutions).

Annexation and merger, of course, were the tools of municipal expansion, and they had been used by even the oldest American cities in their youth. In the nineteenth century, Boston grew from the compact, colonial port town that was besieged by General Washington's rebel forces from Dorchester Heights to a metropolis of 48 square miles. In the process Boston not only absorbed Dorchester Heights itself but the city of Roxbury (1867) and, leaping Boston Harbor in 1874, the city of Charlestown as well.[5]

In one afternoon in 1854, by act of the Pennsylvania General Assembly, the city of Philadelphia grew twentyfold in territory, filling all of Philadelphia County. In the process five of the nation's most populous cities disappeared: Spring Garden (ninth), Northern Liberties (eleventh), Kensington (twelfth), Southwark (twentieth), and Moyamensing (twenty-eighth).

In 1897 the New York General Assembly enacted the most ambitious restructuring of regional governance yet. The state legislature abolished the cities of New York and Brooklyn (the nation's first and seventh most populous cities), combined them with three largely rural counties (Queens, Richmond, and Bronx), and created the 315-square-mile New York City, the nation's first metropolitan government.

By the mid-twentieth century, of course, the territorial expansions of Boston, Philadelphia, and New York were history (and largely forgotten history, at that). In fact, throughout New England, New York, New Jersey, and Pennsylvania, the political boundaries of 6,236 cities, boroughs, villages, towns, and townships were set in concrete. On the threshold of accelerated urban sprawl, the Northeast had become a region of "inelastic" cities.[6]

Growing territorial inflexibility was also settling in over much of the Middle West, which through the Continental Congress's enactment of the Land Act of 1785 had inherited New England's pattern of township government. State laws might provide for municipal annexation, but cordons sanitaires of incorporated suburbs already surrounded many cities, such as Detroit and Cleveland. Throughout the Middle West, townships hastened to incorporate as independent municipalities as to avoid annexation. After 1950 Chicago would succeed only in annexing twenty square miles for the new O'Hare Airport.

Annexation versus Highways

At midcentury, central-city officials in regions other than the Northeast or Middle West could reasonably anticipate that annexation and

Table 3-1. *Territorial Growth of the USA's 50 Most Elastic Cities, 1960–90*
Square miles unless otherwise specified.

City[a]	Area			Percent increase
	1960	*1990*	*Increase*	*increase*
Albuquerque	56	132	76	135
Anchorage-Anchorage	13	1,698	1,685	13482
Austin	50	218	168	339
Bakersfield	16	92	76	474
Birmingham	75	149	74	99
Charlotte	65	174	110	169
Chattanooga	37	118	82	223
Colorado Springs	17	183	167	997
Columbus	89	191	102	114
Columbus-Muskogee	26	216	190	719
Corpus Christi	38	135	97	257
Dallas	280	342	63	22
Denver	71	153	82	116
Durham	22	69	47	215
Fort Worth	141	281	141	100
Fresno	29	99	71	247
Houston	328	540	212	65
Huntsville	51	164	114	224
Indianapolis-Marion	71	362	291	408
Jackson	47	109	63	134
Jacksonville-Duval	30	759	729	2412
Kansas City	130	312	182	140
Knoxville	25	77	52	204
Las Vegas	25	83	59	237

continued

mergers would continue to maintain their "elastic" city status as near-regional governments. They often had other tools available to shape development patterns. Many cities owned and operated regional water and sewage treatment systems; some exercised extraterritorial planning jurisdiction. With such powers, most southern and western cities expected to successfully maintain their "market share" of regional development.

By the 1990s, they had been proven wrong. The highway system decentralized America's metropolitan areas so rapidly and relentlessly that almost no city's annexation or merger efforts were able to keep pace.

Table 3-1 charts the territorial growth of the country's fifty most

Table 3-1. *(continued)*

City[a]	Area			Percent
	1960	1990	Increase	increase
Lexington-Fayette	13	285	272	2088
Little Rock	28	103	75	264
Memphis	128	256	128	100
Montgomery	32	135	103	325
Nashville-Davidson	29	473	444	1532
Oklahoma City	322	608	287	89
Omaha	51	101	50	97
Orlando	21	67	46	219
Phoenix	187	420	233	124
Portland	67	125	58	86
Raleigh	34	88	55	163
Reno	12	58	46	387
Sacramento	45	96	51	114
Salt Lake City	56	109	53	94
San Antonio	161	333	173	107
San Diego	192	324	132	68
San Jose	55	171	117	214
Shreveport	36	99	63	174
Tallahassee	15	63	48	316
Tucson	71	156	85	120
Tulsa	48	184	136	284
Wichita	52	115	63	122
Total	3,383	11,025	7,642	226

Sources: Author's calculations based on census reports.

a. Hyphenation indicates city-county consolidation.

annexation-minded central cities from 1960 to 1990. Each added at least forty-six square miles to its municipal jurisdiction—an area equal to the city of Boston or the city of San Francisco. City-county consolidation was the mechanism for most of the largest expansions: Nashville-Davidson (1964), Jacksonville-Duval (1968), Indianapolis-Marion (1970), Lexington-Fayette (1973), and Columbus (Georgia)-Muskogee (1977). The champion of territorial imperialists was Anchorage, which by merging with Anchorage Borough in the mid-1960s ballooned from 13 square miles to 1,698 square miles.[7] Oklahoma City, Phoenix, and Houston annexed the most territory by conventional means. Collectively, the fifty cities more than tripled their municipal territory in three decades.

Table 3-2. *"Market Share" of Urbanized and Metropolitan Populations for Fifty Most Elastic U.S. Cities, 1960–90*
Percent

City[a]	Share of urbanized population			Share of metropolitan population		
	1960	*1990*	*Change*	*1960*	*1990*	*Change*
Albuquerque	83	77	−6	77	65	−11
Anchorage-Anchorage[b]	n.a.	n.a.	n.a.	100	100	0
Austin	100	83	−17	88	55	−33
Bakersfield[b]	40	58	18	19	32	13
Birmingham	65	43	−23	54	32	−22
Charlotte	96	87	−9	74	34	−40
Chattanooga	63	51	−12	38	36	−2
Colorado Springs[b]	70	80	10	49	71	22
Columbus	76	67	−9	69	47	−22
Columbus-Muskogee[b]	74	81	7	54	68	15
Corpus Christi	95	95	1	76	74	−2
Dallas	47	31	−16	71	38	−34
Denver	61	31	−31	56	29	−28
Durham	93	67	−26	70	16	−54
Fort Worth	25	14	−11	66	33	−33
Fresno[b]	63	78	15	37	47	10
Houston	82	56	−26	75	49	−26
Huntsville	97	89	−8	47	55	7
Indianapolis-Marion	74	80	5	68	53	−15
Jackson	98	68	−30	77	50	−27
Jacksonville-Duval[b]	53	86	33	44	70	26
Kansas City	52	34	−18	46	28	−18
Knoxville	65	54	−11	30	28	−2
Las Vegas	72	37	−35	51	30	−20

continued

Running Hard but Falling Behind

Most of these fifty cities still lost market share of regional growth. Table 3-2 tracks changes in each city's percentage of (1) urbanized population and (2) metropolitan population from 1960 to 1990. As a group, despite tripling their municipal territory, the percentage of the regions' urbanized populations that were city residents dropped from 65 percent in 1960 to 51 percent in 1990. The cities' share of metropolitan population declined more precipitously, from 60 percent in 1960 to 43 percent in 1990.

Table 3-2. *(continued)*

City[a]	Share of urbanized population			Share of metropolitan population		
	1960	1990	Change	1960	1990	Change
Lexington-Fayette[b]	56	102	46	48	56	8
Little Rock	58	58	-1	44	34	-10
Memphis	91	74	-17	79	61	-19
Montgomery	94	89	-5	79	64	-15
Nashville-Davidson[b]	49	85	36	43	50	7
Oklahoma City	76	57	-19	74	46	-27
Omaha	77	62	-15	66	53	-13
Orlando	44	19	-25	33	13	-20
Phoenix	79	49	-30	66	44	-22
Portland	57	37	-20	51	29	-22
Raleigh	100	68	-32	56	24	-31
Reno	73	63	-11	61	53	-8
Sacramento	42	34	-9	38	25	-13
Salt Lake City	54	20	-34	49	15	-35
San Antonio	92	83	-9	86	71	-15
San Diego	69	47	-21	55	44	-11
San Jose[b]	34	55	21	32	52	20
Shreveport	79	77	-1	73	53	-21
Tallahassee	n.a.	80	n.a.	65	53	-12
Tucson	94	70	-24	80	61	-19
Tulsa	87	77	-10	76	52	-24
Wichita	87	90	3	74	63	-12
Average	65	51	-14	60	43	-17

Source: Author's calculations based on census reports.
n.a. Not available
a. Hyphenation indicates city-county consolidation.
b. No loss in share of urbanized and metropolitan populations.

Over the three decades, only nine cities—Anchorage, Jacksonville, Nashville, Lexington, Columbus (Georgia), Colorado Springs, San Jose, Bakersfield, and Fresno—increased their market shares of both urbanized and metropolitan populations. However, the high-water mark for the consolidated jurisdictions' market shares typically occurred at the moment of the city-county mergers. During the 1980s, for example, Jacksonville, Nashville, Lexington, and Columbus experienced slower population growth than surrounding counties.

Even though these fifty most annexation-oriented cities are slowly losing ground in the face of accelerating urban sprawl, there is still strong justification for continued annexation. As suburban subdivisions are built around central cities, elastic cities are able to absorb some of that growth within their expanding municipal boundaries. By capturing shares of new, middle-class subdivisions, elastic cities maintain greater socioeconomic balance. Average incomes of residents in elastic cities are typically equal to or even higher than average incomes of suburban residents. Tapping broad, growing tax bases, elastic-city governments are better financed and more able to rely on local resources to address local problems. Although no community is free of racial inequities, minorities are more evenly spread out within the "big boxes" of elastic cities. Segregation by race and income class is reduced.

By contrast, "inelastic" central cities are frozen within fixed city limits and surrounded by growing, independent suburbs. By the 1990s, the downtown business districts of many inelastic cities may have revived as regional employment and entertainment centers, but most inelastic-city neighborhoods are increasingly catch basins for poor blacks and Hispanics. With the flight of middle-class families, inelastic cities' populations have dropped steadily (typically by one-quarter to one-half). The income gap between city residents and suburbanites steadily widens. Governments of inelastic cities are squeezed between rising service needs and eroding tax bases. Unable to tap areas of greater economic growth (their independent suburbs), inelastic-city governments rely increasingly on federal and state aid. Suburban areas around inelastic cities are typically fragmented into many "little boxes"—multiple smaller cities and towns and "mini" school systems. With, at best, a heritage of exclusionary practices or, at worst, continuing practice of such policies, the fragmented governmental structure of these little-box regions reinforces racial and economic segregation.

Big Boxes versus Little Boxes

A comparison of the fifty very elastic cities with twenty-three "zero-elastic" cities illustrates these characterizations (table 3-3). As a group, in four decades (1950–90), these twenty-three zero-elastic cities expanded their municipal areas by an average of only 3 percent—in sharp contrast to the very elastic cities' record of more than tripling their municipal areas in just three decades (1960–90).

By the 1990 census, the average income of zero-elastic city resi-

Table 3-3. *Comparing Socioeconomic and Fiscal Health of 23 Zero-Elastic Cities and 50 Very Elastic Cities and Their Respective Metropolitan Areas*

Criteria	Zero-Elastic Cities/Metro Areas[a]	Highly Elastic Cities/Metro Areas
Income of city residents as a percentage of suburban income (1989)	66	91
City bond rating (1993)[b]	A	AA
Metropolitan Segregation Index[c]		
Housing (1990)	74	53
Schools (1990)	74	46
Poor households (1989)	42	31

Sources: Author's calculations based on census reports.

a. Zero-elastic cities are New York, Newark, Paterson, Boston, St. Louis, Providence, Detroit, Washington, D.C., Pittsburgh, Cleveland, Baltimore, Hartford, Minneapolis, Rochester, Syracuse, Jersey City, New Haven, Chicago, San Francisco, Philadelphia, Buffalo, Bridgeport, and Cincinnati.

b. Bond ratings are those assigned by Moody's Investor Services in their *1991 Municipal Data Book.*

c. For segregation indexes, 100 = total segregation.

dents had fallen to 66 percent of suburban levels, while the average income of residents in very elastic cities was 91 percent of suburban levels. Zero-elastic cities averaged lower bond ratings (A) than highly elastic cities (AA).

In 1990, by a common demographic measure, African Americans were much more segregated within the metropolitan housing markets in zero-elastic core cities (an index of 74) than within metropolitan housing markets in highly elastic core cities (an index of 53).[8] For the 1989–1990 school year, the school segregation index matched segregated housing patterns in the zero-elastic regions (74 for both indexes), whereas schools were significantly less segregated (an index of 46) than neighborhoods (an index of 53) in the highly elastic regions. Finally, poor households living in zero-elastic regions were more likely to be segregated away from middle-class households (an index of 42) than those residing in highly elastic regions (an index of 31).[9]

Governance Structure Counts

A clear regional trend appears when the two groups of metropolitan areas are compared. Of the fifty very elastic cities, all but Indianapolis and Columbus (Ohio) are located in the South and West, while all twenty-three of the zero-elastic cities are in the Northeast and Middle West, except Baltimore, Washington D.C., St. Louis, and San Francisco.[10]

However, the preceding discussion on racial and economic segregation is not just a disguised way of describing Rust Belt versus Sun Belt sectional differences. Within an urban region, how local governance is organized has an impact on issues of social mobility.

The clearest impact is on school segregation. In the decades after the U.S. Supreme Court declared segregated schools unconstitutional, school desegregation suits were brought in both southern and northern courts. Southern states (such as Florida, North Carolina, and Tennessee) tend to have big-box school districts that often are countywide. Court-ordered school desegregation plans integrated schools not just within elastic central cities but across city boundaries into the central county's suburban areas.

In the North, however, little-box school districts mirror little-box city, village, and town governments. In its 1974 decision *Milliken* v. *Bradley*, the U.S. Supreme Court ruled that suburban school districts would not be required to participate with central-city districts in school desegregation plans unless it could be shown that state action had brought about such segregation. With white, middle-class anxiety about local schools intensifying the lure of new suburban homes, central-city school districts like Cleveland, Rochester, and Minneapolis were left to integrate systems that rapidly became heavily minority enrollment districts.

For example, with 115 independent suburban systems, metropolitan Detroit has the nation's most racially segregated public school systems. It is the unspoken mission of many little school boards to "keep our schools just the way they are for children just like ours"—whoever "our children" happen to be. That mission is more readily achieved with 115 separate school districts empowered to erect walls around themselves—a pattern repeated over and over again in little-box regions.

"Keeping our town just the way it is for people just like us"—whoever "us" happens to be—has also been the mantra of suburban town councils and planning commissions in little-box regions. Exclusionary zoning policies reign. By contrast, because planning commissions and city councils of big-box governments are accountable to more diverse constituencies, they are less likely to implement policies that divide residents as rigorously by income, with the attendant consequences for racial and ethnic segregation.

In the 1990s, southern metropolitan areas are less racially segregated than northern metropolitan areas, but not primarily because "black and white Southerners always lived closer together than Northerners did." That conventional wisdom doesn't stand up very well to historical analysis. In 1970 the average residential segregation index for eighteen major northern metropolitan areas (including San Francisco–Oakland and Los Angeles) was 85 compared to an average index of 79 for fourteen major southern metropolitan areas—hardly a major difference. By 1990 the northern average had edged down 7 points to 78, but the southern average had dropped 15 points to 64.[11] It is the dynamics of housing markets within big-box central cities, reinforced by public school integration policies (and generally growing regional economies), that largely account for the greater pace of residential desegregation in the South.

Maintaining central-city elasticity is important both for the city's economic and fiscal health and for the region's social health. Wherever cities still have annexation powers, they should use them prudently. Whenever state legislatures or local voters can be persuaded to approve city-county consolidations, the effort should be made.[12]

However, even the most elastic central cities cannot hope to maintain their traditional role as quasi-regional governments that largely control regional development. Annexation strategies have been overwhelmed by the sprawl-inducing effect of the federal interstate highway system and the networks of state highways supporting it.

For example, Charlotte, North Carolina, has carried out successfully one of the most sustained annexation programs. From 1950 to 1996, Charlotte expanded from 30 square miles to 225 square miles. In the process Charlotte captured 83 percent of all population growth within Mecklenburg County, the boundary of its 1950 metropolitan area. However, in those same decades, Charlotte's actual metropolitan area expanded beyond Mecklenburg County to embrace seven counties and fifty municipalities covering 3,700 square miles in two states. Charlotte can no longer call the regional development tune. The Queen City must negotiate transportation and land-use issues with other local (and independent) governments.

If Charlotte could not annex new development fast enough to maintain regional hegemony, no elastic city can. Elastic cities of the South and West now face the same phenomenon of sprawling development beyond their grasp that in earlier decades victimized inelastic cities of the Northeast and Middle West.

The Regional Agenda

Don Hutchinson, president of the Greater Baltimore Committee, the area's regional business leadership organization, laid out the regional challenge most succinctly. "If regionalism isn't dealing with land-use, fiscal disparities, housing, and education," the former Baltimore County executive stated, "then regionalism isn't dealing with the issues that count."

In pursuit of that philosophy, in July 1997 the Greater Baltimore Committee issued a policy statement, *One Region, One Future*, that urged adoption of three major initiatives:

— Regional growth management policies that lead to redevelopment and reinvestment in older neighborhoods and reduce the infrastructure costs to the governments and taxpayers of the region.

— Policies that result in a system of tax-base sharing in the region. Any system should focus on the growth in the tax base and could draw upon a number of different models that have been adopted across the country.

— A policy for developing affordable housing throughout the metropolitan area. A key goal of this policy should be to avoid creating concentrations of people living in poverty.[13]

Baltimore's *One Region, One Future* is a policy statement that should serve as a model for business leadership in all metropolitan areas.

Land Use: the Key Issue

Land-use planning is the pivotal issue. Fiscal disparities, lack of affordable housing, and poor public schools all reflect uneven regional development patterns.

Fiscal disparities arise as new subdivisions, commercial areas, and office parks lead to devaluation and abandonment of older property. Wide fiscal disparities typically emerge most virulently in little-box regions where central cities and suburban jurisdictions alike have fixed jurisdictional boundaries. Elastic cities do not suffer from fiscal disparities. Indeed, elastic cities act as an internal revenue-sharing mechanism, taxing wealthier city neighborhoods to maintain adequate service levels in poorer city neighborhoods. (Highly elastic cities such as Charlotte, Lexington, and Albuquerque annex so much high-end new development that they are wealthier than their suburban neighbors.)

Growing economic segregation in most metropolitan housing markets is a reflection of postwar development patterns. Cities always have had richer and poorer neighborhoods. However, many older city neighborhoods contain a greater variety of housing types than typical postwar suburban subdivisions. As a result, many city neighborhoods contain households that range widely in income.

The greater economic homogeneity of suburban subdivisions partly reflects the fact that homebuilding has changed from a retail industry to a wholesale industry. Postwar homebuilders have learned to apply factory-like production techniques to building sites. Specialized crews (foundation layers, framers, plumbing and electrical installers, sheetrock hangers, roofers) move from site to site with factory-like precision. The result is that, within a given subdivision, a builder will erect large numbers of similar homes priced for a relatively narrow band of potential homebuyers.

Suburban planning and zoning policies often magnify the effect of such industry practices. By setting large minimum lot sizes, limiting the location of (or banning outright) townhouse complexes, apartments, and mobile home parks, local governments encourage economic segregation.

In too many urban regions, where a child lives largely determines the quality of the child's school experience. The problem is not primarily fiscal disparities among different local school districts—the target of many education reformers. The core issue is that a child's school performance is heavily influenced by the socioeconomic status of the child's family and classmates. For example, in communities across the country, 65 to 85 percent of the school-by-school variation in standardized test scores is explained by variations in the school-by-school percentage of low-income students.[14] The most effective education reform for improving poor children's school performance would actually be housing reform: mixed-income housing policies that integrate poor children into middle-class neighborhoods and middle-class neighborhood schools.

Target: New State Growth Management Laws

Growth management is rapidly emerging as the top regional issue of the next decade. There are two key targets: state legislatures, which control land-use rules, and federally required metropolitan planning organizations, which shape the allocation of federal transportation grants.

There are only twelve states that have enacted statewide growth management laws. They vary in effectiveness from strong (Oregon) to almost purely exhortatory (Georgia). In 1999, however, the Georgia legislature created a powerful Georgia Regional Transportation Agency to take charge of transportation and land-use decisions in sprawl-choked metropolitan Atlanta.

The two most recent state land-use reform laws have been adopted in Maryland (1997) and Tennessee (1998). Maryland governor Parris Glendening's Smart Growth Act strengthens a weak state planning law adopted in 1993. The Smart Growth Act ostensibly does not place new mandates on local planning, which is controlled almost entirely by county governments in Maryland. However, it restricts state highway, sewage treatment, and other infrastructure grants (and the federal grants they match) to established urban areas.

Tennessee's new state planning law popped forth virtually unnoticed by growth management advocates nationally. It had an unconventional origin—an obscure amendment to another Tennessee law that was adopted by voice vote in the waning minutes of the 1997 legislative session. To the Tennessee Municipal League's consternation, the stealth amendment suspended Tennessee's annexation laws for one year, wiping out existing cities' powers to veto the incorporation of new municipalities within five miles of their city limits. To ensure against annexation, proposals to incorporate mini-municipalities (dubbed "toy towns" by opponents) sprang up like weeds. By the time the Tennessee Supreme Court declared that the amendment was unconstitutionally adopted by the legislature, residents of unincorporated areas had initiated proceedings to create forty-four toy towns (including one that was simply a condominium apartment building near Knoxville).

During the heated controversy, Tennessee's speaker of the house and the lieutenant governor (the presiding officer of the state senate who had created the stealth amendment) appointed a broad-based commission to review the state's annexation laws. Under the urging of the Tennessee Advisory Commission on Intergovernmental Relations, the commission expanded its mission to consider the broader need for regional land-use planning.

The result was enactment of the Annexation Reform Act of 1998—a title that reflects the law's origins but not its broad scope. Through a complex process, the new law requires counties to adopt comprehensive land-use plans. The plans must designate urban growth boundaries for existing municipalities (which will also be their twenty-year annexation reserve areas), rural preservation areas, and "planned growth areas" (which may allow some "new town" development).

Though undoubtedly not as rigorous a growth management directive as Oregon's law, the new Tennessee law has real teeth. Counties that fail to adopt a comprehensive land-use plan by July 2001 will no longer be eligible for a long list of state infrastructure funds, including participation in federal highway grants.

New Allies

Tennessee's new growth management law may have been born under unique circumstances, but there is growing public pressure for anti-sprawl legislation developing in many states, particularly in the Middle West, where no state has yet adopted a statewide growth management law. New recruits to the legislative struggle—business leaders, church coalitions, and inner-suburb mayors—are joining forces with environmentalists and farmland preservationists, growth management's more traditional advocates. Some key examples:

— A new association of business leadership groups in Pennsylvania, the Coalition of Mid-Sized Cities, has targeted enactment of a smart-growth, antisprawl law as its top priority.

— In Missouri a coalition of eighty churches—Protestant and Catholic, black and white, city and inner suburb—is lobbying for a new state growth management law for Greater St. Louis.

— In Ohio the recently established First Suburbs Consortium, initially formed by ten suburban mayors from communities around Cleveland, told the Governor's Task Force on Agricultural Preservation in 1997 that a strong state land-use law might be desirable to save farmland, but it was essential for the survival of older suburban communities.

"Since the late 1940's, policies have consistently encouraged the abandonment of boroughs and cities in Pennsylvania, and discouraged the redevelopment of existing neighborhoods and established commercial and industrial sites," explains Tom Wolf, president of Better York, owner of a multistate chain of builders' supply yards, and a leader of the Coalition of Mid-Sized Cities.[15] In addition to Better York, the coalition includes a dozen business groups such as the Lehigh Valley Partnership, Lancaster Alliance, and Erie Conference on Community Development.

"In the end, no one wins in a system that makes prosperity a temporary and fleeting phenomenon," Wolf continues. "No one wins in a system that has already condemned our cities and older boroughs to economic stagnation and decline. And no one wins in a system that ultimately threatens to do the same thing to our townships. The point is that public policies that encourage sprawl are neither smart nor right.

"We need to change the rules of the game," Wolf concludes. "Most of all we need to change the rules governing land-use planning."

Excess Land, Excess Housing: Formula for Abandonment

Tom Wolf's conclusion is seconded by Reverend Sylvester Laudermill, chair of Metropolitan Congregations United for St. Louis:

> St. Louis has been devastated by a growth machine that empties out our communities. In recent decades developers have consumed land at seven times the rate of our population growth. They've built twice as many new homes as there were new households for them.
>
> That's a guaranteed formula for abandonment. In just twenty years St. Louis City lost 70,000 housing units, but the decline doesn't stop with St. Louis. Many of our older suburbs are also declining.
>
> For years our congregations have fought to stabilize and redevelop our communities. But every month more homes are boarded up, more local stores have closed. We've concluded that we cannot win the battle for our neighborhoods—the "inside game"—unless we fight and win the "outside game" as well.[16]

In February 1997 the Metropolitan Congregations United extracted a pledge from St. Louis area legislators to back their anti-sprawl agenda. The immediate result was the new Legislative Interim Committee on Urban Growth. The hotly debated hearings that fall were headline news in the St. Louis media. The church coalition crafted a bill to vest regional land-use planning power in a new commission under the East-West Gateway Coordinating Council, the region's council of governments. The regional commission would have the power to draw an urban growth boundary for the Missouri side of Greater St. Louis.

The St. Louis coalition is merely the spearhead of an antisprawl crusade mounted by interfaith coalitions in Gary-Hammond, Detroit, Cleveland, Chicago, and a dozen other midwestern regions. The effort is coordinated by the Chicago-based Gamaliel Foundation.

Yesterday's Winners, Tomorrow's Losers

"Yesterday's winners are today's losers" might be the theme of Cleveland's First Suburbs Consortium. Barely two decades ago inner suburbs such as Euclid, Lakewood, and Maple Heights boasted above-average household incomes. Now they have sunk ten to twenty percentage points below the regional average as higher-end households move into new subdivisions farther out in Geauga, Lake, and Portage Counties. Table 3-4 charts this process of decline for many older suburbs of Ohio's major cities.

"Many older suburbs are more vulnerable to sprawl-driven disinvestment than Cleveland itself. They're left with an aging housing stock, older strip shopping centers and first-generation malls that find it hard to compete with new regional malls and new higher end housing developments," explains Dr. Tom Bier, head of housing research at Cleveland State University.[17]

"Many older suburbs don't have the legacy of charming old neighborhoods, fine parks, museums, or big centers of high-quality jobs found in central business districts, hospitals, and universities historically located in central cities. East Cleveland, for example, which is Cleveland's oldest suburb, is in much tougher shape than Cleveland itself," Bier notes.[18]

In February 1998 the First Suburbs Consortium began building a statewide alliance of Ohio's "mature suburbs." One of the alliance's

Table 3-4. *Average Household Income of Older Ohio Suburbs as a Percentage of Regional Household Income, 1970–90*

Suburb	1970	1980	1990
Akron	92	84	80
Barberton	89	80	70
Cuyahoga Falls	111	99	94
Norton	112	109	105
Tallmadge	127	119	114
Cincinnati	82	79	76
Bridgetown North	123	112	101
Forest Park	138	130	111
Franklin	94	85	74
Lebanon	93	91	84
North College Hill	100	94	82
Norwood	85	83	69
Reading	105	102	88
Sharonville	124	113	104
Springdale	128	120	111
Cleveland [a]	72	68	60
Bedford	101	99	87
Bedford Heights	106	96	84
Brooklyn	109	100	81
Brook Park	127	115	101
East Cleveland	77	68	57
Eastlake	103	101	93
Euclid	103	92	82
Fairfield Park	136	118	113
Garfield Heights	100	93	82
Lakewood	99	93	93
Maple Heights	103	96	85
Mayfield Heights	103	90	85
Middleburg Heights	138	126	114
North Olmstead	124	120	115
Parma	111	106	96
Parma Heights	114	101	89
Seven Hills	148	141	121
South Euclid	117	114	106
Warrensville Heights	104	95	84
Wickliffe	109	109	95
Willoughby	104	102	98
Willowick	119	111	93

continued

Table 3-4. *(continued)*

Suburb	1970	1980	1990
Columbus	87	86	85
Blacklick Estates	122	111	103
Gahanna	131	121	112
Grove City	117	110	99
Lancaster	91	92	74
Newark	87	87	76
Reynoldsburg	126	114	109
Whitehall	110	92	80
Dayton	78	70	67
Englewood	127	112	110
Huber Heights	125	113	112
Kettering	151	118	120
Overlook-Page Manor	113	101	91
Shiloh	135	111	99
Vandalia	119	110	105
West Carrollton	109	101	98
Springfield	76	78	74
Fairborn	104	91	88
Xenia	94	83	80
Toledo	95	88	83
Fostoria	87	82	74
Warren	97	93	89
Girard	100	94	88
Niles	99	97	92
Youngstown	81	78	68
Austintown	113	107	100
Campbell	92	86	77
Struthers	94	89	76

Sources: Author's calculations based on census reports.
a. Central city included for comparison and geographic reference.

primary goals is enactment of the proposed Agricultural Preservation Act—once again a state land-use planning law whose impact (like Tennessee's new law) would be much broader than its title.

York, St. Louis, and Cleveland share one characteristic: highly fragmented local government. With 72 municipal governments in York County, 105 local governments in metropolitan Cleveland, and 134 local governments just in the Missouri portion of Greater St. Louis, purely voluntary cooperation will not produce a meaningful regional plan. As York's Tom Wolf says, changing the rules of the game for land-use planning is essential, and only state legislatures can change those rules.

Land-Use Planning: The Portland Model

Across the continent, business and civic delegations, state and local politicians, and professional planners are flocking to Portland to see the practical results of nearly twenty-five years of operating under different rules of the game. In 1973 the Oregon legislature enacted the Statewide Land Use Law. It required that urban growth boundaries be drawn around cities throughout the state. Portland Metro, the nation's only directly elected regional government, is responsible for land-use and transportation planning in the 1.5-million-person metropolitan area. Anticipating a 50 percent growth of population over the next forty-five years, in November 1997 the Portland Metro Council voted 5–2 to add less than 8 square miles to Portland's existing 342-square-mile urban growth boundary. (The two dissenting votes felt the expansion was too little.)

Opposition to greater expansion was led by many local officials, like Mayor Gussie McRobert of suburban Gresham, as well as by many environmentally concerned citizens. Portland's urban growth boundary has succeeded in protecting farmland in Oregon's rich Willamette Valley. If the Metro Council sticks to its plans, over the next forty-five years, only about four square miles of current farmland will be urbanized—as much farmland as is subdivided in the state of Michigan every ten days.[19]

A big bonus is that shutting down suburban sprawl has turned new private investment back inward into existing neighborhoods and retail areas. Mayor McRobert's Gresham as well as Milwaukie, Oregon City, and other older suburbs are booming. Property values in Albina,

Portland's poorest neighborhood, doubled in just five years. As Metro councilor Ed Washington, whose District 6 includes Albina, explained his role for the small boundary expansion, "We are having redevelopment in my district for the first time in forty years; we don't want to lose it."

By the mid-1990s, Portland's economy had become superheated by a high-tech investment boom. With $13 billion in new, high-tech construction underway, workers flocked to the Portland area. From 1990 to 1996, the Portland area's population grew 16 percent, putting extreme pressure on the housing supply. Housing prices shot up 60 percent, and many area homebuilders and other allies launched a campaign against the region's tight land-use controls.[20]

In the midst of an affordable-housing crisis, the Metro Council adopted a wide-ranging package of regulatory actions and incentives to increase the production of affordable housing. A tough, mandatory inclusionary zoning ordinance (patterned on the successful program in Montgomery County, Maryland)[21] was deferred after several legal challenges before the state Land Conservation and Development Commission that regulates local growth management.

Citizen Accountability: The Portland Model

Portland Metro is the joint creation of both the Oregon legislature (1979) and local citizens (through three separate referenda, including adoption of a home rule charter for Portland Metro in 1992). Covering three counties and twenty-four municipalities, Portland Metro is responsible for regional solid waste disposal, regional air and water quality, the regional zoo, and the Oregon Convention Center. In the new home rule charter, the area's citizens affirmed that long-range planning is Metro's "primary" function. Metro's long-range planning function includes responsibility for both land-use and transportation planning.

Portland area citizens know where the crucial decisions affecting the future of their region are made: Metro. They know when and how such decisions will be made: in well-advertised public meetings after extensive public hearings. (In revising the Portland 2040 plan, Metro held 182 public hearings and presentations.) And citizens know who will make the decisions: the seven Metro councilors and Metro chief executive who are directly elected by the region's citizens. Land-use and transportation decisions are the issues that dominate political campaigns for Metro's elected offices. The result is that there is a much higher level of knowledgeable citizen engagement in regional planning issues in the Portland area than in any other regional community in the United States.

Transforming Metropolitan Planning Organizations

A Republican-controlled Congress dominated by self-anointed "conservatives" enacted in 1998 a $217 billion Transportation Efficiency Act (TEA-21). The country is poised for another massive round of federal transportation spending. Over the next six years, the federal government will spend almost one-third as much for highway and transit construction as was spent in the previous four decades. How this new generation of transportation investments will affect the growth and shape of America's urban areas will be determined largely by metropolitan planning organizations (MPOs).

For decades, deciding how federal transportation funds would be used was primarily the province of the Federal Highway Administration and state highway departments. That changed with the Intermodal Service Transportation Efficiency Act of 1991 (ISTEA). In the judgment of the National Association of Regional Councils, ISTEA "marked a radical and visionary transformation of the nation's transportation policy."[22]

Prior to ISTEA, local planning input was largely limited to prioritizing laundry lists of projects within narrow, federally prescribed program allocations. Under ISTEA, MPOs for all urbanized areas with at least 200,000 residents acquired broad discretion to allocate lump-sum federal funds among road, bridge, and transit projects.

About half of all MPOs are "regional councils," voluntary consortia of local governments with a variety of interests beyond transportation planning. Other MPOs are regional economic development organizations, transportation planning agencies, and arms of state highway departments.

In the years since ISTEA was enacted, most MPOs have not had as "radical" and "transforming" an impact as the National Association of Regional Councils originally anticipated. However, transportation planning certainly has acquired a much more local flavor. Had the MPO structure been eliminated (as several key congressional powers proposed), TEA-21 would have dealt a massive blow to the cause of regional planning; instead, TEA-21 will provide continued impetus to the evolution of regional land-use planning.

There has been a uniquely American asymmetry about the relationship between land-use planning and transportation planning. It is inconceivable that a land-use plan could largely ignore an area's network of roads and highways, yet transportation plans often have been developed as if they dealt only with transportation problems.

However, transportation decisions *are* land-development decisions. Who can doubt today that the primary impact of interstate beltways was not to route interstate traffic swiftly and conveniently around major cities (as originally justified) but was rather to generate major suburban commercial, industrial, and residential development? In urban areas the great majority of interstate highway users are local-origin cars and trucks.

Metropolitan planning organizations are federated bodies. Their boards are composed of individuals appointed by member governments and agencies. This raises two problems for organizations faced with increasingly tough, important decisions.

First, the primary loyalty of most board members is to their home jurisdictions. This is particularly true of local elected officials serving on MPO boards (who usually constitute all or a majority of board members). This makes it difficult to achieve an overall regional perspective. Second, federated boards can rarely survive judicial scrutiny when challenged under the "one person, one vote" standard.

Precedents for Elected Regional Organizations

Very limited precedents suggest that voluntary regional structures like MPOs will evolve into limited-purpose regional governments directly elected by the region's citizens. Portland Metro began as the Metropolitan Services District, with a seven-member federated board of local elected officials—one each from the city of Portland and Clackamas, Multnomah, and Washington counties and three representing other cities in each of the three counties. A parallel organization, the Columbia Region Association of Governments (CRAG), started as a federated board of representatives from four counties and fourteen cities and grew to represent five counties and thirty-one cities. As one observer noted, "The difficulty in building consensus around a [comprehensive regional land-use plan] reflected a fundamental tension in using the council of governments model to develop regional policies. . . . [CRAG board members] were often torn between the imperatives of regional issues and the need to protect their own community from unwanted costs, programs, or development initiatives."[23]

In 1977 the Oregon legislature abolished CRAG, assigned its regional planning responsibilities to the Metropolitan Services District, and authorized replacing the federated, appointed board with a directly elected twelve-member council and elected chief executive. In 1978 the Portland area electorate approved the changes. (The voters reduced council membership from twelve to seven and renamed the organization "Portland Metro" when the home rule charter was adopted in 1992.)

During the postwar years, another regional organization had evolved in the Seattle metropolitan area. Seattle Metro was a well-respected regional wastewater and transit authority governed by a federated board. By 1992, however, with the growth of region's population, the Metro Council had grown from its original sixteen members to forty-five.

Controversy increasingly revolved around the makeup and power of the federated Metro Council. After a dozen abortive efforts by the state legislature to reorganize Metro, the debate took a decisive turn in 1990 when a federal district judge ruled that the Metro Council's federated structure violated the constitutional one-person, one-vote guarantee. After further local controversy, legislative debate, and missed court deadlines, Metro Council members proposed merging Metro into King County government. Under the merger proposal approved by voters in November 1992, a single legislative body—the Metropolitan County Council—replaced the King County and Metro Councils, in effect expanding the King County Council from nine to thirteen members elected by district.

To give cities "a voice and a vote" in developing countywide comprehensive planning policies, three new bodies were mandated in a charter amendment to the King County charter: the Regional Transit Committee, Regional Water Quality Committee, and Regional Policy Committee. Each committee has twelve voting members: six Metro County Council members and six members divided between Seattle and suburban cities. The Metro County Council is the only body that is legally empowered to enact plans and policies. However, the County Council can override a regional committee recommendation only if at least eight of the thirteen council members agree. Otherwise, a regional committee's recommendations automatically become law.

A third nationally recognized regional body—the Twin Cities Metropolitan Council—is on the brink of passing from appointed to elected status. Since its legislative creation in 1967, the "Met Council" has been governed by a seventeen-member board appointed by Minnesota's governor. Although members are residents of sixteen districts into which its seven-county jurisdiction is divided, they and their full-time chairman are, in practice, accountable to the governor that appointed them, not to their neighbors. The Met Council functions like another state agency.

For three decades the Met Council carried out land-use planning functions and exercised loose oversight over three regional wastewater and transit agencies. The regional agencies, however, pursued increasingly independent directions. In 1994, seeking greater regional unity, the Minnesota legislature abolished the three agencies and placed their functions directly under the Met Council. The Metropolitan Reorganization Act transformed the Met Council from a planning body with loose supervisory control into an operational agency with a budget of more than $400 million and supervisory control over the $300 million Metropolitan Airports Commission. "After Hennepin County," noted state representative Myron Orfield, leader of the legislature's regional reform bloc, "the Met Council was Minnesota's second largest unit of government in terms of budget, and perhaps its most significant in terms of authority."[24]

A regional public agency with so much authority and spending so many tax dollars, Orfield and other colleagues argued, ought to be directly accountable to the citizens of the region. A bill to convert membership on the Met Council from gubernatorial appointment to direct election was defeated narrowly in the 1996 legislative session but passed in 1997, only to be vetoed by the governor. There are strong prospects that a similar bill will pass and become law in the near future.

Dealing with the Regional Issues that Count

The growing political support for state land-use planning laws and the increasing level of federal transportation grants are leading in the same direction: the evolution of stronger regional planning organizations. In some states existing regional planning organizations are likely to have their planning authority extended into housing policy, regional revenue sharing, and economic development policy. Some may also become vehicles for management of regionwide infrastructure programs formerly carried out by independent authorities.

I would like to offer some crystal ball gazing. Though there is little pragmatic evidence to date, I believe that as regional organizations become more operationally significant and the impact of their planning decisions becomes better understood, public demand may convert some of them into directly elected rather than appointed bodies.

Thus in coming decades, directly elected metropolitan governments are likely to evolve in a growing number of regions. They will not be unitary governments. (Anchorage is the country's only such example covering an entire metropolitan area.) They will not replace the mosaic of local governments as primary providers of local services. Their powers will appear limited but will be vitally important, since they will affect regional land-use and transportation planning, affordable housing, fiscal disparities, and major regional infrastructure investments—the "outside game." These evolving metropolitan governments will deal with the issues that count for the wealth and health of regions and the future of their central cities.

Notes

1. Unless otherwise noted, all data in this article are drawn from the author's calculations based on various decennial census reports; Department of Commerce, *Statistical Abstract of the United States,* various editions; and Department of Commerce, *Historical Statistics of the United States: Colonial Times to 1970* (1975).

2. Executive Office of the President, *Budget of the United States Government, Historical Tables for Fiscal Year 1996,* table 8.7.

3. The outstanding value of all federally aided home mortgages (including Fannie Mae and Freddie Mac's portfolios) was $2.5 trillion in 1995. By contrast, the annual direct federal appropriation for rental housing assistance for low-income households was $26 billion. In 1996 the federal tax code provided $94 billion in tax incentives for homeowners compared to less than $9 billion in tax incentives for investors in rental properties.

4. Over the next three decades, the census recognized another 239 urbanized areas. By 1990, 396 urbanized areas contained 61,000 square miles of urbanized land—about 2 percent of our land mass.

5. By the centennial of the American Revolution, the site of the Battle of Bunker Hill (that is, Breed's Hill) and all other major landmarks of the siege of Boston lay well with Boston's city limits.

6. "Elastic cities" expand their boundaries through annexation or, more rarely, city-county consolidation to absorb many new suburban areas. "Inelastic cities" are trapped within fixed city limits by either bad state annexation laws or being surrounded by incorporated suburbs. For a full discussion of the consequences of city elasticity and inelasticity, see David Rusk, *Cities without Suburbs*, 2d ed. (Johns Hopkins University Press, 1995).

7. As of 1990, less than one-tenth of the land within Anchorage's city limits was classified as "urbanized" by the Census Bureau.

8. The segregation indexes are "dissimilarity indexes" that describe the relative unevenness of the distribution of target populations. On a scale of 0–100, a score of 0 indicates an absolutely even distribution, or complete integration; a score of 100 indicates an absolutely uneven distribution, or complete segregation. The measurements are made on a census tract by census tract basis (that is, largely without regard to political boundaries). Dissimilarity indexes cited are drawn from a report by Roderick J. Harrison and Daniel H. Weinberg, *Racial and Ethnic Segregation in 1990* (Bureau of the Census, Department of Commerce, 1992).

9. With the assistance of the Urban Institute in Washington, D.C., I calculated dissimilarity indexes for attendance zones of all public high schools in 320 metropolitan areas, based on computer tapes provided by the National Center for Education Statistics, for the 1989–1990 school year.

10. The term *South* refers to the seventeen states and the District of Columbia that maintained legally segregated school systems until the U.S. Supreme Court's epochal *Brown* v. *Board of Education* decision in 1954.

11. See David Rusk, *Inside Game/Outside Game: Winning Strategies for Saving Urban America* (Century Fund and Brookings, 1999), p. 73.

12. In the 1990s, voters have approved three new city-county consolidations: Athens–Clarke County and Augusta–Richmond County, both in Georgia, and Kansas City–Wyandotte County, Kansas.

13. Greater Baltimore Committee, *One Region, One Future* (1997).

14. See David Rusk, *Abell Report: To Improve Poor Children's Test Scores, Move Poor Families* (Baltimore: Abell Foundation, July 1998).

15. David Rusk, "Renewing Our Community: The Rusk Report on the Future of Greater York," *York Daily Record* (November 20, 1997), p. 2.

16. Statement at the Leadership Forum of the Metropolitan Congregations United for St. Louis, August 17, 1996.

17. Personal communication.

18. Ibid.

19. The Michigan Society of Planning Officials estimates that Michigan is subdividing farmland at the rate of ten acres an hour.

20. Housing prices escalated rapidly in other regions of the booming Pacific Northwest and Rocky Mountain states. Without any urban growth boundary in effect, Albuquerque, for instance, experienced a similar increase in housing prices and for much the same reason. In both Albuquerque and Portland, Intel was building $4 billion chip factories.

21. In 1973 the Montgomery County Council adopted the Moderately Priced Dwelling Unit (MPDU) ordinance. It requires that in any new housing

development of fifty or more units builders must make at least 15 percent of the units affordable for households in the lowest third of the county's income range. To compensate builders for lost profits from developing 15 percent of their property at less than market potential, the MPDU ordinance provides up to a 22 percent density bonus. In the twenty-five years under the policy, homebuilders have built over 10,000 affordable units in compliance with the MPDU policy. The county's Housing Opportunities Commission, which, by ordinance, has right of first purchase for one-third of the MPDU units, has purchased over 1,500 units as rental properties for very low-income tenants. While economic segregation has increased in most urban areas, Montgomery County's dissimilarity index for poor households has been stable at a low 27 rating—a direct consequence of the county's MPDU policy and other mixed-income housing initiatives.

22. National Association of Regional Councils, *Regional Reporter 3* (January 1992), p. 1.

23. Carl Abbott and Margery Post Abbott, "Historical Development of the Metropolitan Service District," prepared for the Metro Home Rule Charter Committee.

24. Myron Orfield, *Metropolitics* (Cambridge, Mass., and Washington, D.C.: Lincoln Institute of Land Policy and Brookings, 1997), p. 133.

CHAPTER FOUR

The Death and Life of American Regional Planning

ROBERT FISHMAN

The city and its suburbs are interdependent parts of a single community, bound together by a web of transportation and other public facilities and by common economic interests. . . . Increasingly, community development must be a cooperative venture. . .[that] requires the establishment of an effective and comprehensive planning process in each metropolitan area embracing all major activities both public and private that shape the community.

> — President John F. Kennedy's Special Message to Congress on
> Housing and Community Development[1]

A Region, someone has wryly observed, is an area safely larger than the last one to whose problems we found no solution.

> — Jane Jacobs, *The Death and Life of*
> *Great American Cities*[2]

American regional planning in the 1960s underwent the collective equivalent of a near-death experience: an unprecedented, nearly total breakdown of both planning theory and planning practice. To be sure, American planning has never been entirely healthy,

and its history is filled with badly conceived, imperfectly implemented, or wholly ignored initiatives. In the 1960s, however, planning
theory at the regional level aimed at a totalizing comprehensiveness
that only imperfectly masked its pervasive ineffectuality; meanwhile,
urban renewal in the cities mandated "solutions" that were, if possible, worse than the existing problems and imposed terrible costs precisely on those who were supposed to benefit. Nevertheless, planning
survived this crisis, and as a near-death experience is supposed to do
for individuals, American planning emerged from its ordeal with a
new set of values and priorities. These traumatic lessons have continued to shape American regional planning into the 1990s.

The chapter title is, of course, a tribute to the work that above all
others delivered the coup de grace to dying planning ideas and
pointed the way toward revitalization: Jane Jacobs's *The Death and Life
of Great American Cities.*[3] Jacobs's contributions are vital and important,
although her book is neither a full critique of the failures of postwar
American planning nor a complete guide to the new synthesis that
would emerge. Jacobs very deliberately limited herself to the central
cities and indeed, to certain districts within those cities. She believed
that the great city possessed an inherent vitality that made it self-heal-
ing—if only "antiurban" planners, bankers, and bureaucrats would
cease their meddling.

Almost as much as her opponents, Jacobs missed the full structural dimensions of an urban crisis that was radically redefining the
concepts of "city," "suburb," and "region": the decentralization of population that shifted the majority from central city to suburb; the simul-
taneous "urbanization of the suburbs" that brought the majority of
industrial production, retail sales, and eventually office space to the
suburbs; and the creation of a low-density, multicentered or perhaps
centerless region where growth and vitality seemed concentrated at
the edge rather than the former center. Perhaps more surprisingly,
Jacobs's book also virtually ignores the "great black migration," which
in the context of the structural changes to the regions reinforced the
divisions between city and suburb and left the once-dominant central
cities in a perpetual crisis, caught between rising social responsibilities
and a shrinking tax base. (If only the problems of the central city had
been limited to meddling planners!) But Jacobs certainly saw clearly
the extent of the threat to the American city itself. What was tragic was
that other 1960s planners complacently claimed to possess a wholly
"modern" approach to regional problems but failed to understand

that, taken together, the structural redefinition of the region and the great black migration rendered at best irrelevant and at worst horribly counterproductive virtually their whole theory and practice. At the beginning of the 1960s, that theory was still responding to the problems of the turn of the century, when urbanists first confronted the challenge of metropolitan regions that extended functionally beyond the borders of the central cities. Although the plans and drawings of the 1960s looked modern, they unconsciously and anachronistically assumed a city and a region that no longer existed. For this reason, the "death" of planning in the 1960s must be understood as the last gasps of planning theory from earlier in the century. Similarly, planning's new "life" began when Jacobs and others began to face the realities of the postwar American city and region.

This outmoded planning theory took the form of two rival traditions that had both reached their (theoretical) heights in the 1920s: the *metropolitanist* and the *regionalist* traditions. From the first, the metropolitanist tradition was the dominant establishment view and was embodied in two great monuments of American planning: Daniel Burnham and Edward Bennett's *Plan of Chicago* and *The Regional Plan of New York and Its Environs.*[4] The metropolitanists believed that the basic urban form established in the nineteenth century would persist into the twentieth, even if the metropolitan area grew to 20 million people and stretched fifty miles or more from its historic core. This giant city would still be defined by its downtown, the overwhelming economic and cultural focus of the metropolitan area. The bulk of the population would still cluster relatively tightly around the downtown in a massive "factory zone" that would be the productive heart of the metropolis. Beyond this zone would be the residential suburbs— still a refuge for a relatively small elite—and beyond that the "outer zone" of farms, forests, and parklands.

For the metropolitanists the main challenges of planning were to
— create a monumental downtown worthy of a great urban civilization;
— construct a massive network of rail public transit to connect all the residents of the metropolis with the downtown;
— make the factory zones not only the most efficient places on the planet for industrial production, but also decent places for the bulk of the city's population to live;
— maintain the outer zone as a source of fresh air, fresh water, and open space for the metropolis;

— establish parks and other recreational facilities in the outer zone and build the transit lines and parkways that would enable urbanites to experience unspoiled nature.

Between the 1920s and the 1960s, there were two significant modernizations of the metropolitanist tradition, both disastrous and both symbolized by Robert Moses's massive projects for New York. Where the metropolitanist tradition had originally concentrated on rail mass transit investments to knit the region together, Moses and his acolytes believed in the total dominance of the automobile. The city must be rebuilt to accommodate the expressway. The second updating was the embrace of urban renewal as the total solution to "urban blight." Only the complete leveling of whole neighborhoods and their rebuilding in the new superblock "tower-in-the-park" pattern could create a viable modern central city.[5]

Jane Jacobs's critique of urban renewal, urban expressways, and other aspects of this late decadent stage in the metropolitanist tradition constitutes one of the most important and effective polemics in American writing. To her critique one might add the idea that the metropolitanist tradition was built on the assumption that there was a "metropolitan elite" who had a natural interest in the prosperity and growth of their region in competition with others throughout the nation. Where politicians were necessarily parochial in their outlook, the elite could override local interests to sponsor a genuinely regional perspective. The Chicago and New York regional plans were specifically designed to provide such a long-term, unified vision. Whatever the limitations of this easy identification of the elite's interests with the general good, there is no doubt that in the Progressive Era, this kind of regional leadership contributed to the remarkable flourishing of various metropolitan park districts, water districts, and port, rail, and mass transit projects that united cities and their suburbs.[6]

However, by the 1960s it was clear that the metropolitan elites had at best a highly selective attachment to their regions. They still took a great interest in the downtown cores, at least as prestigious corporate and cultural headquarters, but they had no loyalty to the people or the jobs in the now-aging factory districts that surrounded the cores. The managers of national corporations understood very well that the federal government's provision of highways, electric power, and other vital infrastructure in the suburbs and in the Sun Belt meant that the old urban factory zones were no longer the most efficient locales for production. For example, Pittsburgh's Allegheny Conference, the model post-1945 organization for regional business planning, brought together the city's industrial and financial establishment to sponsor the redevelopment of the downtown as a suitable setting for corporate headquarters. Meanwhile, this same establishment oversaw the dismantling of Pittsburgh's industrial base.[7]

Although urban renewal was originally inspired by the utopian design theories of the great masters of modern architecture, the actual practice of urban renewal tended to reflect the elite's real priorities. The older districts near downtown—whose historic structures and eclectic enterprises gave a sense of character and history to the whole city—were usually the first to be declared "blighted" and ruthlessly leveled, especially if their residents were black. Black neighborhoods also were the favored locale for the new highways built to connect the downtown to the suburbs. Finally, as Arnold Hirsch has shown for Chicago, public housing projects were intentionally located to provide a seemingly permanent color line—a "second ghetto," as he calls it—between white and black neighborhoods.[8]

More subtly, the decay of the metropolitanist tradition meant that one could no longer count on the old downtown elite to speak forcefully for the region as a whole. As deindustrialization ravaged the old urban factory zones and especially condemned the black migrants who had recently moved there to long-term unemployment, one would have expected pressure for an urban "industrial policy" comparable to the vast sums that were spent to keep the downtowns prosperous. But this never happened, because it would have challenged the underlying pattern of urban industrial disinvestment that was the real industrial policy of the 1960s. Instead, the 1960s saw a highly subsidized regional shift of industrial production from the cities to industrial parks in the suburbs. As the older impulse toward common regional action decayed, the regional reality turned into a war for tax base and other resources between the central cities and their suburbs—a war that the suburbs were destined to win.[9]

This profound city-suburb split gave an air of unreality to the metropolitan councils of governments and the elaborate regional plans that occupied so much of planners' time in the 1960s. Perhaps the most important of these was the Year 2000 Plan for the Washington, D.C. region. A worthy theoretical successor to the Chicago and New York plans, the Year 2000 Plan advocated channeling growth into six corridors extending out from the hub of downtown Washington, corridors defined by new highway and rail transit lines. Separating the corridors would be "wedges" of controlled open space that kept growth from consuming the whole region. This corridor-and-wedge plan would thus combine an efficient pattern for regional expansion with the preservation of open space close to new development.[10]

The Year 2000 Plan really did look to the future in its advocacy of rail mass transit lines as a focus for controlled suburban development. The plan especially foreshadowed Peter Calthorpe's "transit oriented development,"[11] and its vision for the region was certainly important in winning support for the (much-reduced) transit system that was built as the Washington Metro. The plan's concern for preserving open space was admirable but more problematic. Precisely in advocating "controls" for an area covering five counties in two states and the District itself, the Year 2000 Plan raised the unanswerable question of how the local governments who had the actual jurisdiction over land use could be persuaded or compelled to follow the pattern of open-space wedges that the plan advocated. In fact, with devastating speed, the plan's wedges were invaded by low-density development, and the neat pattern of corridor-and-wedge never took shape.[12]

One might imagine that the regionalist planning tradition would have fared better in the 1960s than that of the metropolitanists because this school had long anticipated and urged the decentralization of the cities. Led by such notable 1920s designers and social critics as Lewis Mumford, Benton MacKaye, and Clarence Stein, the regionalists tried to adapt the doctrines of Ebenezer Howard and the English Garden City movement to American conditions. They saw the crowded cities of the turn of the century as a temporary phenomenon, the inhuman result of the backwardness of nineteenth-century technology and the concentration of power in the hands of a metropolitan elite. In the new age of electricity and the automobile, the big city was, in Clarence Stein's phrase, a "dinosaur city" whose crowding and inefficiency consumed society's resources and stunted its residents' lives.[13]

The twentieth century would see a return to the dispersed settlements characteristic of the early nineteenth century, but with regional networks of highways and electrical power that would bring the benefits of advanced technology to every point in the region. The regionalists criticized infrastructure investments designed to maintain the crowded urban cores and called for a decentralized highway system that would serve a regional network of planned "new towns." As central cities shrank, the urban region would consist primarily of these new towns located throughout the region and set in an open, green environment, each combining both work and residence. This true regional city would occupy, in John Thomas's phrase, the "middle ground" between the old crowded cities and the old isolated rural areas.[14] The middle ground could combine all the economic benefits of living in a technologically advanced society with the human scale, local identity, and community of small-town America.[15]

In the 1930s and 1940s, the federal government's massive investment in roads, regional electrical systems, and other infrastructure went far beyond what the regionalists of the 1920s or 1930s could have hoped. But the federal commitment to new towns—the Greenbelt program of the New Deal—halted after only three prototypes had been started: Greenbelt, Maryland; Greenhills, Ohio; and Greendale, Wisconsin. More important, the postwar years revealed that the sprawling, corporate-sponsored growth that resulted was the opposite of the human-scaled community-building that the regionalists had hoped to promote. With power over land use fragmented among the hundreds of counties and municipalities at the edge of most regions, there was no means to limit or direct the destructive force of large-scale speculation fueled by government subsidies. Regionalists had argued in the 1920s that the cities must decentralize into the regions. Now this tide of decentralization was a reality, but it was simultaneously devastating the central cities and overrunning the regionalists' cherished middle ground.

Nevertheless, the heirs of the regionalists in the 1950s and 1960s still nurtured the hope of an American new-town program comparable to the one launched in Britain after World War II. The new town was, in effect, reinvented—not as a way of depopulating the cities, which was already happening, but as "the alternative to sprawl," a way of preserving open space and channeling low-density development at the edge into bounded, coherent, relatively dense settlements. The new-town idea received an unexpected endorsement when two private developers, Robert E. Simon and James Rouse, both undertook ambitious new towns in the Washington, D.C., area: Simon's Reston in northern Virginia and Rouse's Columbia between Washington and Baltimore. Columbia, backed by Rouse's considerable development and public relations organization, seemed to revive the idea of planned new towns as the best solution to the growth of metropolitan areas. But the financial difficulties that overtook first Simon and then Rouse also seemed to indicate that the new-town concept required more than private enterprise to succeed.[16]

After a decade of debate, Congress included in the 1970 Housing Act a provision for "new communities": Title VII.[17] The concept behind Title VII was that the up-front costs of providing planning and infrastructure for a new town were more than even the largest private developer could handle. Rather than shift responsibility for new towns to a public corporation, Title VII promised that private developers who undertook a HUD-approved new town would receive extensive federal mortgage guarantees, planning subsidies, and coordinated services from other federal and state programs. A year later, nine new-town proposals were approved by HUD for federal aid. It appeared that the regionalist tradition would at last make a significant impact on the American region.[18]

Nevertheless, by the recession years of 1974 to 1976, it was obvious that the Title VII new-town program was in disarray. In the end, only one new town called The Woodlands, thirty miles north of Houston, survived largely because the developer was an oilman with deep pockets in a region that benefited from the oil crisis. If urban renewal represented the failure of the metropolitanist tradition, the Title VII new-town program represented a similar (but less publicized) failure of the regionalist tradition. Indeed, the failure was so complete that it has been virtually erased from the collective memory of the planning profession. Nevertheless, its lessons are perhaps as significant as those of urban renewal.

First, in spite of seemingly generous federal loan guarantees, the difficulty of pursuing long-term, complex goals (especially in a decade of economic turmoil) left new-town developers extremely vulnerable compared to more conventional developers, who could move quickly to catch a rapidly changing market. Second, whatever the inherent merits of 1960s–70s new-town design, it was ultimately a compromise that failed to establish itself as a real alternative to conventional subdivision. Despite talk of "mixed use" local retail and community centers, bike paths, and sidewalks, the plans were almost as spread out and automobile dependent as typical sprawl. (Here, perhaps, the more radical attempts by the 1990s "new urbanists" to create genuine "pedestrian pockets" are in the long run more practical.)[19]

Finally, and perhaps most important, the new towns sought to produce the benefits of metropolitan governance without its reality. Instead, they demonstrated that without some form of metropolitan growth and transportation policy, the new-town ideal is virtually impossible. In Britain the new-town movement was backed by an

activist national government that was able to impose a strictly maintained greenbelt around all of Britain's major cities and to limit
growth to point the greenbelt to new towns (or infill within existing
towns). The new towns fell victim to the same forces of rapid piece-
meal development that had doomed the corridors-and-wedges design
of the Washington Year 2000 Plan. There was no regional land-use
policy that favored new-town development strongly enough to prevent
conventional suburban development from seizing the land around
the new town and enveloping it in an environment of sprawl.[20]

If the failures of both the metropolitanist and regionalist traditions represent the near death of American planning, where then was
its new life? The revitalization of American planning in the 1960s
stemmed from three sources:

— a new appreciation of the fragility and importance of "urbanity," especially as propounded by Jane Jacobs;

— a new appreciation of the fragility and importance of open
space and respect for the environment, best represented in Ian
McHarg's *Design With Nature*.[21]

— the beginnings of an understanding that these two seemingly
dissimilar goals—urbanity and open space—were in fact necessary elements of a new kind of regional plan and above all, a new kind of
regional coalition.

To begin with Jacobs, her book *The Death and Life of Great American
Cities* concentrated on the recent failures of urban renewal but also
criticized virtually all the icons of American planning from the City
Beautiful to the new-town movement. The problem in all these design
strategies, she charged, was that planners responded to what they saw
as the "disorder" of the city by imposing their own designs, but they
completely failed to understand and to respect the far more complex
order that healthy cities already embodied. This complex order—
what she calls "close-grained diversity"—was the result not of big plans
but of all the little plans of ordinary people that alone can generate
the diversity that is the true glory of a great city.[22]

Jacobs brilliantly supported these critiques with an abundance of
detailed observations that contrasted the bleak and dangerous terrain
of the planned public housing project with the vibrancy of traditional
"unplanned" urban streets like Hudson Street in Manhattan's West
Village where she then lived. Although Jacobs's demolition of bureaucratic urban renewal theory was the most brilliant and most necessary
part of her book, there were other aspects of her work that ironically

proved highly useful to a planning revival. By drastically devaluing theoretical expertise, Jacobs was in a sense returning to the eclectic, pragmatic roots of American planning. By trusting the evidence of her own eyes, she countered the academicization of planning and helped to restore the "urban conversation" that had traditionally been at the core of the American planning tradition. Perhaps most important, Jacobs provided what urban planning needed most in an era of decentralization when almost all urban functions were rapidly suburbanizing: she provided a justification for the city.

In her analysis urban density serves a positive function because it provides the rich, complex setting in which individuals and small businesses can best pursue their own plans. A big corporate bureaucracy could function in isolation, but to succeed, a small business needs a multitude of complementary enterprises nearby. The diversity of small urban enterprises sustains and is sustained by a dense and diverse urban population with highly varied tastes and needs. As Jacobs emphasizes, this special urbanity is made manifest in the street life of a great city. For Jacobs, what happens on the sidewalks is just as important as what happens in the buildings. A successful urban street is a complex blend of neighbors and strangers, a constantly changing "urban ballet" of familiarity and chance encounters that both defines a neighborhood and welcomes the outsider. These streets are safe not because they are constantly policed, but because the citizens watch out for each other. Safe, lively, diverse streets are the essence of true urbanity.

In ways that Jacobs herself never foresaw, her analysis of the city became the starting point for redefining the goals and methods of urban planning. She not only indicated the new aim of urbanism— the preservation of the older urban fabric, with its precious legacy of human-scaled streets and other public spaces—but equally important, she identified the limitations of planning. Where urban renewal had sought total control, post-Jacobs planning returned to Alexis de Tocqueville's perception in *Democracy in America* that the American style of governance is most powerful when it steps back and leaves room for the initiative and creativity of the citizens.[23] The areas that urban renewal had targeted for demolition were now identified as the areas to be lovingly protected, and the prime movers for this historic preservation movement were now individuals willing to buy and renovate older structures.

However, planners soon performed more important tasks than just providing brick sidewalks and fancy streetlights in historic districts. Successful historic preservation often involved the adaptive reuse of historic structures, which required the imagination to conceive effective new uses and the ability to recruit private developers who could carry out the transformation. Downtown planning became increasingly a kind of public entrepreneurship, in which the planners brokered deals to attract new investment. The model for this public-private partnership was the 1976 alliance of the city of Boston and the developer James Rouse to transform the 1826 Quincy Market into a contemporary shopping arcade that would soon prove to be one of the liveliest public spaces in the city. Downtown planning today aims at an eclectic mixture of preservation and adaptive reuse with new office towers, atrium hotels, convention centers, and sports stadiums.[24]

If the urban crisis had impelled Jacobs and her successors to rethink and reaffirm the meaning and importance of cities, the explosion of suburban sprawl similarly impelled the regionalists to rethink and reaffirm their commitment to human settlements in harmony with nature. The single figure whose importance for the regionalist tradition comes closest to Jane Jacobs's importance for the metropolitanists is Ian McHarg, the Scottish-born landscape architect and author of *Design With Nature*.[25] Like Jacobs, McHarg understood the fundamental problem to be combating a way of thinking and building that imposed a destructive simplicity on a complex system. For Jacobs, this complexity was the diverse city itself, imperiled by planners seeking to impose a simple pseudo-order. For McHarg, the complexity was the wonderfully varied ecological structure of the region, which was being destroyed by sprawling suburban building patterns that imposed the same destructively simple pattern of subdivisions and highways from the lowlands to the ridge tops.

McHarg's solution was to "design with nature," that is, to allow the ecology of the region to guide building. Only after a profound examination of the land—both scientific and aesthetic—could one identify the right sites for new construction and the form it must take. This "ecological view" would similarly define the areas that would best be used for varied types of agriculture and the areas that must be preserved as wilderness.[26] McHarg thus reexpressed the fundamental ideals of Benton MacKaye and the earlier regionalists in terms the growing environmental movement could understand. *Design With Nature* never attained the canonical status of *The Death and Life of Great American Cities*, but its ideas underlay the powerful upsurge of environmental activism on the regional periphery. Just as important, *Design*

With Nature provided a language that acknowledged the place of human settlements in nature, a language that could accommodate the new coalitions between urbanists and environmentalists that began to emerge in the 1970s.

These new coalitions reflected what was perhaps the major lesson of the 1960s: although the major trends of decentralization and suburbanization were destructive both to urbanity and open space, careful regional planning could counter both trends by simultaneously strengthening regional centers and limiting growth at the edge. These two strategies reinforced each other: a dense, vital center would help decrease the pressure for peripheral development and increase ridership for mass transit; limiting growth at the edge would encourage the kind of infill development at the center that would keep the older central cities alive.

Thus effective regional planning implied a new kind of regional coalition, first seen in the Portland region in the mid-1970s. In the city of Portland itself, Mayor Neil Goldschmidt led a coordinated program of urban revitalization: downtown preservation and upgrading; neighborhood renovation; and improved mass transit. Portland even removed a waterfront highway and replaced it with a park and in 1975 cancelled a proposed highway and used the money for a new light rail line. At the same time, Governor Tom McCall, responding to rural and suburban concerns, sponsored legislation to create the Land Conservation and Development Commission, whose best-known achievement was the 1979 urban growth boundary around the Portland region. The result was a regionalism that balanced urban and environmental concerns, based on a regional coalition that extended from farmers to suburbanites to neighborhood activists to downtown business and civic leaders.[27]

Portland, to be sure, never experienced either the rapid suburbanization of other regions in the 1950s and 1960s or their racial polarization. One need only mention Los Angeles to indicate the difficulties of pursuing a true regional policy, especially a regional mass transit policy, in a larger, more complex, and more divided metropolis.[28] But if the Portland experience does not yield an easy model to imitate, it certainly indicates that the travails of American regional planning in the 1960s were not in vain. Out of the wreckage of outmoded ideas and practices, planners have fashioned both a new vision of the American region and the promise of new coalitions to implement that vision.

This vision may seem vague and tentative compared to the grand designs produced earlier in the century, and the new coalitions seem weak compared to the massive power that Robert Moses and the other masters of the growth machine mustered at midcentury. Nevertheless, these very weaknesses reflect crucial and positive lessons. Planning in the 1960s sought to establish, in the words of President Kennedy's Special Message to Congress (quoted as the epigraph of this chapter), "an effective and comprehensive planning process in each metropolitan area embracing all major activities both public and private that shape the community." Such hubris inevitably brought retribution. American planning today is most effective and comprehensive precisely when it eschews all-embracing powers and works instead within the limits of the pluralistic systems that actually define the American-built environment. These lessons of the 1960s could be summarized as follows:

— Distrust the "grand design."

— Recognize regional diversity and accept local jurisdictions and local concerns.

— Plan as a "regional conversation" rather than as a top-down exercise in power.[29]

These lessons are demonstrated in an exemplar of current planning, the New Jersey State Plan. Established in 1986 by moderate Republican governor Thomas Kean in response to the depredations of the 1980s building boom, the New Jersey State Planning Commission was supported by his Democratic successor James Florio and is currently an important part of the agenda of Republican governor Christine Todd Whitman. The state's Development and Redevelopment Plan is comprehensive in the sense that it embodies the idea of limiting growth at the edge while redeveloping New Jersey's older cities and transit corridors. One looks in vain for a grand design equivalent to the corridors-and-wedges of the Washington Year 2000 Plan. Instead one finds an attempt to zone land use according to a flexible tier system that seeks to identify appropriate uses ranging from wilderness preservation to targeted urban redevelopment.[30]

However, real power over land use lies not at the state level but with New Jersey's 567 municipalities and 21 counties. Under the leadership of Herbert Simmens, the New Jersey State Plan is, in practice, a kind of invitation to each of these local units to engage in a statewide "conversation" to reexamine needs and priorities and bring them into harmony with the plan's regional goals. The plan is also an invitation to have a dialogue with other state and federal agencies about how they can use their resources to advance the plan's goals. Finally (and this is the greatest challenge), the plan is an invitation to a conversation between New Jersey's cities and suburbs to find some common ground—a conversation far more difficult than in the Portland region because of the deep racial divide between cities like Newark and Camden and their affluent suburbs.

Under the direction of architect Carlos Rodrigues, the New Jersey State Plan is also developing a design component, but once again its goals and methods are far more flexible and eclectic than in the 1960s. There is no equivalent here to the self-confident panaceas of the past, either tower-in-the-park urban renewal or suburban new towns. Instead, Rodrigues and his colleagues have drawn largely from new-urbanist concepts of concentrated development mixed with historic preservation to safeguard the cities and towns that already possess the density, transit links, pedestrian scale, and public spaces that new-urbanist theory prizes. Above all, the plan recognizes that planning in practice is a messy process of protracted dialogue—seeking to balance, for example, the need to reduce development at the edge with the need derived from the New Jersey Supreme Court's "Mount Laurel decisions" to provide affordable housing in the suburbs.[31]

This strategy of planning is the exact opposite of the unified, top-down "metropolitan government" that 1960s planners vainly hoped would emerge out of the metropolitan councils of government of that era. But paradoxically this weaker current form of metropolitan regionalism might generate far more effective power in the end. In *Democracy in America*, Tocqueville addresses this very American paradox of formally limited government and surprisingly effective policies. He argues that the very power of a nineteenth-century European centralized government tends to produce apathy and passive resistance among the governed because it operates without public knowledge or discussion.[32] Such a critique anticipates the failures of top-down American planning in the 1960s.

By contrast, Tocqueville identifies the true effectiveness of democratic planning. The absence of a controlling central power, he observes, invites collective action outside a bureaucratic hierarchy. "Under [democracy's] sway, the grandeur is not in what the public administration does, but what is done without it or outside of it. Democracy does not give the people the most skilful government, but it produces what the ablest governments are frequently unable to cre-

ate; namely, a superabundant force, and an energy which is insepara-
ble from it, and which may, however unfavorable circumstances may
be, produce wonders."[99]

Today we need wonders, because regional planning is attempting
to address simultaneously the two most difficult domestic issues that
face this country: first, the great divide of class and race as expressed
physically by the separation of inner city and suburb; and second, the
destructive impact of an ever-expanding technological society on the
natural environment that must sustain our lives. If these issues often
seem paralyzing in their difficulty and complexity, we can at least
hope for the superabundant force that only regenerated democratic
planning can produce.

Notes

1. John F. Kennedy, "Special Message to Congress on Housing and Community Development," March 9, 1961, quoted in National Capital Planning Commission and National Capital Regional Planning Commission, *A Policies Plan for
the Year 2000* (Washington Metropolitan Regional Council, 1961), p. 26.

2. Jane Jacobs, *The Death and Life of Great American Cities* (Random House,
1961), p. 410. Jacobs was a classic "outsider" when she published this seminal
book. Without professional credentials or even a college degree, Jacobs was a
journalist who worked as senior editor at *Architectural Forum*. In 1961 she was
known more for her opposition to Robert Moses's plans to put a highway
through Washington Square Park than for her limited published work. Nevertheless, *Death and Life* was an immediate success (nominated for a National
Book Award), which propelled her into a lifetime of writing. Her other books
include *The Economy of Cities* (Random House, 1969) and *Cities and the Wealth of
Nations* (Random House, 1984).

3. Ibid.

4. Daniel Burnham and Edward H. Bennett, *Plan of Chicago* (Chicago: Commercial Club, 1909); Committee on Regional Plan of New York and Its Environs, *Regional Plan of New York and Its Environs: The Graphic Regional Plan* (New
York, 1929).

5. Robert A. Caro, *The Power Broker: Robert Moses and the Fall of New York*
(Knopf, 1974), part VI.

6. Robert Fishman, "The Regional Plan and the Transformation of the
Industrial Metropolis," in David Ward and Olivier Zunz, eds., *The Landscape of
Modernity* (Russell Sage Foundation, 1992), pp. 106–28.

7. Jon C. Teaford, *The Rough Road to Renaissance: Urban Revitalization in
America, 1940–1985* (Johns Hopkins University Press, 1990), chap. 2.

8. Arnold R. Hirsch, *Making the Second Ghetto: Race and Housing in Chicago,
1940–1960* (Cambridge University Press, 1983).

9. Thomas J. Sugrue, *The Origins of the Urban Crisis: Race and Inequality in Postwar Detroit* (Princeton University Press, 1996), chaps. 5 and 7.

10. National Capital Planning Commission and National Capital Regional Planning Commission, *A Policies Plan for the Year 2000* (Washington Metropolitan Regional Council, 1961), pp. 46–47.

11. Peter Calthorpe, *The Next American Metropolis: Ecology, Community, and the American Dream* (Princeton Architectural Press, 1993), pp. 46–71.

12. Mel Scott, *American City Planning Since 1890* (University of California Press, 1971), pp. 573–80.

13. Clarence Stein, "Dinosaur Cities" (1925), reprinted in Carl Sussman, ed., *Planning the Fourth Migration: The Neglected Vision of the Regional Planning Association of America* (MIT Press, 1976), pp. 28–36. For Stein and his colleagues Lewis Mumford and Benton MacKaye and their debt to Ebenezer Howard, see Edward K. Spann, *Designing Modern America: The Regional Planning Association of America and Its Members* (Ohio University Press, 1996).

14. John Thomas, "Holding the Middle Ground," in Robert Fishman, ed., *The American Planning Tradition: Culture and Politics* (Johns Hopkins University Press, 1999), chap. 2.

15. Ibid.

16. Gurney Breckenfeld, *Columbia and the New Cities* (New York: Ives Washburn, 1971).

17. Urban Growth and New Community Development Act (1970). Title VII of the act provided aid for new towns.

18. American Institute of Architects, *New Towns in America: The Design and Development Process* (John Wiley, 1973).

19. Lloyd Rodwin, "The Next Generation of New Towns," in *New Towns in America*, pp. 126–30.

20. Robert Fishman, "America's New City," *Wilson Quarterly*, vol. 14 (Winter 1990), pp. 24–55.

21. Ian L. McHarg, *Design with Nature* (Garden City, N.J.: Doubleday/Natural History Press, 1969). Born outside Glasgow, Scotland, McHarg was profoundly shaped by the contrast between the rugged countryside and a Glasgow that he called "one of the most implacable testaments to the city of toil in all of Christendom, a memorial to an inordinate capacity to create ugliness, a sandstone excretion cemented with smoke and grime." (*Design with Nature*, p. 1). After serving as a parachute officer in World War II, McHarg studied landscape architecture at Harvard and then joined the faculty of the University of Pennsylvania. There he cofounded the influential Philadelphia planning firm of Wallace, McHarg Associates (the present-day WRT). As faculty member and consultant, he pursued the important case studies of the New Jersey shore, the Philadelphia watershed, and the Washington-Baltimore metropolitan region that form the heart of *Design with Nature*.

22. Jacobs, *Death and Life of Great American Cities*, chap. 7.

23. Alexis de Tocqueville, "Political Activity Which Pervades the United States," in *Democracy in America*, ed. Richard D. Heffner (New American Library, 1956), part I. Originally published in 1835 and 1840.

24. Bernard J. Frieden and Lynne B. Sagalyn, *Downtown, Inc.: How America Builds Cities* (MIT Press, 1989).

25. McHarg, *Design with Nature*

26. Ibid., pp. 99-152.

27. Carl Abbott, Deborah Howe, and Sy Adler, eds., *Planning the Oregon Way: A Twenty-Year Evaluation* (Oregon State University Press, 1994).

28. William Fulton, *The Reluctant Metropolis: The Politics of Urban Growth in Los Angeles* (Point Arena, Calif.: Solano Press, 1997).

29. For the politics of this new regionalism, see especially Myron Orfield, *Metropolitics: A Regional Agenda for Community and Stability* (Brookings, 1997).

30. New Jersey State Planning Commission, *Communities of Place: The New Jersey State Development and Redevelopment Plan* (Trenton, N.J.: Office of State Planning, 1992).

31. The "Mount Laurel decisions" of the New Jersey State Supreme Court in the 1970s and 1980s prohibited this New Jersey suburb and all others in New Jersey from "zoning out the poor," that is, using zoning regulations to exclude affordable housing. To implement the decision, the justices required that each suburb make provisions to include within its boundaries its "fair share" of affordable housing for its region. The decisions and their consequences are discussed in David L. Kirp, John P. Dwyer, and Larry A. Rosenthal, *Our Town: Race, Housing, and the Soul of Suburbia* (Rutgers University Press, 1995) and Charles M. Haar, *Suburbs Under Siege: Race, Space, and Audacious Judges* (Princeton University Press, 1996).

32. Tocqueville, *Democracy in America*, p. 108.

33. Ibid., p. 110.

PART TWO

COALITIONS AND METROPOLITANISM

CHAPTER FIVE

Coalition Building for Regionalism

MARGARET WEIR

For over a century, urban planners and supporters of "good government" have argued in favor of metropolitanism. These advocates have criticized the growth of conflicting and overlapping local political and administrative jurisdictions on grounds of both efficiency and equity. In the postwar era, as suburbs grew and metropolitan political jurisdictions multiplied, a chorus of planners—many enjoying positions of influence within an expanding federal government—called for solutions ranging from outright government consolidations to voluntary cooperation among the maze of metropolitan governments. Despite the persistent complaints from urban experts about the irrationality and unfairness of metropolitan fragmentation, their ideas have had very limited practical impact on postwar American cities and suburbs. The wave of expert enthusiasm for metropolitan regionalism in the 1960s and 1970s left only a handful of city-county consolidations and a legacy of weak regional organizations with few resources and even less power.

There were two important exceptions to this pattern of failure: Oregon adopted effective land-use regulation that provided a basis for strengthening metropolitanism in the coming decades; Minnesota created a Metropolitan Council for the Twin Cities area and passed fiscal disparities legislation that helped compensate for the financial consequences of metropolitan political fragmentation. It is revealing to compare the successes in Oregon and Minnesota with the failures to adopt comparable measures in Illinois and California, states that faced significant metropolitan fragmentation and suburban sprawl in the 1960s and 1970s. In the former two states, coalition building in state politics was the key to success. Studies of metropolitanism have focused on federal initiatives and on features of particular metropolitan areas, but the examples of Oregon and Minnesota illustrate the central role of states in enacting or blocking legislation needed to promote metropolitan regionalism.

The successful cases had three common elements: at least one politically powerful interest that saw metropolitan regionalism as a way to address its concerns, bipartisan coalition building, and relatively weak opposing groups. In Oregon, farmers, the environmental movement, and Portland city leaders, for different reasons, all supported the land-use legislation enacted in 1973. Oregon's Republican governor, Tom McCall, was pivotal to success. In Minnesota, Minneapolis city leaders pressed for legislation to create the Metropolitan Council and found support in a sympathetic governor. As in Oregon, moderate Republicans were critical to the victory. In both states the groups most likely to oppose metropolitan initiatives—developers and suburban interests—were unusually weak or quiescent.

The politics of Illinois and California looked much different on each of these dimensions. The availability of alternative goals and resources meant that environmental and urban interests in these states did not look to metropolitanism as a way to achieve their objectives. Thus even though a strong environmental movement existed in California and both states experienced significant sprawl and urban decline, those concerned with these problems sought other ways to address them. In addition, given the nature of political party divisions in these states, bipartisanship and gubernatorial support for metropolitanism were most unlikely. The election of Ronald Reagan as governor in 1966 effectively ruled out such an alliance in California; longstanding animosity and partisan division between city and suburb in the Chicago metropolitan region blocked the way in Illinois. Finally, opponents in these states were stronger. In California the political system magnified the power of developers, who staunchly opposed land-use regulation. In both Illinois and California, racial divisions between city and suburb promised that any serious efforts to promote metropolitan cooperation or to "open up the suburbs" could trigger venomous political fights that few politicians wanted to confront.

The conditions for building coalitions around metropolitan-oriented legislation were clearly much more favorable in Oregon and Minnesota during the early 1970s. Yet even in these cases, favorable legislation was not inevitable. It took the political effort of environmental and urban interests (and agricultural interests in Oregon) and sympathetic politicians to enact the charter legislation. The divergent fate of the initiatives in Oregon and Minnesota underscores the importance of political coalition building at the state level as key to successful metropolitanism. In Oregon ongoing political mobilization of supporters created a "virtuous cycle" in which the initial legislation provided a springboard for strengthening the regional approach and winning new support. In Minnesota, where there was much less mobilization, the virtuous cycle came to a halt when the politically weak Metropolitan Council lost support in the legislature in the 1980s. In fact, the Metropolitan Council was nearly moribund until recent efforts to build legislative coalitions between the Twin Cities and less affluent suburbs. Thus, while the particular political configurations that enacted regional initiatives in Oregon and Minnesota two decades ago are unlikely to be reproduced in other states, many aspects of their coalition-building and mobilization strategies offer valuable lessons for proponents of metropolitanism today.

Metropolitan Regionalism in Oregon and Minnesota

The successful legislation in Oregon and Minnesota in the early 1970s reflected the unusually favorable social and political conditions in both states. However, each followed a different political path: In Oregon important social and economic groups mobilized in favor of reforms and created a broad political debate. In Minnesota the process was much more elite driven—a practical good-government response to problems facing the Twin Cities metropolitan area. In both states the initial legislation provided a wedge for expanding the scope of regional efforts, but the continuing strength of regionalism in Oregon and its growing weakness in Minnesota highlight the need for broad and ongoing political mobilization to support regional approaches to urban issues.

Two Paths

In Oregon state regulation of land use provided the essential framework for metropolitan regionalism. The critical piece of legislation was a 1973 law that created a new Land Conservation and Development Commission (LCDC), appointed by the governor and charged with formulating goals for land use across the state.[1] The law required counties and cities to draw up comprehensive plans that conformed to the LCDC goals. What put teeth in the act—and distinguished Oregon's land-use legislation—was the LCDC's power to reject local plans. In the year after its creation, the LCDC formulated goals that had important implications for the pattern of urban growth in Oregon. It required cities and counties to create urban growth boundaries, areas within which the cities could be expected to grow over the next twenty years and in which development would be encouraged. Outside these boundaries, land was zoned exclusively for farm use, making development much more difficult. The aim of the growth boundaries was to limit sprawl by making urban growth contiguous and stopping leapfrog patterns of development.

Bowing to political realities, the law did not create a new state agency responsible for drawing up plans but rather delegated planning responsibility to counties. The one exception was the Portland metropolitan area, which was designated as a special planning district ranging over three separate counties. Like many metropolitan regions, the Portland area in 1969 had established a council of local governments, the Columbia Region Association of Governments (CRAG), to meet federal requirements for a metropolitan planning district. As in other metropolitan areas, the organization operated on a voluntary basis and was composed of local governments, each of which had an equal vote. In 1973, however, the state legislature gave CRAG the legal authority to require the counties to comply with its land-use plans (including the urban growth boundary) and made membership mandatory for the three counties in the Portland metropolitan area. It also weighted voting within the association by population, thus giving the more densely populated city of Portland 40 percent of the votes.[2] Local voters approved this delegation of power in a referendum. The strong city support for the agency and its dominant voice within the organization gave the city unusual leverage in metropolitan politics.

State-level initiatives for land-use planning were thus critical in supporting metropolitan planning efforts already under way in the Portland area. In 1969, with a local transportation system on the verge of bankruptcy, Portland had pressed the state legislature to establish a regional transportation agency that would allow it to tap into the suburban tax base. In return, the city agreed to the creation of a Metropolitan Services District, whose initial responsibilities included solid waste disposal and a financially precarious zoo.[3] In 1978 the Metropolitan Service District (MSD) took over the responsibilities of CRAG, which was abolished, and in a departure from the usual organization of regional bodies across the county, the new MSD commissioners were to be directly elected, not appointed. Over time the responsibilities of the MSD grew to encompass authority over metropolitan land-use policies, including the urban growth boundary, as well as key metropolitan services and facilities ranging from garbage disposal to a major convention center. In 1992 the MSD was redesignated "Metro" and given even more authority with the status of a home rule government.

One of the most striking political features of these initiatives was the broad range of active support they generated. On the urban side, it was not just planners and good-government groups but politicians with substantial constituencies, such as Portland mayor Neil Goldschmidt, who strongly supported the land-use law and the other metropolitan initiatives associated with it. Likewise, environmentalists, an important new force in politics in the early 1970s, focused on the land-use regulation law as the central means of achieving their goals. This intertwining of urban and environmental interests and their support of a single legislative agenda was the only one of its kind across the nation. At the same time that Oregon was debating its land-use law, Congress was considering a land-use bill that provided incentives for states to engage in precisely the kind of planning Oregon was considering. In stark contrast to the political coalition that backed Oregon's bill, the national legislation never attracted strong support from either environmental groups or urban interests, who did not see their agendas as intertwined.[4] Perhaps most unusual, agricultural interests were key initiators of the 1973 Oregon legislation.

What facilitated this unusual political cooperation between urban, environmental, and agricultural groups? Part of the answer lies in Oregon's distinctive geography. With nearly half of the state's population concentrated in the Willamette Valley, which contains the state's major cities as well as its richest agricultural land, the trade-offs between urbanization and the limited supply of rural land were much more starkly drawn in Oregon than in most states. In fact, the land-use legislation of 1973 only passed because of strong support from leg-islators in the Willamette Valley. Forty-nine of the sixty legislators from the valley backed it, whereas only nine of the thirty legislators from eastern and coastal regions supported it.[5] This distinctive geography and the sharp trade-offs it posed accounted for the critical support of agricultural interests. In places where land is more plentiful, agricul-tural interests either have shown little interest in land-use regulation or have opposed it, fearing that it would strengthen state government at the expense of local decisionmaking. Moreover, in most places farmers have sought to preserve the right to dispose of their land as they wished—including the right to benefit from the higher land prices that come with development. Such sentiments also existed in Oregon, especially from rural interests outside the Willamette Valley.[6] However, the limited supply of land in the Willamette Valley altered the perspective of its farmers because of the obvious threat that urban sprawl posed to the entire agricultural industry there and the way of life it supported.

Key interests were thus predisposed to endorse land-use regula-tion; however, such predispositions had to be mobilized if they were to unite and become politically powerful. In this task Oregon governor Tom McCall played an important role. A moderate Republican and a long-time leader on environmental issues, McCall wanted to make Oregon the "environmental model for the nation."[7] Such sentiments were on display in his 1972 address to the legislature, which castigated the "unfettered despoiling of the land" by "sagebrush subdivisions, coastal condomania, and the ravenous rampage of suburbia." McCall's galvanizing role helped ensure that support for land-use reg-ulation would be bipartisan. But the geographic basis of support also made bipartisan support possible: cities in the Willamette Valley tended to be Democratic, while the rural areas voted Republican. Both, however, shared a concern about sprawl that provided the basis for cooperation.

In addition to these favorable political conditions, the interests that posed the greatest opposition to metropolitan regionalism else-where in the country were unusually weak in Oregon during the 1960s and 1970s. Suburban interests were particularly weak. Oregon's slow growth in the 1950s and 1960s meant that it had few full-service suburban governments and not much of a distinct suburban agenda when land-use regulation and metropolitan regionalism came under consideration.[8] Oregon's racial homogeneity also played a role. In such racially homogenous metropolitan areas, the division between city and suburb is much less fraught with tension and conflict. For all of these reasons, suburban interests played little role in blocking state land-use legislation or in contesting the development of metropolitan government in Portland.[9] The other major interests generally opposed to land-use regulation—developers and the housing industry—indeed did work against the 1973 legislation, but slow suburbanization left them weaker than in other states. Moreover, because other commercial interests with a stake in Portland supported metropolitan regionalism, business did not speak with a single voice on this issue. Together the broad support for land-use legislation, gubernatorial initiative, and bipartisan cooperation overwhelmed the weak opposition.

In Minnesota metropolitan regionalism took a different form and stemmed from distinct political impulses. Two key pieces of legislation in Minnesota created the Metropolitan Council in 1967 and the Fiscal Disparities Act of 1971. The immediate impetus for establishing the Metropolitan Council was a crisis over water and sewer lines in growing suburban areas, a problem that had become so severe that the federal government was threatening to withhold its home mortgage insurance from these areas. The legislature initially charged the new council with finding solutions to the sewage problems and later extended its purview to include a broad range of regional issues, including the sewers, solid waste disposal, and regional parks.[10] Although early discussion had called for an elected board, the legislature ultimately decided that the governor would appoint board members. As the board worked to define its role during its first year, it became clear that it would function as a general policymaker and overseer of regional concerns rather than as a direct operational agency.

Most histories of the Metropolitan Council stress the practical problem-solving orientation that its initial supporters shared. Indeed, the debate about metropolitanism in Minnesota was much more technocratic and elite oriented than in Oregon. One of the most important groups pushing for the creation of the council was the Citizens League, a nonpartisan civic organization that sponsored research on metropolitan policy concerns. With close ties to elites in business and politics, the Citizens League was a politically influential organization but not one that mobilized grass-roots support. In fact, the debate over metropolitanism in Minnesota displayed very little grass-roots organization of the kind that occurred in Oregon. The environmental movement was not much of a presence in Minnesota in 1967 when the legislation passed, and rural interests, who feared the expansion of metropolitan power, were largely opposed. Most important in creating the Metropolitan Council was the state legislature, where one-person one-vote reapportionment finally broke the rural stranglehold on the legislature and gave the Twin Cities region nearly half the seats in 1967. The long tradition of progressive politics in Minnesota, the well-organized civic elites of the Twin Cities, and the new dominance of the region in the legislature all made the creation of the Metropolitan Council a largely uncontroversial affair.[11]

More sharply contested was the 1971 fiscal disparities bill. As passed, the act established regional tax-base sharing.[12] Forty percent of the tax income from new commercial and industrial development would go into a common pool to be redistributed among political jurisdictions throughout the six-county metropolitan region on the basis of their commercial and industrial wealth. Drawing on ideas developed by the Citizens League, a Republican representative from a low-tax-capacity suburb led the effort to pass the bill. Driving him was the fear that the movement toward regional land-use planning and development would prevent districts such as his from developing more taxing capacity in the future. Representatives of affluent suburbs bitterly contested the bill, denouncing it as "communistic," "Robin Hood" legislation. These opponents nearly defeated the bill in the state senate. Only a political alliance with rural Republicans, forged through longstanding personal ties with the bill's author, allowed the fiscal disparities legislation to pass. Suburban cities immediately contested the act in the courts, where it was upheld.

Thus the Twin Cities experienced conflicts between city and suburbs, but these disputes were not broad enough to block the development of regional legislation. The ease with which the Metropolitan Council was created suggests that as in Oregon, cities and suburbs did not have the separate and conflictual identities characteristic of more racially divided metropolitan areas.[13] The line between city and suburb was not perceived as a racial line, and this homogeneity allowed the legislature to treat the problems surrounding metropolitan service provision as practical or technical concerns that did not invoke highly charged political issues. Moreover, as in Oregon, the Twin Cities had no tradition of the machine politics that made suburbs in many other metropolitan areas suspicious of any forms of cooperation with the city. Racial homogeneity also made it easier for Republican representatives from lower-tax-capacity suburbs to join with Democratic representatives from the city in support of the fiscal disparities legislation. Common economic interests could not be overshadowed by racial divisions. A history of bipartisan compromise in the legislature further facilitated political coalition building as rural Republicans were persuaded to support the bill despite opposition from Republicans representing affluent suburbs.

Political Mobilization and Virtuous Cycles

In both Oregon and Minnesota, initial legislation provided little more than an opening for further developments. The scope and content of metropolitan regionalism depended on how these initial achievements were defined and expanded over time. In both states the scope of metropolitanism expanded significantly in the 1970s, as regional bodies assumed authority over key decisions about land use, public services, transportation, and housing. But in Oregon this growing authority developed into a virtuous cycle in which policy and politics reinforced one another: as regional decisionmakers moved into new areas, the political coalition that supported them actually grew stronger. In Minnesota, by contrast, after an initial ten years of growing authority and accomplishment, the Metropolitan Council began to languish. The difference was that Oregon's approach to land-use planning was inherently more political and was accompanied by ongoing mobilization and coalition-building efforts, whereas Minnesota's approach remained more narrowly technocratic and dependent on the political winds in the legislature.

In both states the scope of regionalism grew from rather ambiguous beginnings, but because so many regional issues were interrelated, action in one area often led to efforts in new areas. For example, in Oregon the LCDC initially focused on stopping development in rural and agricultural areas. However, the commission quickly realized that effectiveness on this issue required that development be free to occur in other areas. Thus the commission began to press for the removal of barriers to development within urban growth boundaries. This meant directly challenging local efforts to establish large-lot zoning, building moratoria, and other measures designed to limit development. In its first such case in 1977, the LCDC struck down a zoning ordinance in the city of Durham that increased minimum lot sizes. The commission ruled that the zoning ordinance violated the housing goal that all localities accommodate housing to meet the needs of all their citizens. The zoning restrictions would, in the words of the commission, promote "economic and social homogeneity" at odds with the housing goal.[14] Similar pressures directed the LCDC's attention to the development and location of large public facilities, such as convention centers. In the Twin Cities the Metropolitan Council gradually took on a similar range of responsibilities as the legislature added responsibilities that went far beyond the initial charge of addressing the sewage problem. By 1977 the council bore responsibility for establishing regional policy on transportation, waste control, airports, affordable housing, and land use. While it did not have direct operational authority in these areas, the council had significant leverage over the operational commissions because it had the power to approve their capital budgets and, in most cases, to appoint their members.[15]

The loosely similar policy trajectories in Oregon and Minnesota belie important underlying political differences. From the start Oregon's law required far more grass-roots political engagement. The 1973 legislation charged the new Land Conservation and Development Commission with drawing up a set of goals to guide counties as they devised their land-use plans. The commission developed these goals in a year-long process of statewide public meetings. Nineteen goals emerged, covering a broad range of housing, transportation, environmental, and service issues. Number one was the requirement for broad citizen participation in all future planning. By contrast, in Minnesota the newly created Metropolitan Council reported to the legislature; it had no charge to engage in grass-roots discussion about regional matters, but rather was expected to recommend the best policy solutions to the legislature. The fiscal disparities legislation was more controversial and reliant on a distinctive political coalition, but the self-executing nature of the legislation meant that it did not require ongoing political mobilization to operate.

In addition, in Oregon, as Governor McCall left office in 1975, he helped to create a nonprofit organization, 1,000 Friends of Oregon, to monitor the implementation of land-use legislation. Since its inception 1,000 Friends of Oregon has functioned in a wide range of arenas to defend and expand the scope of land-use legislation and to build political support for it. One of its major activities has been to file lawsuits strategically aimed to establish precedents that strengthen and extend the law. But its activities have not been confined to the legal arena; 1,000 Friends also mobilizes grass-roots support, lobbies the legislature, provides timely studies designed to bolster its arguments, and assists le coalition in drawing up their land use plans.[16] Minnesota's Metropolitan Council had no comparable defender. The Citizens League, which had been so important in its creation, had never viewed its mission as that of building political support or devising legal strategies to extend the council's authority. Moreover, in the 1980s the Citizens League became increasingly cautious and unwilling to go out on a limb in support of regional initiatives. Created by the legislature, the Metropolitan Council did not have any independent grass-roots political allies to bolster its political standing or advance the metropolitan agenda. In contrast to Oregon, no Minnesota governor stepped forward to champion the regional agenda. The council remained dependent on the goodwill of the legislature, which it had little power to influence. Nor did it seek legal authority to bolster its power: the council never brought a lawsuit to enforce its land-use powers.[17]

The support behind Oregon's law has made it increasingly effective, which in turn, has helped to curb the political power of potential opponents. The urban growth boundary has helped to stem speculative development in the suburbs and as a consequence, has "discouraged the emergence of suburban 'super developers' with overwhelming political clout."[18] At the same time, deliberate political compromises further strengthened support for the legislation. An important role was played by 1,000 Friends of Oregon by pressuring local governments to eliminate restrictions on development and in the process winning the support of the homebuilding industry.[19] This ability to create common interests through a political process is one of the most striking features of the implementation of land-use law in Oregon. It has allowed the law to withstand five major challenges in statewide initiatives. During the second such challenge, in 1978, the growing base of support was evident when the Home Builders of Metropolitan Portland voted to oppose the initiative, providing vital support for land-use law and dividing the business community.[20] The LCDC has also maintained political support by strategically compromising on its goals on occasion. For example, it agreed to a substantially larger urban growth boundary for the Portland area than it believed justified in order to avoid a major political conflict that could have caused severe political damage.[21]

Despite these strategic political actions designed to sustain political support, the land-use law has come under heavy fire in recent years.[22] Pressures for economic development, combined with the rise of a "property rights" movement, and a much more highly polarized political setting produced a major assault on land-use laws in the 1995 legislature. Oregonians In Action, a new organization dedicated to rolling back land-use restrictions, had formed in the early 1990s and worked to elect a Republican legislature, where its views enjoyed a warm reception. In this setting, a long history of organized support, capable of mobilizing a broad base of allies, made all the difference for preserving the land-use law. Groups such as 1,000 Friends of Oregon, the Oregon Conservation Network, and others mobilized grassroots supporters among organizations of urban advocates and environmentalists, activated their supporters in the Portland business community, and stepped up lobbying and research efforts to challenge their opponents. In the end the land-use legislation remained largely intact, although protected on some measures only by the governor's veto. The future of land-use legislation in Oregon thus rests very much on the back of its organized supporters.

In contrast to this virtuous cycle of growing authority and political support, Minnesota's Metropolitan Council became less effective over time and lost political backing. Lacking the kind of active advocacy that sustained Oregon's law, the Metropolitan Council grew timid and its opponents grew stronger. The council did little to resist heavy political pressure to accommodate growth in outlying suburbs. Likewise, it had little say in major development decisions that would shape the entire metropolitan area, such as the siting of a race track, a domed stadium, and the largest shopping mall in the country (the Mall of America).[23] By 1991 the council was widely viewed as so ineffective that newly elected governor Arne Carlson threatened to abolish it. The elite base that had supported its activities in the 1970s had eroded significantly in the intervening decade. The Citizens League, as we have seen, had pulled back from its once active support. Corporate restructuring left much of the urban business community with a reduced stake in local government issues.[24] This was an important shift in the Twin Cities, where local business leaders formerly had played a key role in civic affairs and had supported a regional perspective as a way to strengthen the urban core. Moreover, the Metropolitan Council now had new competition from the county governments, which had grown stronger and viewed any efforts to bolster the authority of the council as a threat to their own power. Finally, the prospects for metropolitanism weakened still further as political parties in the legislature became sharply polarized in the 1990s. In this more highly charged political environment, the kind of bipartisan alliance that had supported metropolitan initiatives in the past was much harder to orchestrate.

Only through concerted attempts at new coalition building in the 1990s did metropolitanism in the Twin Cities begin to revive. State representative Myron Orfield, a Democrat from Minneapolis, put metropolitan issues back on the political agenda with a series of legislative initiatives.[25] These linked bills included proposals to give the Metropolitan Council operational power over transit and waste control, implement a policy of "fair share housing" throughout the metropolitan area, enlarge the base of the regional tax scheme, and enact stronger land-use controls. To support this agenda, Orfield sought to build a new coalition between the cities and less affluent inner-ring suburbs on the basis of common economic interests: the political goal was to split the suburbs along economic lines. Confronted with evidence that their tax dollars were subsidizing development in the outer suburbs and that they shouldered more than their fair share of low- and moderate-income housing for the region, representatives of these tax-poor suburbs began to see their own problems from a regional perspective. Although such common economic interests are the core coalition-building strategy, efforts have been made to expand the base to include environmental groups, social justice organizations (including churches), and good-government groups. The political process departed from the good-government, elite orientation of the past in two ways: it mobilized political support primarily on the basis of economic interest and it deployed a much more participatory bottom-up strategy. As Orfield noted in connection with the fair-share housing proposals, "Solution and design of the proposal came from the bottom up, not the top down. It was a legislative solution with broad community input, not a litigation-based court decision lacking grassroots input."[26]

These coalition-building efforts have thus far produced only limited legislative victories. Partisan division has been part of the problem: the few Republican representatives of inner-ring suburbs have been reluctant to support the initiatives, and representatives of rural areas have been suspicious of them. More important were the vetoes of the Republican governor. Several of Orfield's key proposals, including the increased tax-base sharing and fair housing, passed the legislature only to be vetoed by the governor. Others, however, including increased powers for the Metropolitan Council, have been enacted.

The shifting fate of metropolitan regionalism in Oregon and Minnesota highlights the importance of ongoing coalition building. Regionalism cannot be considered secure once legislation is enacted. The economic and political pressures for growth and local (rather than regional) decisionmaking are too strong. Challenges will come from developers concerned that land-use controls will hurt business and from communities aiming to preserve local prerogatives—even at the expense of their neighbors. As state legislatures have become more dependent on private campaign money, the power of monied groups, such as developers, has grown. Yet the cases of Oregon and Minnesota show that the base of potential support for regionalism is broad; with political mobilization it is possible to build coalitions of common economic interest and shared ideals to support metropolitan regionalism.

Sprawl and Localism in California and Illinois

The failed efforts to create forms of metropolitan regionalism and land-use controls in California and Illinois in the 1960s and 1970s stand in marked contrast to the successes in Minnesota and Oregon. Yet Californians expressed intense concern about environmental degradation and urban sprawl,[27] and in Illinois growing sprawl and urban flight sparked new interest in metropolitan regionalism in the early 1970s. Why did these sentiments not produce either elite-oriented or broad-based coalitions for metropolitan regionalism as in Minnesota and Oregon? A comparison of these states shows that California and Illinois adopted particularistic and often exclusionary solutions to the kinds of problems that had sparked the coalitions for metropolitan regionalism in Minnesota and Oregon. These decisions deflected pressures and diverted energies away from coalition building toward alternative, less encompassing political and policy strategies. The different patterns and timing of urban-suburban development as well as distinctive partisan alignments in the state legislatures help explain why metropolitan regionalism remained so weak in California and Illinois.

The Politics of Particularism

Suburban development exploded in California in the decades after World War II and with it concerns about service delivery and the impact on cities. These problems usually were attacked with remedies that not only were ineffective in controlling sprawl, but also exacerbated fragmentation and exclusionary barriers in the suburbs. Two key examples are the 1954 Lakewood Plan, which was designed to address the suburban services problem, and the Local Agency Formation Committee (LAFCO), formed in 1963 to oversee incorporations and annexations.

The Lakewood Plan approached the problem of suburban services in Los Angeles County in a way that promoted political fragmentation, class stratification, and racial exclusion. The plan allowed smaller cities to contract with the county to receive basic services such as fire and police protection. Prior to the plan's adoption, incorporating as a separate city was economically infeasible for most developing suburbs.[28] The high cost of providing local services meant that such new cities would have to charge very high tax rates. If these areas remained unincorporated, they could receive services from the county but would lack local control over such essential matters as land use, zoning, and services. Moreover, unincorporated areas remained vulnerable to annexation by neighboring cities. Although earlier incorporations had already hemmed in the city of Los Angeles, making further annexation impossible, other cities in the county, such as Long Beach, were annexing large new tracts of the developing suburbs. By making small cities economically viable, the Lakewood Plan stymied this annexation strategy and set off a wave of new municipal incorporations. Over the next fifteen years, thirty-two new cities incorporated, thirty-one of them contracting with the county for services.

As Gary Miller's careful study shows, the Lakewood Plan created a sharp stratification by class among Los Angeles County municipalities, dividing the metropolitan area into jurisdictions of "service seekers" and "tax avoiders."[29] These divisions followed racial lines as well. In the fifteen years after the Lakewood Plan went into effect, the county's black population became concentrated in just a few cities, and the number of nearly all-white jurisdictions grew. As Miller notes, "The Lakewood Plan cities were essentially white political movements."[30] By allowing contracting, Los Angeles County had provided the means for separation and exit from broader political arenas rather than for building a common purpose throughout the metropolitan areas. Instead of linking the problems of the suburbs and the cities as Minnesota had sought to do, Los Angeles County widened the gulf.

Concern about metropolitan political fragmentation and unchecked growth in California lay behind the creation of LAFCO in 1963. In 1960 both the state legislature and Democratic governor Pat Brown launched studies of the proliferation of local governments and its impact on California's metropolitan areas.[31] Prior to 1963, decisions about annexation and incorporation had to be approved by the counties alone, subject to electoral approval by the affected districts. One group in the state legislature, echoing the governor's commission, wanted to create a strong state agency that would have power over local boundaries. A second group, supported by the counties, wanted the power to reside with the counties. The compromise legislation called for county-level LAFCO boards composed of two representatives from cities, two county supervisors, and a fifth member to be chosen by the other four. In contrast to Oregon, California failed to create any new statewide or multicounty authority over local boundaries and growth. The highest level of decisionmaking was the county.

The new county-level LAFCOs did little to control the pace and direction of growth, nor did they stem jurisdictional fragmentation. Instead, the LAFCO process set off a power struggle among cities, counties, developers, and homeowners with the result that "rational analysis of issues like sprawl, efficient service provision, and fiscal equity has been no more apparent than in the days before LAFCO."[32] With few resources for drawing up plans to guide growth and riven by political disputes, the LAFCOs have been reactive agencies with little independent impact on land-use patterns.[33]

In 1970 the California legislature once again considered a spate of proposals for regional approaches to land use, all of which failed.[34] In Oregon the burgeoning environmental movement had provided one pillar of vital political support for land-use legislation. By contrast, California's environmental movement played a negligible role in debates related to metropolitan regionalism in the 1960s and 1970s. The debate about LAFCO in California occurred before the emergence of the modern environmental movement, but even in the late 1960s and 1970s, California's environmentalists showed little interest in metropolitan regionalism. Instead, they focused their concern on wilderness and coastal areas. Moreover, as a new social movement that had grown by leaps and bounds, environmentalists were riven by factionalism and ideology. A 1971 report by Ralph Nader's organization on the politics of land in California characterized the state's environmental movement as congeries of small ideological and parochial organizations that "usually don't know what their counterparts in the next city or county are doing."[35] Even the venerable Sierra Club, long organized in California, was so divided that even on important matters it could not effectively mobilize its membership.

Not surprisingly, environmentalists in California lacked the skills of coalition building and legislative bargaining. Their biggest success—the creation of the California Coastal Commission, which delegated strong regulatory powers over coastal development to new regional commissions—reflected the distinctive orientation and capabilities of the environmental movement. The new law was concerned with the natural environment, not metropolitan areas, and it was the product of a statewide initiative held in 1972, at the crest of broad enthusiasm for environmentalism. Even so, fearing the weakness of environmental groups, the initiative campaign stressed the issue of public access, not environmental protection. As an initiative campaign, played out largely in the media, the new legislation did not involve environmentalists in ongoing legislative bargaining or coalition building.[36]

Although California failed to devise a regulatory process to manage metropolitan growth, the issues of land use, development, and housing did not disappear; instead, their politics played out in different arenas using different tools. Local political NIMBYism enacted through lawsuits and the initiative process became the central way that disputes over metropolitan land use were adjudicated. The impulse to manage development became intertwined with localism and exclusivism as slow-growth initiatives spread throughout California in the 1980s. The slow-growth movement proposed initiative after initiative, aiming to lodge growth controls at the most local levels of government.[37] Many of the same impulses that led to coalition building and statewide legislation in Oregon were thus localized and much more narrowly cast in California. The civic elites, who took a rational problem-solving approach to metropolitan issues in Minnesota, were mostly invisible on land-use issues in California.

What made the politics of metropolitan regionalism so different in California? Most important was the central place of land-development interests in the California economy and in the political system. In much of the Southwest, land development and local boosterism provided the key to economic growth during the twentieth century.[38] In contrast to Oregon, the power of land interests was well established long before the modern environmental movement appeared on the scene. And in contrast to Minnesota, most local elites were closely intertwined with development interests, who sharply opposed restrictions in the pattern of growth. The importance of money in California's political system magnified the power of development interests. In the 1960s the California legislature led the nation in the number of lobbyists and in the role of interest-group money in electoral campaigns.[39] Land interests predominated in both. The power of land interests permeated both political parties, but their impact was especially significant for Republicans, because it effectively blocked the emergence of a moderate Republican leadership around metropolitan regionalism that was so important in Oregon and Minnesota. The much more partisan politics of California—intensified with the 1966 election of Ronald Reagan as governor—further hampered any coalition building around land-use policy in California. With environmentalists and land interests taking an all-or-nothing stance on policy and with a legislature awash in interest-group money and sharply divided on party lines, neither rational technocratic legislation nor broad compromise approaches stood much chance of enactment in California.

In Illinois, despite growing suburban sprawl and urban decline, metropolitan regionalism and land-use regulation did not draw the same kind of political attention they attracted in Oregon, Minnesota, or California. Broad regional organizations had existed in the Chicago area since the 1950s. The Chicago Area Transportation Study formed in 1955 to draw up transportation plans for the metropolitan area. Two years later the state created the Northeastern Illinois Regional Planning Commission to develop a comprehensive general plan for the region.[40] In the mid-1960s, a group of prestigious civic, business, financial, and educational leaders in the Chicago metropolitan area revived the call for metropolitan government. But the achievements of these organizations remained largely on paper, as they had little real authority to guide development. Instead, a maze of special districts with operational responsibilities carved up the region into functional areas for water, parks, and waste disposal. For the most part, the problems of growing suburbs were addressed through these ad hoc and functionally specific entities, among which there was little coordination and no overarching vision.[41]

The contrast with Minnesota is striking. Although some elites showed an interest in devising a regional perspective, these ideas never made any headway in the state legislature. To understand why, we must examine both how the city of Chicago operated in the state legislature and how political divisions between Chicago and its sub-urbs made metropolitan cooperation a political nonstarter. Of critical importance was the power of the Chicago Democratic political organization. Although Chicago never commanded a majority in the state legislature, the tight organization of its delegation allowed the city to make legislative deals in its favor. For example, in 1966 Minneapolis mayor Arthur Naftalin bemoaned his state's failure to make the county, rather than the city, responsible for local welfare costs; Chicago, by contrast, had succeeded in pushing these costs up to the county a decade earlier.[42] Likewise, when necessary, Chicago was able to get state approval for major development initiatives, such as convention centers, designed to ensure its primacy in the metropolitan region. Thus concern about the fate of the central business district—which had spurred Portland mayor Neil Goldschmidt and his allies in the business community to support state land-use regulation—had no counterpart in Illinois. Chicago had little interest in regionalism, because it could generally get what it needed from the state and accordingly, saw no real threat to its dominance in the region. Moreover, through the Democratic organization, Chicago's mayor effectively controlled political arenas outside the city, including Cook County. Any new regional organizations would only dilute the city's power—and more important, that of the Democratic organization.[43]

If the city was uninterested in regionalism, the suburbs abhorred the idea. In contrast to Minnesota, Chicago suburbs had a longstanding and deep animosity toward the city. With a tradition of reform that prided itself on efficient, honest government, suburban Chicago viewed the city as a pit of political corruption rife with dishonesty. Compounding this animosity were sharp partisan differences: most of the suburbs had long been dominated by Republicans. Any form of regional government threatened to disrupt the political balance in the metropolitan area.

Finally, proponents of metropolitan regionalism in Chicago ignored the way racial divisions affected their proposals. By the 1960s, as ethnic whites began to leave Chicago for the suburbs, race became a key factor dividing city from suburb, choking off suburban interest in any regional initiatives that might be linked with racial equity. Moreover, race cut two ways. Black leaders in Chicago had little interest in new forms of regional governance that would simply dilute black political power. As Gilbert Steiner, commenting on proposals

for metropolitan government in 1966, noted, "The prospects for success in planning Chicago metropolitan area development will be
pretty slim unless some explicit case can be made to support the
proposition that there is a community of interest between the Negro
on Chicago's South Side and the white commuter from the North
Shore suburb."[44] Ignoring the racial issue, proponents of metropolitan government did not even begin to make the case.

These political realities left little room for the state legislature to
consider measures promoting metropolitan regionalism. Although
regional organizations continued to exist, they had no power. Instead,
as George C. Hemmens notes in his study of the Chicago area, discussions with implications for the region occurred in two unconnected
arenas: "Side by side, at the same time, with minimal interaction,
there is a highly rational, civil, public process working on regional
infrastructure decisions, and a highly political, combative, political
process working on regional infrastructure decisions."[45] The political
process, driven by particularistic local interests as opposed to a
broader regional vision, was the one that counted.

Politics and Vicious Cycles

The triumph of more particular and narrow approaches to urban
problems and land-use concerns in California and Illinois exacerbated the problems of urban decline and suburban sprawl. As a consequence, some of the political barriers to metropolitan regionalism
became more deeply entrenched. White flight from the cities made
race an even more central division in metropolitan areas than it had
been in the 1960s, when city populations were more racially diverse.
The continuing development of the suburbs led to the creation of
more capable full-service suburban governments, making suburbs
even more formidable as political forces. Likewise, the power of developers and other land interests continued to grow, while some defenders of urban interests, especially urban-based business concerns,
became less visible. Yet the gathering force of unregulated metropolitan growth also generated opposition. Much of this opposition has
taken a defensive form that does little to build alternative coalitions.
But these same forces have also created new possibilities for coalition
building around metropolitan regionalism.

In California the interest in metropolitanism in the 1960s left a
meager legacy. Weak regional agencies continued to convene and

churn out reports, but they had little real power. The regional council of governments in southern California, the Southern California Asso-
ciation of Governments, could not even retain the membership of many local governments.[46] In place of any regional approach, the politics of land use occurred at the county level, where formal authority was lodged. Yet California's political process made it difficult to engage in coalition-building politics even at the county level, because decisionmaking occurred by the initiative process, which made compromise nearly impossible and tended to push opponents further apart.[47] Moreover, the importance of money in such campaigns favored well-funded development interests. In Orange County, for example, a slow-growth movement emerged in the 1980s to challenge decades of unrestrained growth. Viewing the county government as hopelessly tied to developers, the movement sought to restrict growth by a countywide initiative. The "Citizens' Sensible Growth and Traffic Control Initiative" would have forced developers to widen roads and undertake other measures to reduce traffic problems before they could develop unincorporated areas. Despite widespread dissatisfaction with the pattern of growth and a large early lead, the initiative lost. Land development interests had poured some $2.5 million into the campaign, the most ever on a growth initiative.[48]

In Illinois Chicago's go-it-alone strategy in the state legislature became less successful as suburbs gained population and power. When suburban Republican leaders took over the state legislature in 1993, they made their desire to advance a low-tax, anti-Chicago agenda clear. As the new Senate president, Pate Philip, declared, "[Suburbanites have] always been paying for Chicago, they've been doing it forever. . . . The day of the free ride is over."[49] This sentiment took political form as Republican legislators successfully blocked key Chicago development initiatives, such as a third regional airport, that required legislative approval.[50]

But suburban expansion has raised a new set of issues in many older suburbs. The residential profile of the inner-ring suburbs has changed as more lower-income minorities, especially Latinos, have left Chicago or immigrated directly to suburban locations. The initial response of many such suburbs has been to resist the influx of poorer residents or to try to contain the costs they present. For example, one Chicago suburb, Mt. Prospect, sought to impose a special tax on an area of apartment buildings after they had attracted a substantial number of Latino families.[51] Strict enforcement of building codes and occupancy limits in apartments is another common tactic aimed to reduce the number of low-income Latino families in suburbs. But such defensive tactics are likely only stopgaps: on their own, inner-ring suburbs cannot control the powerful economic and demographic shifts that are weakening their tax bases and making their residents more needy.

The slow-growth movement in many California communities and the defensive measures taken by Chicago's inner suburbs are evidence of the strains that the pattern of unregulated growth has engendered. Thus far the responses to these strains have largely been narrow defensive measures. But, as the case of Minnesota shows, it may be possible to build new kinds of coalitions that take a broader, more regional perspective on metropolitan development. "Urban" problems are no longer the province of cities alone, suggesting that it may be possible to reproduce Orfield's city-suburban coalition in other metropolitan areas. Many cities that were once confident that they could go it alone are more attentive to the need to find allies in state politics. Moreover, as sprawl has continued to eat up farmland and encroach on natural settings, environmental and some agricultural groups have shown more interest in policies to manage growth. These elements of an alternative approach to metropolitan problems are as yet faint and unassembled, but discontent from many quarters with the older model of metropolitan growth and urban abandonment suggests new possibilities for the future.

Lessons for the Future

The diverse experiences of Oregon, Minnesota, California, and Illinois suggest some lessons for advocates of metropolitanism today. Changed social and economic forces have altered the metropolitan landscape, but key aspects of the experiences of two decades ago are still relevant today.

First, ongoing political mobilization must accompany efforts to create metropolitan regionalism. The contrasting experiences of Minnesota and Oregon show the importance of building widespread grass-roots support for regional initiatives as well as using the courts. The initial legislation in Oregon simply created a "foot in the door" for establishing meaningful metropolitan regionalism. It took ongoing involvement in the implementation process to make it a reality.

Likewise, a readily mobilized base of support was essential for preserving the legislation from the many political challenges it attracted over the past two decades. Oregon's experience also suggests that much can grow from even modest initial legislation. Metropolitan regionalism is best conceived as a political process that develops over time rather than something that is achieved in a single blow.

Second, it is possible to turn enemies into allies in the course of creating metropolitan regionalism. Because metropolitan regionalism is a compromise strategy that manages growth rather than imposing blanket restrictions, it can be beneficial to development interests, who most often tend to oppose it. By removing local barriers to growth and creating more predictability, growth management can ease development. While it is unlikely that all homebuilding and development interests will be converted into allies, it is possible that the positive experience of some will at least split this opposition.

Third, go-it-alone strategies do not work. In the 1970s environmental and urban interests sought to achieve their goals on separate tracks. Environmentalists sought federal regulation, while urban advocates relied on a growing pool of federal grants. Each of these strategies has run into barriers in the past decade and a half. Coalition-building strategies in which cities and environmental interests combine forces and work to build a common agenda are needed to effectively address future problems in each domain. It is important that these efforts at coalition building occur at the local level and build up to the statehouse. Too often in the past, cities and environmentalists neglected the states. Yet that is where constitutional authority for land use is lodged; these interests have ignored the states at their own peril.

Fourth, land-use controls and other measures associated with metropolitanism need not be partisan issues. In recent years, a strong property rights movement, hostile to any land-use regulation, has emerged within the Republican party, especially in the West. It is a mistake to make measures associated with metropolitan regionalism a partisan issue. In the face of strong opposition to unregulated growth and concern about the consequences of urban decline, such a narrow interpretation of constituents' interests is doomed to failure in the long run.

Fifth, metropolitanism has different implications across racial groups, and this cannot be ignored. Metropolitan regionalism can only succeed as a strategy for building common interests and accommodating diverse needs, not as a way of cutting out the "inconvenient" concerns of racial minorities. Accordingly, the institutional goals of regionalism and the legislative initiatives it embraces must be designed to work toward building common interests in a racially inclusive decisionmaking process.

Notes

1. On the development and early implementation of Oregon's plan, see H. Jeffrey Leonard, *Managing Oregon's Growth: The Politics of Development Planning* (Washington, D.C.: Conservation Foundation, 1983).

2. Paul G. Lewis, *Shaping Suburbia: How Political Institutions Organize Urban Development* (University of Pittsburgh Press, 1996), pp. 105–06; Carl Abbott, *Portland: Planning, Politics, and Growth in a Twentieth Century City* (University of Nebraska Press, 1983), p. 257.

3. Abbott notes that Portland city officials were not enthusiastic about Metro because they feared it would take over responsibility for the city's profitable water supply system, *Portland*, p. 254.

4. Margaret Weir, "Planning, Environmentalism, and Urban Poverty: The Political Failure of National Land Use Planning Legislation, 1970–1975," in Robert Fishman, ed., *The American Planning Tradition: Culture and Policy* (Washington, D.C., and Baltimore: Woodrow Wilson Center and Johns Hopkins University Press, in press).

5. Abbott, *Portland*, p. 251.

6. See the discussion in Gerrit Knaap, "Land Use Politics in Oregon," in Carl Abbott, Deborah Howe, and Sy Adler, eds., *Planning the Oregon Way: A Twenty-Year Evaluation* (Oregon State University Press, 1994), pp. 6–7.

7. Abbott, *Portland*, p. 250.

8. Carl Abbott, "The Capital of Good Planning: Metropolitan Portland, Oregon since 1970," in Fishman, *The American Planning Tradition*; Leonard, *Managing Oregon's Growth*, p. 89.

9. Also, as Abbott notes, the election of MSD commission members made Metro more palatable to suburbanites, *Portland*, p. 262.

10. John J. Harrigan and William C. Johnson, *Governing the Twin Cities Region: The Metropolitan Council in Regional Perspective* (University of Minnesota Press, 1978), p. 33.

11. There was opposition from some suburban areas and from the counties. See Arthur Naftalin and John Brandl, *The Twin Cities Regional Strategy* (St. Paul, Minn.: Metropolitan Council of the Twin Cities Area, 1980), p. 24.

12. Myron Orfield, *Metropolitics: A Regional Agenda for Community and Stability* (Cambridge, Mass., and Washington, D.C.: Lincoln Institute of Land Policy and Brookings, 1997), pp. 143–44.

13. Harrigan and Johnson, *Governing the Twin Cities Region*, pp. 23–24; see also John J. Harrigan, "The Politics of Regionalism in the Twin Cities," paper

prepared for HUD Roundtable on Regionalism, Washington, D.C., December 8–9, 1994, table 2; Judith A. Martin, "In Fits and Starts: The Twin Cities Metropolitan Framework," in Donald N. Rothblatt and Andrew Sancton, eds., *Metropolitan Governance: American/Canadian Intergovernmental Perspectives* (University of California, Institute of Governmental Studies, 1993), pp. 205–43.

14. Leonard, *Managing Oregon's Growth*, pp. 17–18, 119.

15. Harrigan, "The Politics of Regionalism in the Twin Cities," p. 10.

16. Leonard, *Managing Oregon's Growth*, pp. 20–25.

17. On the governors, see Naftalin and Brandl, *The Twin Cities Regional Strategy*, pp. 25–26; Orfield, *Metropolitics*, p. 102.

18. Abbott, "The Capital of Good Planning," pp. 17–18; see also Nohad A. Toulan, "Housing as a State Planning Goal," in Abbott, Howe, and Adler, *Planning the Oregon Way*, pp. 91–120.

19. Leonard, *Managing Oregon's Growth*, pp. 109–10.

20. Ibid., p. 110.

21. Ibid., pp. 103–04.

22. See Robert Liberty, "The Battle over Tom McCall's Legacy: The Story of Land Use in the 1995 Oregon Legislature," *Environmental and Urban Issues*, vol. 23, no. 3 (Spring 1996), pp. 1–12.

23. Judith A. Martin, "Renegotiating Metropolitan Consciousness: The Twin Cities Faces Its Future," in Donald N. Rothblatt and Andrew Sancton, eds., *Metropolitan Governance Revisited: American/Canadian Intergovernmental Perspectives*, (University of California, Institute for Governmental Studies, 1998), pp. 245–53; Harrigan, "The Politics of Regionalism in the Twin Cities," pp. 13–15; and Orfield, *Metropolitics*, pp. 173–80.

24. Harrigan, "The Politics of Regionalism in the Twin Cities," pp. 17–18.

25. Orfield, *Metropolitics*, pp. 104–55; Judith A. Martin, "Renegotiating Metropolitan Consciousness," pp. 243–44.

26. Orfield, *Metropolitics*, p. 111.

27. See Francine F. Rabinowitz and James Lamare, "After Suburbia What? The New Communities Movement in Los Angeles," in Werner Z. Hirsch, ed., *Los Angeles: Viability and Prospects for Metropolitan Leadership* (Praeger Publishers, 1971), p. 189.

28. For a careful analysis, see Gary J. Miller, *Cities by Contract: The Politics of Municipal Incorporation* (MIT Press, 1981).

29. Ibid., chaps. 6 and 7.

30. Ibid., p.135.

31. Jon C. Teaford, *Post-Suburbia: Government and Politics in the Edge Cities* (Johns Hopkins University Press, 1997), pp. 103–05; Stephanie Pincetl, "The Regional Management of Growth in California: A History of Failure," *International Journal of Urban and Regional Research*, vol. 18, no. 2 (June 1994), pp. 256–74.

32. Miller, *Cities By Contract*, p. 124.

33. Teaford, *Post-Suburbia*, pp. 105–08. See the case study of Irvine, California, by Martin J. Schiesl, "Designing the Model Community: The Irvine Company and Suburban Development, 1950–88," in Rob Kling, Spencer Olin, and

Mark Poster, eds., *Post Suburban California: The Transformation of Orange County Since World War II* (University of California Press, 1991), pp. 55–91.

34. Robert C. Fellmeth, *The Politics of Land* (Grossman Publishers, 1973), pp. 391–92; "Environment," *California Journal* (August 1970), pp. 228–29.

35. Fellmeth, *The Politics of Land*, p. 462.

36. On the Coastal Commission, see Melvin B. Mogulof, *Saving the Coast: California's Experiment in Intergovernmental Land Use Control* (Lexington, Mass.: D.C. Heath, 1975); Paul A. Sabatier and Daniel A. Mazmanian, *Can Regulation Work? The Implementation of the 1972 California Coastal Initiative* (Plenum Press, 1983), chap. 2.

37. See Mike Davis, *City of Quartz: Excavating the Future in Los Angeles* (London: Verso Press, 1990), chap. 3; Pincetl, "The Regional Management of Growth," pp. 267–72.

38. On politics and land development interests in the Southwest more generally, see Amy Bridges, *Morning Glories: Municipal Reform in the Southwest* (Princeton University Press, 1997).

39. See Fellmeth, *The Politics of Land*, chap. 12; Lou Cannon, *Ronnie and Jesse* (Doubleday, 1969).

40. See George C. Hemmens and Janet McBride, "Planning and Development Decision Making in the Chicago Region," in Rothblatt and Sancton, *Metropolitan Governance*, pp. 111–52.

41. These arrangements also benefited the city. See Ester Fuchs, *Mayors and Money: Fiscal Policy in New York and Chicago* (University of Chicago Press, 1992), pp.192–200. On the Metropolitan Sanitary District, see Judith A. Martin and Sam Bass Warner, Jr., "Local Initiative and Metropolitan Repetition: Chicago 1972–1990," in Fishman, *The American Planning Tradition*.

42. See Arthur Naftalin, "A Mayor Looks at the States," in James H. Andrews, ed., *The State and Its Cities*, University of Illinois Bulletin, vol. 64, no. 108 (April 28, 1967), p. 110. On public assistance in Chicago, see Edward C. Banfield, *Political Influence* (Free Press, 1961).

43. Milton Rakove, *Don't Make No Waves, Don't Back No Losers: An Insider's Analysis of the Daley Machine* (Indiana University Press, 1975), chap. 5 and pp. 234–56.

44. See Gilbert Y. Steiner, *Metropolitan Government and the Real World: The Case of Chicago* (Loyola University, Center for Research in Urban Government, 1966), p. 12.

45. George C. Hemmens, "Planning and Development Decision Making in the Chicago Region," in Rothblatt and Sancton, *Metropolitan Governance Revisited*, p. 151.

46. Teaford, *Post-Suburbia*, p. 125.

47. For an argument about the effects of the initiative process on California, see Peter Schrag, *Paradise Lost: A California Experience, America's Future* (New Press, 1998).

48. See Spencer Olin, "Intraclass Conflict and the Politics of a Fragmented Region," in *Post Suburban California*, pp. 238–41.

49. See Margaret Weir, "Central Cities' Loss of Power in State Politics," *Cityscape*, vol. 2, no. 2 (May 1996), pp. 23–26.

50. For a discussion of the dispute over the third regional airport, see Hemmens, "Planning and Development Decision Making in the Chicago Region," in Rothblatt and Sancton, *Metropolitan Governance Revisited*, pp. 110–19.

51. See Philip Franchine, "Mt. Prospect Debates Plan for 'Crime Tax,'" *Chicago Sun-Times*, September 20, 1993, p. 6. The plan was ultimately defeated by the owners of the apartment buildings.

CHAPTER SIX

Business Coalitions as a Force for Regionalism

ROSABETH MOSS KANTER

In Kansas City, Missouri, on August 20–21, 1998, hundreds of regional business leaders met with public officials, civic activists, and academics for the first Greater Kansas City "Going Global" conference, designed for "partners and players in the region's international future." The region referred to spanned the borders of Missouri and Kansas. The conference unveiled for discussion regional economic development plans, a neighborhood improvement and transportation initiative, and "The World Comes to Kansas City," a briefing about tourism and trade promotion efforts. Participants heard success stories about regional cooperation and international strategies from the Research Triangle in North Carolina, the Trade Development Alliance of Greater Seattle, and the European Union. The event concluded with a family-oriented "ethnic enrichment" festival for the general public.

Ranging from broad global issues to the most local of concerns, regional consciousness-raising events like this are increasingly common throughout the United States and in other countries. They are a response to a widespread perception that strong communities in the global economy must have a regional focus—that neighboring cities and towns must join forces to present a unified image to the rest of the world. They can promote the region, secure its economic future, and muster the will to tackle local problems important to mobile global businesses, foreign visitors, and citizens who do not want to fall behind in a more global economy.

In addition to promoting a regional identity, such events build support for a regional political agenda—one that is led by new coalitions. These coalitions, often business oriented and almost universally containing business executives in key roles, constitute new governance frameworks that cross political jurisdictions. There are many of these coalitions in every metropolitan area. They have diverse agendas but overlapping leadership and membership, and they often come together as coalitions of coalitions to support specific initiatives.

Convening the Kansas City event was a new entity, the International Alliance, which itself was a coalition of coalitions. Members included major business associations (the Greater Kansas City Chamber of Commerce), quasi-public entities (the Mid-America Regional Council, an organization of local government officials from cities and towns in Missouri and Kansas), ethnic business associations (the African Chamber of Commerce), traditional voluntary groups (the International Relations Council), niche-oriented trade groups (the International Visitors Council), colleges and universities, and federal agencies (the U.S. Department of Commerce and the Small Business Administration). Financial support came from large companies that reflected a range of local-to-global positions and interests: Commerce Bank, which had a local market; Sprint, a locally headquartered company serving national and international markets; and Hoechst Marion Roussel, a global pharmaceutical giant with a German owner.

International trade has been an important part of the American economy since the country's founding. BankBoston, perhaps the oldest chartered bank in the United States, grew as it financed New England's wool trade with Argentina for the region's textile business. What is different about the global economy of the last decade is reflected in the Kansas City example: the extent to which private economic associations are playing a leadership role in crossing, blurring, or breaking down political jurisdictions to create new metropolitan regional identities that market themselves to the world and maintain direct international relations—in essence, creating city-states with their own foreign policies.

In 1993 I undertook a series of projects to understand the impact of today's economic globalization—travel, trade, information technology, and communications media that link the world—on businesses, workplaces, and communities in the United States at the cusp of the new millennium. Research in 1993 and 1994 for my book *World Class: Thriving Locally in the Global Economy* included surveys of 2,600 business heads in five American regions, extensive interviews with community leaders and activists, and site visits, supported by an overview of developments in other regions in the United States and elsewhere.[1] In the fall of 1995, I visited twenty-six American cities, often to speak to a regional coalition or business association about my findings, and these trips provided me with reports, documents, and discussions about the plans of those metropolitan regions, large and small. In 1997 and 1998, a team of M.B.A. students working on my Harvard Business School project on "Business Leadership in the Social Sector" conducted telephone interviews with over fifty officials, journalists, and leaders in ten cities about the activities of businesses and business associations in urban investment, public education reform, and welfare-to-work programs.[2]

This work clarified the role that new or reinvented business coalitions play in addressing the problems of metropolitan regions. Nearly absent twenty-five years ago or discredited as a civic force with the public's interest in mind, these coalitions now are driving a renewed appreciation for metropolitan approaches to issues such as economic competitiveness, human resource development, infrastructure investment, and protection of unique environmental or civic assets.

However, these groups have not yet addressed fiscal disparities among towns, jurisdictional boundaries, or other distributional and political issues within metropolitan regions—nor is it apparent that they wish to—and they have only begun to focus on recalcitrant problems associated with inner cities, public education, affordable housing, or racial and economic segregation. Such matters tend to enter the agenda of business coalitions when they can be framed as economic development problems—for example, affordable housing or transportation for low-wage workers from cities to suburbs as ways of addressing labor shortages in regions with low unemployment.

Furthermore, it is difficult to prove what difference business coalitions make, except by anecdote. The problems of metropolitan regions are complex, and there are many variables that can make a difference. Still, the turnaround in Cleveland during the manufacturing recession of the 1980s, even before midwestern manufacturing enjoyed a resurgence in the 1990s, can be contrasted with the slower progress (some would say stagnation) of Detroit. Cleveland's success can be attributed directly to public-private partnerships led by a strong business coalition with an integrated focus and clear strategy.[3] Yet Cleveland still lags behind Boston on a number of key economic and social indicators, despite a much weaker and more fragmented set of business coalitions in Greater Boston.[4]

The role and contributions of business coalitions vary with regional circumstance; they are more important during times of industrial transformation or when other institutions, such as higher education, are weaker.[5] Some are permanent civic associations with public transparency and a continuing flow of issues on their agenda; others are ad hoc or time-limited groups that form for a particular purpose or event and then disband.

There has been little detailed research on the range or role of these groups across cities, and some will be surprised to see them included as a topic in a book on regionalism. Therefore, it is important to clarify what this chapter does not cover. It does *not* discuss the activities of individual businesses, such as the impact of Disney in Orlando or General Motors in Detroit; instead it focuses on *associations of businesses* claiming to act in the public interest. It does *not* explore public-private partnerships in their entirety; rather, it focuses on the growing role played by business coalitions in shaping a *regional agenda*, as well as some of the limits of that role. And as an overview of the rise of one force for regional identity, it does *not* offer solutions to every metropolitan problem. To regional planning professionals, the business coalitions examined here may occasionally seem irrelevant to some of their issues, such as land use or urban sprawl, except when those issues have an economic development angle. Some critics, suspicious of business motivations, may write off as boosterism any accounts of public interest activities undertaken by chambers of commerce (a view that reflects the historical antagonism between business elites and public interest advocates in some American communities). But the growing prominence of business-backed coalitions, and their increasing collaboration with public officials, makes it important to begin to examine their goals and activities. This chapter is such a beginning.

Regionalism in a Global Economy

The "new regionalism" recognizes that political jurisdictions do not match operative economies and social systems. Economic develop-

ment groups find that traditional geographic boundaries do not
reflect the economic and social interests that span cities, counties,
states, and nations or that concentrate within them. Indeed, the
National League of Cities has called the United States the world's first
common market of separate economic regions. Although metropolitan planning commissions have long existed in some parts of the
nation (Minneapolis–St. Paul's efforts to cooperate have been noteworthy), and the private sector has always played a major role in local
civic and political life, a more global economy has engendered a mul-
tiplicity of policy bodies and governance mechanisms at many levels,
beyond and within the nation-state. Often nongovernmental in the
traditional sense, such entities carry on functions once associated with
government. Instead of being the twilight of sovereignty, an argument
made by globalists such as retired Citicorp chairman Walter Wriston,
this is the dawn of multiple overlapping sovereignties.

Nation-spanning superregional groups include government-initi-
ated trade blocs, such as NAFTA or Mercosur in South America, and
also groups such as APEC (Asia Pacific Economic Cooperation),
which began as a voluntary association and was later embraced as a
forum by government leaders. Subregions within countries also are
developing bodies for policy and trade promotion. At the New England Council, a business coalition that links six states, it was an
oft-cited mantra that "if America had been settled from West to East,
New England would be a single state"—and therefore, the interests of
the whole region should be joined, and businesses should view all
twelve senators as their representatives in Washington. Sometimes
national borders are crossed to create a regional identity apart from
national affiliations, such as the vision of "Cascadia" as a region
including Oregon, Washington State, and British Columbia. Raymond
Barre, a former premier of France who returned to his home city of
Lyon as its mayor, has led the development of regional plans to link
adjacent portions of France, Germany, Switzerland, and Catalonia,
Spain, with Lyon as the regional center. Regional economic planning
can have political consequences. Scottish Enterprise is perhaps
unique among regional development authorities in the United King-
dom in that this business booster enhanced a regional identity that
preceded the formation (or reconstitution) of a political body, the
Scottish Parliament.

The growth of regional consciousness at the metropolitan level—
a center city and its surrounding territory—is said to constitute the

rebirth, in new form, of something like medieval city-states.[6] Metropolitan regions in Europe and North America are creating public-private partnerships to pursue cross-jurisdictional agendas; like Kansas City's, some cross state lines. (Another example is the Greater Philadelphia growth plan, which encompasses southern New Jersey.) Eurocities, formed in 1986, is an association of fifty-eight European regional centers that facilitates its member cities' international linkages and represents their interests at European Union deliberations in Brussels. In the United States, the National League of Cities has long advocated regional cooperation.

Such groups struggle for new language to describe their purpose. A growth plan widely circulated in Houston by business associations reconceptualized Greater Houston as a "federation of neighborhoods," each maintaining its distinct character but joining together for the common infrastructure and educational needs of the whole region—an argument now used by proponents of annexation of suburbs by the central city. Although coalitions of business and government leaders are often the forces behind these plans, it is striking to see other organizations take the lead: in southeastern Massachusetts a group of twenty-two churches developed a regional improvement plan for two neighboring cities suffering from deterioration.

Because transportation is an obvious aspect of regionally shared infrastructure, intercity metropolitan authorities have long been common for both ground transportation and airports. But the global economy has increased the number of items on the regional agenda. In recent years competition among cities to attract and retain businesses has highlighted other common concerns. Business location decisions are based not on single cities and towns, but on the facilities and amenities of several. There is growing recognition of the resources that businesses draw from the central city, even if they are not in it. Site planners, particularly those from other countries, seek one-stop shopping services that inform them about many places within a region at the same time; competition between adjacent towns is confusing and often dysfunctional, but proposals that link several jurisdictions are effective. Thus business coalitions focused on marketing the region are often among the most prominent—and sometimes the first effective—regional forces. The greater the marketing efforts and international outreach, the more likely that these coalitions will represent the whole region, linking many businesses, public sector officials, chambers of commerce, and trade promotion groups.

Leadership in Shadow Governments

It is clear that more groups, at more system levels, with overlapping boundaries and membership are working on regional strategies. But one striking aspect of the new regionalism is that these efforts are often business led or dominated by business thinking. It is taken for granted in many places that the problems of metropolitan regions will not be solved without business involvement, and many informal or unofficial public leadership roles have been handed to the private sector, reflecting an assumed primacy of the economy over the polity.

In many American cities, private coalitions act as shadow governments, making public policy by their investment decisions, such as hiring consultants to report on the state of the public schools (as happened in Denver). Such coalitions sometimes include public officials as members but often transcend them in long-term importance. In Spartanburg, South Carolina, a succession of anonymous mayors has been forgotten, but the long-serving Chamber of Commerce president, Richard Tukey, was immortalized in the call letters of the local public television station, WRET. These private groups sometimes have greater organizational continuity than political regimes: their leaders can occupy their positions longer than elected officials; they can mobilize substantial resources and talent faster than the public sector; their meetings can occur behind closed doors; and they can be regional from the start, their activities unconfined by city limits.

Some groups have long histories that predate World War II, such as the Citizens League (Cleveland) or the Bay Area Council (northern California). The Greater Baltimore Committee was created in 1955; the Minnesota Business Partnership, in 1977.[7] Some government-mandated groups seed other regional initiatives, for example, the private industry councils under the Job Training Partnership Act of 1981. Some regional groups are linked to national associations, such as the National Alliance of Business or the Business Roundtable. CEO-to-CEO groups meet to link the largest employers in a region; sometimes they are convened by a powerful chief executive with a particular stake in the region, such as former Knight Ridder CEO Alvah Chapman in Miami. And chambers of commerce, once merely pamphleteers and civic boosters trying to help small companies drum up business, have been setting longer-range regional agendas, often in collaboration with other, more specialized associations. The power of these groups has grown in the last half century, waxing and waning with the rise and fall of particular industries in particular cities. The most powerful are not merely discussion forums but also mobilize resources in support of visible projects, and they are encouraged in their role by elected officials.

After World War II, corporate money gradually supplanted family money as the chief underwriter of social and cultural activities in many American cities. This accelerated in the 1950s, once courts permitted corporate philanthropy for reasons other than direct shareholder interest.[8] Corporate chieftains became more important public figures than a city's heirs to family fortunes or, sometimes, than its elected officials. The dominance of business as an urban institution was reflected in the shifting patterns of urban architecture—from churches and cathedrals as a city's most important landmark buildings to city halls and public buildings to corporate headquarters buildings and office towers for the business elite.

Starting in the late 1950s, the transformation of South Carolina's upstate region from hillbilly country to a global manufacturing center exemplified the changing role of private sector leadership. When Roger Milliken moved the headquarters of his textile company from New York to Spartanburg in 1954, he started systematically encouraging German and Swiss companies that supplied the textile industry to set up facilities in the region to be close to their customers. Richard Tukey, executive director of the Greater Spartanburg Chamber of Commerce from 1951 until his death in 1979, got on board quickly to support this effort. Milliken's individual actions, stimulated by business self-interest, started a chain reaction of regional improvements: upgrading education and training in cooperation with the state and community colleges, creating or renewing community amenities, developing a new regional airport, and marketing the region to European and eventually all international companies. The last culminated in a joint regional effort—supported by most major business and community leaders across the region—to land BMW's first-ever factory outside Germany. "Foreign industry has created regionalism more than the Greenville Chamber or the Spartanburg Chamber," a leader said, because international companies in the area, such as Michelin, spread their activities and used suppliers across many counties. Now twelve chambers of commerce in the seven-county region are moving toward common messages and publications. However, regional cooperation has not yet touched some of the inner-city problems still facing Spartanburg and Greenville, even in the midst of stunning economic prosperity.[9]

Business coalitions proliferated in the 1980s, largely to address economic development issues. Three examples demonstrate the range of organizational forms and activities. Interviews with community leaders in their cities indicate that these entities are considered effective by a range of nonbusiness interests, even if they are not endorsed in every respect.

Miami's Beacon Council

Created in 1986 to help make Greater Miami a leading center for international business, culture, education, health care, and recreation, the Beacon Council is an award-winning, nonprofit, business-supported economic development agency. Financed by a large number of member companies, it can get government contracts and foundation grants. It offers databases and business assistance services, recruits companies to locate in the area, and organizes marketing events (including nearly forty international trade missions in 1994 alone) and strategic alliances with economic development organizations in over a dozen countries. The Beacon Council received federal funds to assist in the cleanup after Hurricane Andrew and thus was able to offer $11 million in bridge loans to over 500 companies. It also has developed communitywide working teams in collaboration with the Greater Miami Chamber of Commerce. For example, Black Team Miami obtained commitments from eighteen of Dade County's major employers to procure goods from minority businesses; Latin Team Miami assisted in the development of videos and brochures in Spanish to market the area internationally. The Beacon Council has been considered a stabilizing force in a fragmented, politicized, multiethnic region with few large established institutions, many tiny political jurisdictions, and public officials who have only narrow support from interest groups rather than widespread public support.[10]

Greater Denver Corporation

Denver provides another example of business-led regional change. In 1988 Denver's petroleum-dependent economy was in deep economic depression. Twenty large corporations donated $1 million each to the Greater Denver Corporation, whose mission was to diversify the economy, attract new high-technology jobs, and encourage new business start-ups. One of the founders was the CEO of Denver's main public utilities company—an industry that had a direct stake in the prosperity of its community. Among the offshoots was a partnership to integrate business, government, and cultural organizations to create a district for scientific and cultural facilities. Later the Greater Denver Chamber of Commerce raised $350,000 for a consulting firm to study the management of public schools. Business coalitions were major forces behind the push for the new regional airport outside Denver and for Coors Field, a new baseball stadium in a rundown part of Denver.[11]

Cleveland Tomorrow

Severe urban decline propelled the formation of a remarkably effective business coalition in Cleveland. Often referred to as the Turnaround City, Cleveland has enjoyed much success and progress since its recovery and revitalization that began in the 1980s. Once a thriving manufacturing center, Cleveland suffered the downturn of the Midwest Rust Belt throughout the 1960s and 1970s. The city became increasingly economically depressed and defaulted on its loans in 1978. Cleveland was in crisis, and business leaders were disappointed by aspects of city administration and concerned about the negative national and international image of Cleveland, which had an adverse effect on corporations' business activities and recruiting efforts. At the turn of the 1980s, Cleveland Tomorrow was incorporated as a not-for-profit, CEO-only organization to address these issues. Newly elected mayor George Voinovich joined with Cleveland Tomorrow to focus on economic development and the revitalization of downtown. Projects launched or supported by members included Gateway Stadium, the Rock and Roll Hall of Fame, Jacobs' Field, transforming a rundown industrial area into a lively entertainment center, rebuilding neighborhood housing, and creating investment entities to fund new businesses.[12]

With over fifty-five CEOs as members, Cleveland Tomorrow is at the pinnacle of business coalitions in Greater Cleveland. However, the city and region are characterized by a wide array of groups cooperating to improve the area. The Greater Cleveland Growth Association, formerly the Chamber of Commerce, involves large numbers of small companies in civic projects. Leadership Cleveland, a network of leaders from many institutions, focuses on community service. The Business Volunteerism Council matches corporate resources with community needs. But Cleveland's education system is still in disarray and was taken over by the state in 1995. By 1998 a Corporate Partnership Program founded by the Cleveland Initiative for Education had matched 90 out of 117 public schools with a corporate partner or deployed its business skills to improve school management; for example, Continental Airlines provided leadership training for teachers and school administrators.

These activities in Miami, Denver, Cleveland, and other cities are all the more remarkable because of events that have weakened the leadership infrastructure of many communities.

Trends Undermining Leadership

In the 1950s and 1960s, populist politicians and leftist critics decried power elites that dominated community decisions in their own interests.[13] By the 1980s, communities became alarmed about the loss of these groups, as locally headquartered companies were caught in the takeover boom and had their centers of leadership displaced to suburban and exurban campuses in new "edge cities," to other regions, and sometimes to locations outside the United States. Banks, utilities, retailers, and professional service firms were often the only businesses left downtown, while nearby manufacturing plants and corporate offices were closed or relocated in suburbia. Industry consolidations, mergers and acquisitions, and globalization of markets and supply chains continued to reduce the number of locally owned firms or turned them into satellites of rootless global companies. Meanwhile, central cities were suffering from lost resources, deteriorating schools and neighborhoods, a growing welfare burden, and loss of leadership.

Some cities have faced a civic leadership crisis as shifting business conditions caused a loss of corporate headquarters. Traditionally, a hometown bias brought extra benefits to cities housing the headquarters of large, prominent companies. Even today, locally headquartered companies contribute more to their communities, standing out even among the largest employers. Allison Hughes, as part of my research group, analyzed the community involvement of 180 companies in Boston, Cleveland, and Miami. The twenty largest employers in each city were categorized by headquarters location—local, nonlocal but domestic, or foreign—and compared. Locally headquartered companies did the most for the community on every measure; they had the largest corporate contributions to the United Way (averaging about $75,000 more annually than non-locally-headquartered companies), the largest average contributions by individual employees to the United Way, and the most active involvement by their leaders in prominent local civic and cultural organizations.[14]

Companies often have a larger stake in the quality of their headquarters city (or the central city of their headquarters region) than elsewhere, above and beyond the numbers employed there (which can be small compared to places housing production facilities), because of the flow of executives and customers through it. In larger companies international recruitment of talent in a global labor market means that the headquarters city must meet international standards, with maximum amenities and minimum problems. Companies often place showcase operations or pilot ventures in the headquarters region for convenient visits by top management, customers, or suppliers.

A Gillette executive explained why his global company makes such large contributions to local cultural and social service organizations in Boston, even though Boston is only a miniscule part of the market or employment base for Gillette (which has two-thirds of its sales outside the United States): "Management people are sophisticated. It is important that we can move people worldwide in and out of our headquarters, that they can educate their kids well, find good housing and cultural attractions here. It is important that we don't have slums or crime. For this reason, we are a major contributor to the Boston social structure, way beyond the proportion of our business here."[15] But when headquarters shrink in importance, advantages for the community decline. Texaco Latin America headquarters in the Miami suburb of Coral Gables were downsized in 1993, when more control was given to field centers in Rio de Janeiro and Bogota. Once a major contributor to Miami-area cultural and civic groups, Texaco reduced its involvement in regional causes considerably, to the consternation of local groups. The big donations went to Brazil, home to 1,600 employees. "From now on," the regional president said, "we will make contributions in South Florida that are more in line for a company with less than 200 employees in the community."[16]

The large businesses that remained in urban areas—downtown banks, utilities, newspapers, retail stores, and professional firms—continued to be acquired by outside companies. Regional general managers for companies headquartered elsewhere lost power as companies reorganized around product or customer type, not geography.

For example, the state president for the phone company was once the powerful overseer of all activities in his or her state; now he or she is a figurehead, while the real power is held by a systemwide line of business managers. Local budgetary authority and flexibility are reduced when resource allocation decisions are made elsewhere.

In Boston this industrial transformation was manifested in reduced contributions to charities such as the United Way and in a growing inability to find chief executives who could make significant commitments to civic causes. Today, a handful of the "usual suspects" serve on every board; for example, Chad Gifford, CEO of Bank-Boston, was associated with nearly every major regional activity, although he was often represented by former External Affairs vice president Ira Jackson. But there is a wide gap in interests between Boston's downtown banks and utilities, whose markets are local or regional, and high-tech companies in the suburbs and beyond that are "born global." Newer technology companies are cosmopolitans that must be industry innovators and pacesetters; they compare themselves to companies everywhere in the world and plan expansions out of the region and into international markets. They often complain about the local political and civic environment but are not really dependent on it. When Robert Palmer moved to Massachusetts to become CEO of Digital Equipment Corporation, once the world's second-largest computer company, he expressed a desire to get involved in the region and signed up for committees; then he became unavailable for service as internal business problems overwhelmed the company, which has since disappeared into Compaq.

Yet global competitiveness, sometimes viewed as undermining local community loyalties, can actually cut two ways. Certainly, large businesses supplying global customers have weaker ties to specific regions and can often locate facilities anywhere, especially as communities compete to attract them. But businesses also need much more from the places in which they operate in order to remain competitive: higher skills for their work force, a good education for their executives' children, and access to research facilities. And banks, utilities, real estate developers, midsize companies, and professionals (lawyers and money managers) remain dependent on local markets and local goodwill. So some businesses, at least, have an interest in strengthening the regional economy and infrastructure, and those tend to be overrepresented in the leadership of business coalitions. In addition, the increasing prevalence of coalitions reduces the dependence of a region on any one business; thus today's business leadership in the community is more likely to be a group effort.

Public Primacy of Business

What is remarkable today is not simply that such business coalitions exist or that they embrace regional development causes. The noteworthy issue is that business leadership is held in such high public esteem that some public functions are ceded to it, as though business is "above politics."

This role of business coalitions in the new regionalism derives from changing attitudes toward business and government. Public systems, including school systems, are considered dysfunctional and in need of "reinvention." Business culture—which needed its own heavy dose of reinvention in the 1980s—is now considered innovative and entrepreneurial. Business is seen as setting the standards, and, in the view of such public officials as Mayor Stephen Goldsmith of Indianapolis, only business understands the measures and accountability that can ensure positive outcomes from improvement programs. Mayor Goldsmith has made the business community his ally in fighting for privatization of municipal services, school vouchers, and welfare-to-work programs.

Business language increasingly pervades public discourse. Observers of civil society have noted a decline in political participation. Perhaps, in a real as well as metaphoric sense, the role of the American public is shifting from "citizen" to "customer." National and state "reinventing government" initiatives describe the public as "customers" for government services, and consolidated services are referred to as "one-stop shopping." According to reports, many residents of Disney's new town of Celebration, Florida, seem more comfortable as customers of a developer than as voters in a self-governing polity. Business tools, techniques, methods, and language are being applied to any issue, well beyond their proven limits. Among the most popular business tools transported to the public sector are private sector incentives and measures. A business group in New York City has created a fund for performance pay for superintendents and principals for improving test scores; however, use of monetary incentives for students in Cleveland did not work, and the widely touted Boston Compact did not have the desired result.

The belief in the virtues of the private sector over the public sector is a Reagan-era legacy. Indeed, many business coalitions that started in the Reagan era took on urban issues that had long been considered government concerns. In 1984 Cardinal Bernard Law and the Boston Globe's owner and publisher, William Taylor, started Boston's Challenge to Leadership, which brought together business, nonprofit, and government leaders to create a shared agenda on crime, teenage pregnancy, and education, as well as economic development. The hope was that both public and private sectors would do their share to implement the agenda. Fourteen years later, in 1998, Challenge to Leadership orchestrated a transition, disbanding to form the Metropolitan Affairs Coalition to serve as a Greater Boston economic forum for long-range metropolitan planning.

It is now assumed by many Democrats as well as Republicans that "government can't do it alone" and that the private sector must get involved. The division of labor among urban institutions is being reorganized. Sometimes private sector involvement is financially motivated, as strapped government entities or civic groups need to raise additional funds for worthwhile community endeavors. Money is clearly one way that businesses and their associations shape the civic agenda: public funds for large projects are more likely to be appropriated when private money has already been raised (and used to campaign for public appropriations), as in the case of baseball and football stadiums. But money is not the only, or even always the primary, contribution.

Increasingly, public officials of both parties turn to business leaders for ideas and management talent, not just for financing campaigns, and they expect to work with business coalitions through public-private partnerships. The defining moment for Cleveland occurred when Republican George Voinovich (later governor of Ohio) succeeded antibusiness populist Dennis Kucinich as mayor of Cleveland. Voinovich's cooperation with the CEOs of Cleveland Tomorrow set a standard for business coalition influence that his successor, Democrat Michael White, upheld as a matter of course. Many regional efforts today enjoy joint sponsorship by the central-city mayor or other politicians and one or more key business associations. In Greater Miami the "One Community, One Goal" project to lure high-growth industries to Dade County was cochaired by the head of the chamber of commerce and the mayor. In January 1997 Chicago mayor Richard Daley and Cook County President John Strozier formed the City/County Welfare Reform Task Force, which included executives from large corporations, foundations, public schools, colleges, and local welfare service providers. The intent was to build on work by the Chicago Workforce Board, the Chicago Civic Committee, and the decidedly private Commercial Club.

Private sector involvement is now mandated for some public issues. In Florida, for example, schools must have school improvement teams consisting of teachers, administrators, parents, and community leaders (which essentially means business leaders). There are an estimated 200,000 business–public school "partnerships" in the United States, according to the Business Roundtable, most of which are in the realm of traditional charity and individual volunteerism. But increasingly, business coalitions are setting the agenda for public school reform in many cities: as elected school boards are replaced by ones under mayoral control, business leaders are appointed as board members and chair search committees for school superintendents.

Public-private partnerships, with business coalitions in the ascendant, reflect the complicated nature of many issues—it is true that no one institution can change a complex system by itself. But what is striking is that business leaders, through their associations, are the ones assumed to confer legitimacy on regional projects. National surveys and focus groups indicate that for many people the public sector is associated with politics, and politics is the enemy of change. These same people feel that business efficiency and emphasis on results are the only hope for change. Some community officials join members of the public in considering business a "neutral convenor" that is above politics—a phrase heard from a senior Democratic official. Another common belief is that CEO "star power" can bring people together, make sense of good intentions, and ensure that action plans are effective.

It seems that business, and not a duly-elected government, now confers legitimacy on civic agendas. Groups and actions are not credible without business support. In Philadelphia the involvement of Greater Philadelphia First, a thirty-five-corporation coalition, helped convince David Hornbeck to become superintendent. Consider this comment by Terry Peterson, counselor to U.S. Secretary of Education Richard Riley, in a November 1997 interview: "The mayor or governor can bring people together once, but business is seen as a neutral convenor that can continue the process without politics intruding." Business, he argued, can build excitement for a vision and convene interest groups to act on it. Is not that leadership role precisely the one that elected officials were once expected to play?

Business may be a convenor, and even a contributor, but the idea that it is "neutral" is worth pausing to ponder. It is true that the agenda brought forth by civic business associations is increasingly broader, more proactive, and less reactive. The business-led Boston Municipal Research Bureau moved beyond its founding role as fiscal watchdog to examine the future and lead discussions about a regional vision. The Massachusetts Software Council added to its member-focused marketing and training roles a set of projects to get public schools wired for the Internet and to increase their technological sophistication. Joint Venture: Silicon Valley, a business coalition in a region known for apolitical entrepreneurial companies serving global markets, made public education its number one priority because of a shortage of well-trained workers in a tight labor market. Because many of the competitiveness problems facing businesses today involve work-force skills, there is a convergence, perhaps temporary, of business and regional social agendas.

As long as the regional agenda focuses on economic competitiveness, the dominant role of business coalitions makes sense. Businesses have a clear stake and expertise in these issues and a willingness to contribute their own resources, and there is a long tradition of business associations promoting their areas through chambers of commerce and other organizations. Indeed, it is not clear that government should use taxpayers' money for business boosterism, even in the interest of job creation. The state of Florida has privatized its economic development department, establishing Enterprise Florida (run by the former head of Miami's Beacon Council) as a private-public partnership.

However, the current wave of social problems facing metropolitan areas, such as faltering public education, are not as clearly suited to business tools and techniques as is economic development—although they clearly benefit from the attention business leaders lavish on them and from business lobbying local and state governments for improvements. Although public education is now considered a core economic development issue by coalitions such as the Greater Philadelphia Chamber of Commerce, such groups are often dealing with the consequences of other business coalitions' previous tax-cutting efforts. In Massachusetts high-technology companies in software and telecommunications are involved through coalitions in projects to wire the schools, putting Boston public schools well ahead of those in other parts of the country. But in the 1980s, the same high-technology community was instrumental in weakening the tax base that supported public education.[17]

It is instructive to look at other periods in which the public sector has turned to business for solutions. In 1913 Frank Spaulding, the superintendent of the Newton, Massachusetts, public schools, spoke at a National Education Association convention about the successful introduction of scientific methods drawn from business for efficient management, bolstered by the expertise of businesspeople on school boards. During the Depression, business leaders were directly involved in broad efforts to reshape public budgets. Another wave of applied business techniques occurred during the 1960s and 1970s, as public schools adopted program planning and budgeting systems from businesses and defense contractors; by 1970 three-fourths of the states either had mandated or were considering requiring school districts to report in a program budget format. During the early 1970s, some aspects of school management were privatized via performance contracting. But failure to make permanent improvements or even achieve stated goals created a backlash against each of these sets of experiments.[18]

Weighing the Pros and Cons of Business Leadership

To assess the role, contributions, sustainability, and impact of regional business coalitions, it is first important to understand the motivations behind corporate involvement in regional activities. Corporate community service was once a matter of signing up top executives for boards and boosterism, as a kind of club to which their peers belonged. Corporate philanthropy, which took hold in the 1950s, began largely as an automatic form of noblesse oblige to any group in the company's neighborhood; it was diffuse and reactive. Companies often gave small amounts of time or money to large numbers of groups, and executives dutifully showed up for the right civic luncheons and charity balls. Causes came looking for money more than companies went searching for causes.

Today's globalization of business, dispersion of headquarters to more distant locations, and entry of foreign companies and outside managers, combined with business belt-tightening, make the old way harder to sustain. Community service is now another set of weapons in the strategic arsenal, more intimately connected with the business mission, more highly integrated with a variety of business functions, and often not even local in scope. Cosmopolitan companies with national and international customers look for national or international causes to sponsor. Reebok, located outside of Boston, is known for receiving international human rights awards but not for making contributions in its headquarters area.

Corporate community service has many functions: development of political connections and good will, marketing of products and services through their association with a good cause, and market building through increased community prosperity. It also serves as an employee benefit to attract, motivate, and retain people who like the company's association with good causes. In short, it is increasingly strategic. Businesses seek focus and impact; they want their names associated with important results. This means that the agenda for business coalitions must be action oriented and show results, often in the short term, or businesses will lose interest. One coalition head remarked, "To keep members motivated, we need action." This biases the agenda toward big new projects, such as real estate development. Surveys by *Fortune* magazine in the early 1990s showed waning business support for school partnerships because results were so difficult to achieve. Business concern for the quality of public education has waxed again in the late 1990s but could suffer the same fate.

After interviewing business and civic leaders in Chicago, Rebecca Davis, from my research team, observed that "there is a limit to the contribution the business community can make; this is not a bottomless well of support. The dollars and time businesses dedicate to community activities are spread across many functions: cultural and social events, social service activities, and programs that strengthen the internal employee community. Some business leaders feel the pressure of the 'voluntary tax' of participation. Some leaders suggest that community-based organizations and public officials should pick their battles, thinking more strategically about the funding and support they want to request from the business sector."[19]

Thus the success of regional projects often depends on the extent to which they can be framed in ways that address the self-interest of business. This can skew the agenda toward economic development projects that bring specific financial benefits to specific businesses, such as convention centers, or toward marketing efforts that promote the region. Also, softer "human capital" issues need to be characterized as matters of direct, short-term business interest. For example, the Success by Six program in Philadelphia, a United Way initiative for early childhood education, initially did not receive business support. Subsequently, new child-care programs were framed in terms of their positive effect on employee productivity, and this encouraged businesses to become advocates for programs such as full-day kindergarten in public schools.

Given the self-interest issue, getting many businesses to work together on a shared agenda in the public interest is a tricky undertaking. The degree of cooperation in Cleveland is considered unusual. A community leader told Jennifer Min, from my research team, that "corporate involvement in community issues is 'faceless' in Cleveland," a collective strategy not intended for the aggrandizement of particular companies. Nearly twenty years of effort, starting from extreme crisis and producing tangible bricks-and-mortar developments that increased civic pride, have cemented a strong partnership and commitment among member corporations as well as between corporations and the city.[20]

But today, even in Cleveland, some of the appeals for business involvement are anticoalition, such as "strategic philanthropy" and "cause-related marketing" in which businesses put their brand name on an initiative. Rivalries among businesses can mean that when one gets involved, others stay out. In one large city, two leading banks vie to be the most community-minded. For one of them it is a long-standing commitment to the health of the region; for the other, a relatively new entrant from outside the region that bought up local banks, it is a marketing ploy. To present unified support for important initiatives, the public affairs head of the first bank bends over backwards to include his counterpart from the other on boards of major projects and makes sure that they appear in public together, but relationships are often tense.

Coalitions make most sense when "public goods" are created that many businesses share, that are too costly for any one to fund alone or require the resources of many institutions, and that have longer-term time horizons and benefits. It is thus not surprising that coalitions focused on tax reductions, improved public services, economic development, or shared infrastructure (for example, airports) tend to be the most prevalent and effective. These efforts bring new shared benefits but do not ask anyone to give up anything. They also focus on concrete, tangible projects with clear and measurable results.

Because businesses have divergent interests, it can be difficult to agree on a few priorities. And because business coalitions are voluntary associations, there is generally no mechanism for sorting it out; the board can vote, but a vote that alienates too many members risks the pocket veto of lost members and withdrawal of support. A bank president in Boston tried to rally the business community around an effort to bring the Olympics to Boston, but among the businesses that declined to support this was the leading investor in sports promotions, a company that sponsored the World Cup because it was more valuable than Olympic affiliation for its global markets. Priority setting also can be complex in communities with a great deal of civic activity because of the proliferation of organizations—for example, community development corporations, investment funds, school reform coalitions—each seeking support for its own agenda.

The most pressing improvements needed in many American metropolitan areas do not necessarily lend themselves to the big development projects—convention centers, stadiums, mass transit, airports, or neighborhood revitalization—that once were characteristic of urban renewal. Human capital issues are at the forefront, including public education and welfare-to-work programs. Business coalitions that have been effective at regional marketing and economic development have not yet addressed disparities between center cities and suburbs, attracted much development to the inner city, or fixed public education. Changing a large institution like the public schools is not only a more difficult task than a bricks-and-mortar real estate development project; it is also an urban core problem rather than one with clear regional impact for companies located outside the boundaries of the central city.

Achieving Objectives

There are a number of important lessons to be drawn from the experiences of those business coalitions that have achieved their objectives and are regarded by public officials and community leaders as having made a positive contribution to a region.

Agenda Setting is First and Foremost

Many leaders in my research group's 1997–98 interviews cited the power of dialogue between key people as more important than money in getting things done in their community. In many regions the initial challenge is one of focus: sorting out priorities and achievable goals from the huge number of problems that face every region. The most effective coalitions serve as convenor and catalyst, not as an operating entity. They get leaders in key roles in key institutions who have something to offer with respect to a problem to talk together, agree on priorities, communicate a vision to the broader community, and stimulate action, which is then carried out by public sector entities, individual corporations, or nonprofit organizations with a traditional focus on that issue or newly formed to act on it.

This does not mean that business coalitions or other civic associations spring spontaneously from market forces; they may play their wider, agenda-setting role because a concerned individual or small group has articulated an issue persuasively enough to bring other leaders to the table. For every Roger Milliken in Spartanburg, Alvah Chapman in Miami, or Chad Gifford in Boston, there are public officials and heads of community organizations making proposals to capture the attention of such prominent business leaders, who then put the matter before a somewhat larger group—an existing organization, a set of fellow CEOs, or the press—and turn an issue into an opportunity for dialogue. The dialogue then creates the agenda. To use the example that opened this chapter, the mayor of Kansas City may have had the bully pulpit, but it was the Kansas City International Alliance that ran the conference.

Crisis Enlists People, Success Retains Them

Some effective business coalitions and their activities, such as Cleveland Tomorrow or the Spartanburg chamber's international initiatives, were undertaken during periods of distress, when industrial transformation weakened the economy, deteriorating infrastructure threatened the companies that remained, or other economic, political, and social challenges affected quality of life. Early successes and quick wins through tangible projects with immediate and visible benefits deepened the commitment of leaders to further efforts, earned credibility with critics and skeptics among community activists, helped reelect friendly local officials, and proved that collaborative efforts could bring results. Success breeds success. Miami's Beacon Council grew in influence because of its effectiveness in the Hurricane Andrew cleanup.

Involve Not-for-Profit and Community-Based Organizations

Business coalitions take on formal organizational status by incorporating as nonprofit organizations, and that helps provide a governance structure for shared decisionmaking and rotation of leaders. In a sense, becoming a public interest nonprofit organization helps institutionalize the coalition qua coalition so that it is not excessively dominated by the interests of just one major business. But beyond this narrow connection with the not-for-profit sector, business-led coalitions also are entwined with other major civic and nonprofit groups; the heads of such organizations (often large employers themselves) sit on the board and at the decisionmaking table. Coalitions also benefit from the key role of nonprofits as intermediaries that encourage exchange of information, relay information, assimilate resources, and serve as brokers for all involved parties.

Nonprofits sometimes become the operating entity for the projects stemming from the business coalition's agenda. In Boston a coalition of coalitions created a vision for Year 2000 projects that would prepare the region for the next century. Mayor Thomas Menino appointed a Boston 2000 Commission of regional business and nonprofit leaders, and the nonprofit Fund for Boston Neighborhoods, which was linked to the mayor's office, served as the initial vehicle for contributions and foundation grants. Boston 2000 then incorporated as a nonprofit organization. The focus and commitment of the nonprofit or community-based organization and its staff—who become dedicated to the effort full time—often sustain efforts that would otherwise depend on corporate CEOs twisting each other's arms for voluntary contributions of scarce time.

Great Staff Work Counts

The leadership skills of the staff to whom volunteers from the business community delegate responsibility make a critical difference.[21] The most effective actions come from issue-focused organizations with strong professional personnel, who build credibility through their leadership and actions. Greater Philadelphia First, for example, was cited by leaders in the region for the professionalism of its staff, which identified needs, motivated businesses to get involved, and matched resources with needs.

Business Resources Should Fit Community Needs

Effective coalitions find an appropriate balance between collective and individual effort and understand what specific businesses have to offer. They do not expect the same model to work for everyone. Thus they create broad umbrellas under which a variety of projects can be accomplished in different ways by different businesses. The highest-impact community service projects undertaken by individual companies tend to involve the core competence of a business, entail market building or technology development, and bring specific business benefits as well as community solutions.[22] It is not surprising that the presence of many high-technology companies in the region enabled the Boston public schools, with the support of business coalitions and industry councils, to create a five-year technology plan with $76 million in public and private money behind it. By October 1998, two years into the school technology plan, each of the city's big schools was wired for high-speed Internet access, and 60 percent of the system's 4,800 teachers had basic training for computers in their classroom.

Avoiding Pitfalls

Even the most effective business coalitions cannot do everything. Leaders must beware of potential problems surrounding the role of business coalitions.

Overreliance on Single Powerful Organizations

Centralization of power gets certain things done, but it can weaken the development of other leadership ready for changing times, and it can create a vacuum if the main business coalition deteriorates. Elite CEO-only groups that are still at the center of many cities' regional business coalitions are harder to sustain as companies change hands and CEOs come and go. CEO-only activities and meetings behind closed doors no longer fit the public role played by business leadership groups. Boston's Coordinating Committee (informally known as "the Vault" after a preferred meeting place) dwindled into irrelevance in the 1990s, while new, more diverse and open groups became players in regional leadership circles. In Cleveland some community leaders worried about overdependence on Cleveland Tomorrow. In other cities there were worries that the very strength of a business leadership group in getting things done prevented the region from cultivating other leaders or encouraging people to go into public service. If it is possible for a business executive to have informal public power, why should he or she run for office?

Sustaining Commitment

Community organizations worry about the sustainability of corporate contributions. According to some regional leaders, once the excitement of an agenda or an announcement goes away, the problem is to ensure that the project gets rolled out. In the era of strategic community service, companies often get their major benefits up front, from the public relations value of the press conference or the tax deductibility of a financial contribution. Coalition leadership then has the problem of getting volunteers to take responsibility. Without a broad base of leadership, turnover can be a problem. Bernard Reznicek moved from Oklahoma to head Boston Edison in 1990, initiating several business coalitions for economic development of particular interest to utilities, but he left the company and Boston in 1994. The groups atrophied until the efforts were revived a few years later by the next CEO.

Lack of Accountability

In 1997 at a meeting of the World Economic Forum in Davos, Switzerland, business and government leaders listened to glowing reports of business contributions to their communities until a critic burst the bubble of goodwill by arguing that this was a very bad thing for democracy. Such unelected groups, he argued, subvert the public process, turn the public sector into a tool of business, and lack accountability to anything other than the self-interest of member corporations. This was a harsh criticism in light of the needs communities have for business resources, expertise, and involvement. After all, business coalitions represent a new form of social capital and interest in civil society that could reverse the decline of participation in public life. But unless the wider public has a voice, powerful groups representing economic interests alone could distort the public agenda in their interests—which can be benign and even highly beneficial in

some circumstances but potentially harmful to some public constituencies in others.

The fears stem from two sources. One is the legacy of the Reagan
years, when well-organized business groups in some parts of the
United States were so adamantly antitaxation that it was assumed that
their power would undermine public investments in public services.
Community leaders should be wary of single-issue groups, instead
favoring broader coalitions interested in dialogue rather than pushing a single point of view. The second source of fears is that business
coalitions might be quiet cartels, operating behind closed doors to
carve up desirable civic territory and elect captive politicians. But
groups that try to operate that way are increasingly discredited. In
Boston a watchdog reporter leaked information from behind the
scenes at a CEO-only coalition and ridiculed it in print, placing the
final nail in the coffin of a group that had become irrelevant just
because it was closed and exclusive. To get things done, business-led
coalitions must increasingly reach out to the leadership of many other
community groups and show that they are inclusive and transparent,
or their agendas will lose credibility.

Business coalitions have a clear and positive role to play in
public-private partnerships, and they serve as a force for regional consciousness and action. But we should not embrace the private side of
these partnerships to the neglect of the public side. Strong public sector leadership is essential to marshal resources beyond the feasible
contributions from individual corporations (who must serve their
shareholders), protect the public interest, extend the dialogue to a
wider array of institutions, and use the bully pulpit of campaigns and
elected office to argue for a shared vision and agenda. The initial case
studies from *Business Leadership in the Social Sector* show that the most
effective business contributions are made in places where public leadership—from civic activists as well as elected officials—is strong,
visionary, respected across interest groups, and change oriented.

The most effective business coalitions collaborate with elected
officials and convene public forums at which many community voices
can be heard. As a force for regional problem solving, they help
elected officials from many jurisdictions work together, and they
reach across organizational lines to include leaders from many parts
of the community. Did Kansas City's "Going Global" conference in
August 1998 solve any problems? Of course not. It was just another
conference and another party. But it helped create an occasion in

which business leaders and average citizens could talk together about international exports and local neighborhood improvements in the same breath. It served as one more reinforcement of regional identity and the need for dialogue and collaboration.

Notes

1. Rosabeth Moss Kanter, *World Class: Thriving Locally in the Global Economy* (Simon and Schuster, 1995).

2. Rosabeth Moss Kanter, "Business Leadership in the Social Sector," in *Proceedings of National Forum*, Harvard Business School, April 1998. Interviews were conducted by Michelle Renbaum, Rebecca Davis, Sukyana Lahiri, Catherine Lovejoy, Stephanie Lowell, Jennifer Min, Randi Reich, Joshua Solomon, and Sarah Vickers-Willis.

3. James E. Austin, "Business Leadership Lessons from the Cleveland Turnaround," *California Management Review*, vol. 41 (Fall 1998), pp. 1–21.

4. Boston was first in education and health care in a benchmarking study and was far ahead in venture capital and new business startups. See Cleveland Citizens League, *Rating the Region* (1994).

5. Rosabeth Moss Kanter, *World Class*.

6. Neil Peirce, Curtis W. Johnson, and John Stuart Hall, *Citistates: How Urban America Can Prosper in a Competitive World* (Washington, D.C.: Seven Locks Press, 1993).

7. Frey Foundation, *Taking Care of Civic Business: How Formal CEO-Level Business Leadership Groups Have Influenced Civic Progress in Key American Cities* (March 1993), as cited in James E. Austin and Stephanie Woerner, "Social Purpose Business Leadership Coalitions," paper presented at Business Leadership in the Social Sector Forum, in *Proceedings of National Forum*, Harvard Business School, April 1998.

8. Jerome L. Himmelstein, *Looking Good and Doing Good: Corporate Philanthropy and Corporate Power* (Indiana University Press, 1997).

9. Kanter, *World Class*, chap. 9.

10. Ibid., chap. 10.

11. From interviews by Sukyana Lahiri for Kanter, Business Leadership Forum.

12. Austin, "Business Leadership Lessons from the Cleveland Turnaround," paper presented at Business Leadership in the Social Sector Forum, in *Proceedings of National Forum*, Harvard Business School, April 1998.

13. John Logan and Harvey Molotch, *Urban Fortunes: The Political Economy of Place* (University of California Press, 1987).

14. Allison K. Hughes, *Corporate Impact on the Community: A Study of Charitable Contribution Patterns for Corporations with Local, Non-Local Domestic and Foreign Headquarters in Three U.S. Cities*, honors thesis, Harvard University, Department of Economics, 1994.

15. Kanter, *World Class*.

16. Ibid.

17. Elizabeth Useem, *Low Tech Education in a High Tech World* (Free Press, 1986),

18. Craig E. Richards, Rima Shore, and Max B. Sawicky, *Risky Business: Private Management of Public Schools* (Washington, D.C.: Economic Policy Institute, 1996); David Tyack and Larry Cuban, *Tinkering towards Utopia: A Century of Public School Reform* (Harvard University Press, 1995).

19. Kanter, "Business Leadership."

20. Ibid.

21. Austin and Woerner, "Social Purpose Business Leadership Coalitions."

22. Kanter, "Business Leadership."

PART THREE

RACE AND REGIONALISM

CHAPTER SEVEN

Gentleman's Agreement: Discrimination in Metropolitan America

KENNETH T. JACKSON

Almost as old as cities themselves, walls have a long and useful history. For centuries in Europe, walls offered protection against invading armies and rampaging bandits. During times of danger, residents from miles around would race toward the gates, there to find shelter within the city. Indeed, the walls of medieval and early modern towns even formed a spiritual boundary, preserving those within from the evil outside.

During most of its history, the United States has had a different experience. On this continent the very absence of walls was part of its lure. Whereas the Old World was bounded and limited, the New World was expansive, open, and limitless. After all, what was the need for walls in a country where land was inexpensive, and potential enemies were far away? For that matter, what is the use of walls today? The American republic currently stands astride the world like a colossus—vast, rich, powerful, and without external enemies capable of making war against it in a serious way.

Robert Frost put it well in his poem "Mending Walls":

Before I built a wall I'd ask to know
What I was walling in or walling out,
And to whom I was like to give offense.

Something there is that doesn't love a wall,
That wants it down.[1]

Unfortunately, since 1914, when Frost published his complaint against walls, the United States has come to be filled with them. In our time the most obvious manifestations of this trend are gated communities, those residential areas with fences, guardhouses, and restricted access designed to privatize normally public spaces. Like the medieval cities of old, they feature visible walls. Across the nation, in new suburban developments and in older inner-city areas retrofitted to provide security, perhaps 4 million Americans have found this new form of refuge. Not only are new communities "forting up," but existing neighborhoods are increasingly using barricades to isolate themselves.[2]

This essay is not on gated communities and visible walls, but rather on the invisible fences that surround entire municipal jurisdictions in the United States. We may not see them, but they are as real and effective as both the fortifications of medieval Europe or the gated communities of our own time. These are the boundaries between our cities and our suburbs. As the mayor of St. Louis noted a generation ago, the walls between his city and its suffocatingly surrounding suburbs in 1961 were more secure and inviolable than the wall that then divided East and West Berlin.[3]

To be fair, invisible fences are not unique to the United States. All communities in all societies have boundaries—the definition of a city requires it. Thus Beijing has a legal or corporate limit, as does London, Tokyo, Paris, Siena, or any city. But American walls are more numerous, effective, and insidious than those of other countries for four reasons.

First, economic inequality is greater in the United States than in other advanced nations. It is true that the Dutch, British, and French have recently become accustomed to derelicts camped in tunnels, under highways, along fashionable shopping streets, and inside train stations, and that in Tokyo the Shinjuku train and subway station, like many others, fills up at night with homeless people. And even the Germans, long noted for their neatness and generous social services, now occasionally see broken glass or encounter beggars as they walk along their streets. But the American people now accept squalor, slums, and misery as inevitable. And nowhere in the developed world are slums and poverty more noticeable than in the United States.[4]

Second, the rich and poor are not evenly divided across the American landscape. The typical pattern, understood even by young children, is that suburbs are rich and central cities are poor. Indeed, so common and well understood is this "North American pattern" that the opposition between wealth and poverty in the shared urban space of a single metropolitan region has become a classic theme of sociology. The concept was first developed at the University of Chicago in the 1920s, when Louis Wirth and Robert E. Park transformed the way scholars looked at social pathology.[5] From their work came social stratification theory, which posits that the geography of the large metropolis is socially, economically, and racially differentiated in terms of residence and amenities.[6]

Third, the United States is more suburbanized and balkanized than European and Asian nations. Its metropolitan regions stretch over hundreds and sometimes thousands of square miles, dwarfing the geographic spread of even the largest agglomerations elsewhere. Because municipal annexation has not kept up with the outward movement of the American population, the number of little governments in metropolitan regions has proliferated. The New York metropolitan area alone is dotted with more than 1,400 separate taxing authorities.[7]

Fourth, political balkanization is more important in the United States than in comparable nations, because land-use controls, public education, and police and fire protection are *local* responsibilities in the American system of decentralized authority. Indeed, this arrangement is practically enshrined in the Constitution. Thus when middle-class families move from cities to suburbs, they take with them needed tax revenues. In Europe and Japan, by contrast, outward population movements have little effect on schools, crime, or fire protection. Similarly, municipalities, landowners, and small businesses in the United States have successfully resisted the centralization of land-use controls, which remain mostly under local jurisdiction. Other nations have local planning and zoning boards, but they are typically subservient to regional or national bodies.[8]

These American "peculiarities" have long been well understood by scholars. In fact, the causes and consequences of inequality have been occupying them for generations. Similarly, municipal boundary changes have been an important political issue since the nineteenth century. Finally, we now understand in a general sense the suburbanization process and why it is that the American landscape does not look like that of Germany, England, or Australia.[9]

But why do communities in the United States differ so much among themselves and so much more than is the case in other nations? Of course, there is no reason to believe that all places should be similar, especially given the importance of region, class, economic structure, and dominant transportation system in place at the time of a community's greatest growth. Perhaps municipal differences are part of the natural order of things, like the rising sun, the barking of dogs, or the mutual attraction of male and female. But this essay posits that the socioeconomic variation in American towns and cities is not random or natural. Rather, it is determined by government, and especially by those who have controlled it. And it is not fair. Every metropolitan region offers examples of disparate communities. Ladue outside St. Louis, Winnetka outside Chicago, Beverly Hills outside Los Angeles, Park City outside Dallas, Germantown outside Memphis, Grosse Pointe outside Detroit, and Atherton outside San Francisco are at one economic extreme. Ford Heights outside Chicago, East Orange outside Newark, Camden outside Philadelphia, and Compton outside Los Angeles are at the other.

Why is this so? Why are some places commercial and others residential, some full of promise and others full of despair? How have public policy decisions influenced the trajectory of individual communities? How has the American system of rewards and punishments shaped municipal choices? My hypothesis is that the peculiar confluence of four separate issues—residential deconcentration, social inequality, governmental balkanization, and local control and support for education, fire, and police—inhibits the search for solutions to such basic problems as poverty, crime, environmental destruction, and excessive energy consumption. If history demonstrates anything, it is that what happened was not inevitable and that the range of potential choices at any given time has always been broader than it appears in retrospect. One role of a historian is to reveal how one particular kind of thing happened and other kinds of things did not happen and which things could not have happened. Hopefully, through that process we arrive at a place where we can define more broadly the options that are available to us in the situations we face now.

This chapter focuses on the thirty-one-county, three-state, 20-million-person New York metropolitan region and especially on three small areas within it: a 36-square-mile swatch of Fairfield County, Connecticut, comprising the towns of Darien and New Canaan; the 23.6-square-mile city of Newark, New Jersey, in Essex County; and a 10-

square-mile section of Westchester County, New York, that makes up the entire city of White Plains. Each of these areas was originally settled in the seventeenth century, each is within fifty miles and an hour's commute of midtown Manhattan, each has long been suburban and subordinate to the same great metropolis, and each has included African Americans and other minorities among its population for more than three hundred years.

There the similarities cease. In fact, few places could be more unlike than Darien, New Canaan, Newark, and White Plains. Darien and New Canaan are separate and adjacent communities with a similar demographic and economic profile. They are exclusive, affluent suburbs in the richest part of the richest state in the United States. Darien is the older and smaller of the two. Indeed, at 12.9 square miles, it is the smallest town on Fairfield County's Gold Coast. A sailing mecca, it has a gorgeous shoreline with coves, bays, and ice-skating ponds. New Canaan, which since 1899 has called itself "the next station to heaven," comprises twenty-two square miles of heavily wooded and rolling countryside. Together, they had a combined population of 38,000 in 1990, when each ranked among the most affluent communities in the United States. Both are among the top ten communities in the nation, based on the number of *Who's Who in America* entries per capita. They boast expensive shops, fleets of Mercedes and BMWs, gracious homes, prestigious and well-equipped public schools, and attractive and well-kept parks. But the price of admission to their quiet precincts is steep: in 1999 new houses in both communities typically sold for more than $1 million, available building lots were priced at $700,000, and several builders specialized in tearing down older homes to make room for massive luxury structures costing between $2 million and $4 million. Incredibly, much of this building was speculative and without buyers on hand.[10]

Predictably, Darien and New Canaan citizens live in relative peace, free from most urban ills. With the exception of two widely publicized acquaintance rapes in 1989, for which a star local athlete was finally convicted eight years later, the police there are mostly concerned with teenage parties and with the various depredations of skunks, raccoons, and deer. Virtually no one is on welfare, and there is little public housing. Darien and New Canaan have few poor and minority residents (each has a sprinkling of live-in, African American servants), and they have long been regarded as inhospitable to Jews. In fact, the chapter title, "Gentleman's Agreement," is borrowed from the 1947 novel of the same name (later made into a movie starring Gregory Peck) that dealt with anti-Semitism in Darien.[11] In short, these two suburbs have been and are exclusionary in almost every sense of the term.

Newark is also a statistical leader, but not in categories most persons would find desirable.[12] By almost any measure, it is among America's most troubled cities. In the past half century, it has lost most of its job base and 40 percent of its total population. Two-thirds of those that remain are African Americans, and a staggering one-third are on some form of public assistance. Its once bustling commercial streets are now ghostly thoroughfares of burned-out and boarded-up buildings, littered with blowing paper, used condoms, liquor bottles, and tattered plastic from the hidden dens of the homeless. Newark's once legendary theaters and nightclubs are closed, and its schools are so bad that they were taken over by the state in 1996. The city suffers from extraordinary rates of slum housing, property taxes, venereal disease, and infant mortality. It typically ranks at or near the top in most categories of the annual FBI Uniform Crime Reports, and the head of the police department was himself arrested, indicted, and convicted in 1996 for stealing public funds. Crack and heroin drops along Springfield Avenue are known even to children, and the illegal drug trade is among the biggest employers of Newark's young and desperate.[13]

Finally, White Plains is a paradigm of yet another kind. Located halfway between the Tappan Zee Bridge and Long Island Sound, the city is a commuter's dream, with direct access to three major highways and to the busy Metro North commuter rail line. It includes four separate malls within a short walk of each other. Indeed, in New York State it ranks second only to Manhattan in retail sales. As Mayor Sy Schulman noted early in 1995, "White Plains is a place that is carefully trying to straddle polar opposites of city and countrified suburb."

Few American cities anywhere, however, have changed as quickly and radically as White Plains in recent years. Partly as a result of a gigantic urban renewal effort, dozens of major buildings, including the Galleria Mall and the Westchester Mall, have transformed the physical landscape since 1970. The population of White Plains is now racially and economically mixed, and its neighborhoods include mansions as well as public housing projects. The well-funded White Plains schools spend about twice the national average per student, and both the middle and the high schools have been named Schools of Excellence, a federal designation based on the quality of the curriculum and teaching staff. In 1993 the district was rated among the top ten in the nation by *Expansion Management Magazine*, a publication for families involved in corporate relocation.

Although these communities are just small parts of a continental nation, they represent a larger national pattern. Any of the two dozen largest metropolitan areas in the United States could have provided similar examples. In Philadelphia, for example, Camden could have substituted for Newark, King of Prussia for White Plains, and Bryn Mawr for Darien and New Canaan. Similarly, Chicago could have provided Gary, Schaumburg, and Winnetka; the St. Louis area might suggest East St. Louis, Clayton, and Ladue. The questions would be similar: Why do communities differ? How do wide demographic disparities among small governmental jurisdictions affect the nation?

In 1870 New Canaan and Darien were rather ordinary places. During the course of the next century, they adopted restrictive zoning ordinances, refused public housing, and turned away the poor and the weak. In other words, they built invisible fences to transform themselves into elite residential areas of wealth, prestige, beauty, and gracious living. Similarly, Newark in 1870 was a prosperous and successful city with enormous potential. It had beautiful parks, distinguished public schools, a solid economy, and a thriving central business district. Indeed, as late as 1911, the superintendent of schools could remark that "I doubt whether there can be found anywhere in the world a population of 365,000 souls more universally happy, contented and prosperous than the residents of Newark." But it welcomed ethnic and racial minorities, allowed industry to grow, refused to adopt restrictive residential zoning, and encouraged public housing. For its efforts Newark lost the confidence of the middle class and of federal agencies that encouraged home ownership. Finally, in 1870 few people could have foreseen that White Plains would be, on a proportionate basis, a bigger magnet than Manhattan.

Darien and New Canaan

The first persons to settle what is now Darien arrived about 1641. The area was originally part of Stamford, but it became Middlesex Parish in 1737 and was incorporated as the town of Darien in 1820. For more than two centuries, it was a quiet farming and commercial fishing village, replete with millers, carpenters, blacksmiths, tanners, and teamsters. By the middle of the nineteenth century, a town center had developed near the railroad station, with a general store, a blacksmith shop, and a coal yard.[14]

New Canaan developed along relatively similar lines. Initially settled late in the seventeenth century, it was established by the Connecticut legislature as Canaan Parish, a religious entity. The right to form a Congregational Church was granted to the families there so that they might avoid having to travel long distances to churches in Norwalk or Stamford. It was finally incorporated as a separate town in 1801.

Early in the nineteenth century, New Canaan became a center for shoemaking. Indeed, by the 1820s, the town was among the top half-dozen shoemaking places in the United States, and it maintained its industrial status for many decades. The 1850 census, for example, revealed that there were more shoemakers in New Canaan than farmers and that its factory work force was proportionately as large as that of any other community in Connecticut. By the 1870s, however, the 50,000 handmade pairs that New Canaan produced annually could not compete with the new machines of bigger companies in bigger places. Shoemakers soon began to move away from New Canaan to make a living. The Excelsior Shoe Factory on Linden Avenue was the last remnant of that once flourishing industry.

In sum, a century and a quarter ago, neither Darien nor New Canaan was particularly pretentious or successful. What happened to change their circumstances?

Demographics

An influx of wealthy weekend and summer residents began around the turn of the century; this especially affected Long Neck Point and Tokeneke along the Darien waterfront and Oenoke Ridge along the high ground in New Canaan. Although these new, rich families never made up more than a small percentage of the total town populations, they employed a large number of blue-collar workers as gardeners, maids, chauffeurs, and cooks and began to set the tone for the community.

Zoning Restrictions

Both towns were quick to adopt zoning and use it to limit residence to families in comfortable circumstances. Zoning in the United States began in New York City in 1916 as a method of controlling the height of buildings and the use of commercial and industrial space. Although it represented an extraordinary growth of government power, nearly everyone supported zoning, in part because it seemed a convenient way of preserving class segregation and property values. It surely was popular: by 1926 seventy-six communities, Darien among them, had adopted ordinances similar to that of New York; by 1936 an astonishing 1,322 towns and cities (85 percent of the national total) had zoning laws, and they were affecting more property than all national laws relating to business.[15]

Darien was on the bandwagon early and adopted the new methodology in 1924. Over the decades it slowly ratcheted up restrictions so that apartments, condominiums, and other relatively affordable units were effectively excluded from the community. For New Canaan the pivotal zoning moment came on February 27, 1932, when a town meeting voted to create a zoning commission. Amazingly, that commission drew up a zoning code in less than three months, and the town approved New Canaan's first zoning map on May 23, 1932. The classification of land was important, because there were still about thirty-five farms in the town in at that time, totaling more than 4,000 acres. How would this open space be zoned for future development? Town leaders set aside a small space for industry and zoned the town center for commercial development. For virtually everything else they decreed *two-acre-minimum* lot sizes, an astonishingly high figure for the time. Moreover, within a few years they added a *four-acre-minimum* lot zone and eliminated industrial space altogether.

Transportation Investments

Public investment in railroads and roadways on a scale unknown by outlying locations in other nations transformed all of Fairfield County, Connecticut. The New Haven Railroad, for example, provided a dependable and speedy commute to Manhattan, and by 1923 *National Geographic* magazine could write that "even Connecticut, as far as Stamford, Greenwich, and New Canaan is peopled by those who work in Gotham by day and sleep in the country by night." Moreover, the opening of the Merritt Parkway in 1938 and Interstate 95 in 1958 made automobile travel more attractive. By 1950 Connecticut had the most extensive road system in the United States with 3,000 paved miles, an unusual total for a state with fewer than 5,000 square miles of territory.

Lending and Tax Policies

Discriminatory use of various forms of Federal Housing Administration (FHA) and Veterans Administration (VA) loan and mortgage
guarantees, coupled with America's unique practice of allowing the
deduction of mortgage interest and property taxes from total income,
encouraged the suburbanization of the wealthy. In June 1933 Congress established the Home Owners Loan Corporation (HOLC), and
in June 1934, the Federal Housing Administration. Together they low-
ered interest rates for potential homeowners and made possible the
long-term, self-amortizing mortgage with uniform payments spread
over the whole life of the debt. Their impact on the United States was
immediate and enormous, although their greatest influence was felt
after World War II.

When federal HOLC appraisers evaluated Darien and New
Canaan in the 1930s for the relative safety of mortgage loans made
there, they liked what they saw, and they colored the secret Residential Security Maps they prepared for the two towns mostly with green
and blue. There was none of the red or yellow that dominated Newark
and other places with "inhospitable racial or minority groups."[16]

Discrimination

Both Darien and New Canaan were inhospitable to persons who
were racially, religiously, or culturally different from the white Protestant establishment in both towns. In fact, socioeconomic homogeneity
was one of the reasons that federal appraisers rated them so well. To
be sure, there was a small Italian and Irish community that comprised
most of the "townies": the grocers, cleaners, gardeners, and plumbers
who kept Darien and New Canaan running. But these groups scarcely
affected the Waspish image of either place.

Jews and blacks were another matter entirely, and until recently,
both groups were routinely discriminated against in the area. In the
1930s, when African Americans represented less than 1 percent of the
population, they were not welcome in stores, restaurants, or the
Darien Playhouse, and doors were slammed in their faces when they
tried to rent places to live. One person recalled, "The negro minister's
wife used to tell me stories where people who were maids used to
come and gather in her house and used to sit there in rocking chairs
on their day off because they were not welcome in the stores." Simi-

larly, a Jewish attorney in New Canaan recalled that in 1940 his father agreed on the price of a home and put down a deposit. His money was then returned when the owner decided against transferring the property to a Jew. As late as 1974, a young white couple was in a New Canaan realty office looking for a home when the telephone rang. The realtor seemed exasperated and then said to the waiting pair, "My mother just wants to make sure I am not showing any houses to Jews."[17]

Avoiding Low-Income Housing

Another cause of the current situation in Darien and New Canaan has been extreme class discrimination, brought on partly by the fact that neither community has exploited the possibilities for low-income or affordable housing. In 1937, for the first time in American history, the federal government accepted responsibility for the construction of decent, low-cost homes. The legislation empowered the United States Housing Authority to develop public projects by funding local housing agencies. So enthusiastic was President Franklin D. Roosevelt about the new possibilities that when work began on the first five projects in 1938, he wrote to his chief housing official, "Today marks the beginning of a new era in the economic and social life of America. Today, we are launching an attack on the slums of this country which must go forward until every American family has a decent home."[18]

On one level, public housing was successful. By the end of 1938, thirty-three states had passed enabling legislation, and 221 local authorities had been established. By the end of 1962, more than 2 million people lived in the half-million units built under various public housing programs. Even if the quality and design of the new structures frequently invited derision, they were usually superior to the dilapidated hovels they replaced.[19]

Unfortunately, federally assisted public housing never achieved the high purposes set out for it by its founders. One major reason was the decentralized nature of the program. Essentially, every American community had to make its own decision as to whether or not a need existed. The resulting application for federally subsidized housing had to be *voluntary*. Because municipalities had discretion on whether, when, and where to build public housing, the projects almost always reinforced racial segregation. An exclusive suburb, or one that wished to become exclusive, did not have to tarnish its image

by providing shelter for the needy within its boundaries. The preferred method was simply to refuse to create a housing agency. In
such circumstances, no national or state official could force a town to
do otherwise. By contrast, in Great Britain the municipality is itself the
"housing authority," and in Japan the national government typically
buys land on the *periphery* as the best means of acquiring space for
public housing projects.[20]

Needless to say, Darien and New Canaan avoided most of this federal largesse, and whenever housing projects were proposed, they
were the subject of intense scrutiny. The towns scarcely even considered low-income, public housing. Their only discussion was about
moderate-income programs for divorcees, empty-nesters, grandpar-
ents, teachers, and fire and police officers.

In the 1950s, on the grounds of the old Fitch's Soldiers' Home,
Darien did build fifty-three units of moderate-income housing for
returning World War II veterans, and in 1987 it built thirty units of
low-income housing specifically for the elderly. That was it. Otherwise,
every attempt to build affordable units was beaten back by coalitions
of concerned residents. Even housing for town employees or the elderly was typically rejected. In 1984, for example, a Darien referendum
killed a proposal for thirty apartments for fire and police officers,
teachers, and the elderly. Similarly, litigation against using park lands
and funds for anything other than public open space stopped the proposed Cherry Lawn Project (thirty units) in Darien.

New Canaan was similar. The eighteen-unit Millport apartment
complex was for low-income families, but only if they were already residents of the town. Such local residency preferences, administered by
suburban officials, functioned as a mechanism for discrimination. By
giving preference to town residents, equally qualified out-of-town families were effectively excluded, particularly when the number of qualified local applicants exceeded the number of units available, which
was virtually always the case.

In both Darien and New Canaan, as most citizens see it, the question has not been housing for the regional poor, but whether *any*
apartments or condominiums should be permitted. In 1987 Darien
became one of the last places in the Northeast to permit any condominium construction, on the theory that the persons who would
occupy such dwellings might degrade the community. But this did
not mean that the needy were about to breach the invisible fences of
the bucolic suburb. Instead, new "affordable" units were sold at mar-

ket rates, which meant hundreds of thousands of dollars for the smallest condominiums. As the president of a local real estate firm remarked, "There is a need for affordable housing, but the minute the town acquires a piece of property, the term 'affordable' goes out the window."

Newark

Founded in 1666 on the banks of the Passaic River by Puritans from Connecticut, Newark is, after New York and Boston, the third-oldest major city in the United States. But it remained mostly agricultural until 1800, largely because it was cut off from New York City by vast salt marshes and three large rivers. Slowly it became a transportation hub, as the Morris Canal from Phillipsburg to Newark opened in 1831 and the Morris and Essex Railroad opened from Newark to Dover in 1845. With improved transport facilities came industrial opportunities, which were exploited by master shoemakers who hired farmers who were underemployed in winter. By the time of the Civil War, Newark was among the American urban leaders in manufacturing.[21]

The economic boom continued after the Confederate surrender at Appomattox, and Newark soon solidified its ranking as the largest city in New Jersey and one of the dozen largest in the United States. By 1890 it also had become a major center for banking, insurance, legal, and government services. The Prudential Insurance Company, for example, began in Newark as the Widows and Orphans Friendly Society, while the giant Ballantine Brewing Company became one of the largest single enterprises in the Northeast. By the turn of the century, more than 90 percent of the patent leather in the United States was produced in Newark, and the city was also a leader in manufacturing trunks, drugs and chemicals, electrical machinery, jewelry, and varnish and paint.

In many respects Newark continued to grow and prosper into the 1930s. By 1910 its population had risen to 450,000 (eighth largest in the United States). Port Newark opened in 1915, Newark Airport in 1928, and Newark's Pennsylvania Station in 1935. By 1931 both the airport and the local intersection at Broad and Market Streets were touted as the busiest in the world. The city had become a leader in hats, hardware, jewelry, leathers, brewing, thread, carriages, and insurance, and the thriving central business district featured three big department stores, several elegant movie theaters, and such outstanding cultural institutions as the Newark Museum and the Newark Public Library. The cherry blossoms and shade trees of Branch Brook Park and the spacious houses along High Street around Military and Washington Parks were as attractive as any anywhere. Newark boasted of exciting nightclubs and of a sports team that was legendary. Indeed, the 1937 Newark Bears baseball club is widely regarded as the finest minor league team of all time.[22]

Not surprisingly, confidence and euphoria were in the air, and local boosters confidently predicted that Newark would one day rival New York as a world city. A 1925 futuristic portrait of Newark, for example, predicted that by 1975 its central business district would be as prominent as any on earth and would be chock-a-block with impressive skyscrapers. In fact, as late as the 1930s, Princeton economist James G. Smith predicted that Newark had potential "comparable to the phenomenal growth of Los Angeles."[23]

Obviously, Newark did not fulfill such expectations. In fact, it deteriorated so far so fast that in 1970 incoming mayor Kenneth Gibson remarked that "wherever urban America is going, Newark will get there first."[24] It was a prescient comment. By 1998 the city counted only 260,000 residents, barely half the number that had been there a half century earlier. The job loss was equally stark. Some firms, like the once imposing Ballantine Brewery, just closed their doors. Others, like the Spring Air Mattress Company or the Barton Press, moved out of town. Still others, like the Prudential Insurance Company, technically remained in Newark while shifting many operations to other locations.

In the end, however, statistics are less revealing than individual experience. For example, Philip Roth's best-selling novel *Goodbye, Columbus* was written in the late 1950s, when the Jewish exodus from Newark was reaching its peak. The journey west was toward the "promised land," which in terms of the protagonist Neil Klugman meant suburban Short Hills, where Brenda Potamkin lived. Similarly, in 1991, when the South Orange High School Class of 1961 held its thirtieth reunion, one young woman thanked her parents for getting her out of Newark in the 1950s.[25]

There were as many reasons for Newark's transformation as there were people hustling out of town in the great suburban land rush of the postwar era. But six issues have been of particular importance.

Failure to Expand

Newark's city fathers at the beginning of the twentieth century were unable to secure the necessary space for future growth. Like all cities, Newark had grown by 1900 from its tiny beginnings into a larger municipality. In 1869, for example, Newark added Clinton to its boundaries, and in 1871 it added Woodside. The remainder of Clinton Township followed in 1897 and 1902, and Vailsburg became part of Newark in 1905. That ended the era of Newark's expansion. While other ambitious American cities were turning suburbs into neighborhoods, Newark remained stuck at a miniscule twenty-three square miles. Even St. Louis and San Francisco, the smallest of other major American cities, became twice as large as Newark.

This public policy failure was the result of poor municipal leadership. During the 1890s, for example, adjacent Harrison and Kearny were willing to join Newark. But the mayor and council delayed, and by the time their annexation plans had solidified, the two Hudson County towns had industrial strength of their own and spurned Newark's marriage proposal. Still, Newark leaders were confident, and in 1900 the mayor, not foreseeing the day when his booming city would be surrounded by hostile suburbs, said, "East Orange, Vailsburg, Harrison, Kearny, and Belleville would be desirable acquisitions. By an exercise of discretion we can enlarge our city from decade to decade without unnecessarily taxing the property within our limits, which has already paid the cost of public improvements."

But the wish did not father the fact, and Essex County came to be filled with small, independent municipalities—Maplewood, Glen Ridge, Milburn, Caldwell, Montclair, Irvington, Nutley, and the Oranges—that might otherwise have been simply neighborhoods within an enlarged city. Thus when wealthy and middle-class Newarkers began moving away from central areas, they took their tax dollars to independent suburbs. Not surprisingly, historian Paul Stellhorn found that more than half of the members of the elite Newark Chamber of Commerce had left the city by 1930.[26] As Frank Kingdon gloomily noted in 1936, "The more people with money move into residential areas outside the city, the less money will be available from highly assessed properties and for privately maintained social agencies. Either the city will have to maintain such agencies or else it will pay a heavier bill for crime. In either case taxes will rise. As taxes rise, business will move out to avoid them."[27]

The situation was also costly for African Americans. For those black Newarkers who experienced financial success and bought larger homes, their quest typically took them outside the city's boundaries, often to East Orange. Thus their leadership skills were lost to those who remained behind.

Weak Land-Use Control

Unlike Darien and New Canaan, which excluded industries, and unlike other cities, which typically required more cleanup efforts from polluting factories, Newark allowed obnoxious enterprises to coexist in proximity to residential neighborhoods. Leather goods and tanning, paint and varnish manufacture, and brewing caused enormous pollution problems.

As a consequence of its industrial orientation, Newark became progressively lower middle class as the nineteenth century gave way to the twentieth. The city typically did not enforce even the minimal environmental ordinances that were on the books. As early as November 1, 1883, the *Newark Evening News* complained, "In consequence of the widespread reputation for nuisances of this city, its property is mainly of a poor and cheaply-constructed class, there being very few first class dwellings within the city limits. Even the manufacturers will not build for themselves good houses, for before they are finished it is more than probable that some vile nuisance will be located in the neighborhood, destroying the investment."[28]

"Nuisance" was an understatement. Industries were poisoning the inhabitants before the turn of the century. Sewers were also inadequate. There were 10,000 cesspools in Newark in the 1880s, "each one of them a generator of disease and the cause of much of the sickness and death in the city." On August 2, 1883, the *Newark Daily Journal* described how three residents had been overcome by carbolic acid fumes in a fatal attempt to eliminate an intolerable stench emanating from a thirteen-foot cesspool that was shared by several families living in two adjacent buildings. Their bodies were drawn to the surface with grappling irons, "the three ghastly corpses making up a picture that will never be forgotten by those who witnessed it."[29]

The situation did not soon improve. Asked if she were troubled by an unpleasant aroma, one woman remarked in 1884, "Unpleasant! That don't begin to describe it. It is a perfect barrier against a breath of pure air." Another resident echoed, "No matter how sultry the night might be we are compelled to have all the windows closed." An investigator from the *Newark Evening News* offered this first-hand account: "The odor became stronger as each succeeding step brought this reporter nearer to the ditch and when it was reached the stench arising from the black and sluggish water was so overpowering that only a strict sense of duty prevented a hasty retreat. At the opening from which the sewer empties at the railroad crossing, the bloated carcasses of two large dogs were floating, upon which a cloud of flies was banqueting, the surrounding atmosphere being poisoned with a sickening stench."[30] In 1883, when the Republican mayor was beaten for reelection by former schoolteacher Joseph E. Haynes, he said he "was glad to be defeated; it was no honor being Mayor of Newark."[31]

Industrial pollution increased in the twentieth century as chemical plants increased in complexity and size. During World War I, for example, Newark's vaunted reputation for making almost everything brought to the city a variety of military contracts for hardware, munitions, paint, clothing, uniforms, machine parts, and truck components, the production of all of which created toxic agents that found their way into the air or the ground. The problem continued into the modern era. One of the worst local polluters was the Diamond Alkali Company, which made pesticides along the Passaic River from 1951 to 1969, as well as ingredients for the chemical defoliant Agent Orange. During the Vietnam War, when the firm was operating twenty-four hours a day, Diamond Alkali and other companies released dioxin, a cancer-causing compound that is a byproduct of chemical processing, into the water, putting the lower Passaic River on the Environmental Protection Agency's list of the nation's most endangered waterways.[32]

Redlining

The FHA and HOLC, discussed earlier with regard to Darien and New Canaan, also contributed to the contemporary Newark crisis. The HOLC and FHA initiated the policy of residential "redlining." When government appraisers looked at Newark in 1939, for example, they did not regard a single neighborhood as worthy of an "A" rating. So-called "high-class Jewish" sections like Weequahic and Clinton Hill, as well as non-Jewish areas like Vailsburg and Forest Hill, all received a second grade or "B." Average Newark neighborhoods were rated even lower: the well-maintained and attractive working-class sections of Roseville, Woodside, and East Vailsburg were given third grade or "C" ratings. The remainder of the city, including immigrant Ironbound and every African American neighborhood, was redlined as fourth grade or "hazardous." As might be expected, Essex County FHA commitments went in overwhelming proportion to suburbs.[33]

Not only did the HOLC damage Newark through its own actions, but it influenced the appraisal decisions of private banking institutions. During the 1930s, for example, the Federal Home Loan Bank Board circulated questionnaires to banks about their mortgage practices. Those returned by savings and loan associations in Essex County indicated a clear relationship between public and private redlining practices. One specific question asked, "What are the most desirable lending areas?" The answers were often "A and B" or "blue" or "FHA only." Similarly, to the inquiry, "Are there any areas in which loans will not be made?" the responses included "red and most yellow" or "C and D" or simply "Newark." [34] Obviously, private banking institutions were privy to and influenced by federal residential security maps. This meant that it was difficult to secure even ordinary loans for residential properties in Newark itself, even while suburban areas were being treated generously. Meanwhile, Washington's income tax policies of mortgage interest deductions and its transportation policies of subsidizing the private motorcar also damaged Newark while benefiting the suburbs.

Poor Governance

The fourth cause of Newark's difficulties has been a long tradition of incompetence and corruption in its own government. For example, Louis Danzig, the long-time director of the Newark Redevelopment and Housing Authority, ruled his domain with both an iron fist and an iron brain. Between 1949 and 1962, he received seven times as much federal urban renewal money per capita as the legendary Robert Moses in New York City. But Danzig was even more ruthless than the "Power Broker" in his slum clearance programs, and he destroyed entire neighborhoods, some of them healthy and vibrant, in a vain and ultimately unsuccessful effort to "modernize" the city.[35]

Danzig's personal corruption was never proven, even if his arrogance and misjudgments soon became apparent. But other Newark officials were caught with their hands in the till. In 1970, for example, Mayor Hugh J. Addonizio and other high city administrators were convicted of extortion and income tax evasion. In 1996 the commissioner of the Newark Police Department was himself indicted in federal court for thirty-seven counts of theft and fraud. Various members of the city council were taking payoffs, and the chief aide to Mayor Sharpe James resigned in disgrace because of similar charges. Such revelations have been particularly damaging because they have given ammunition to those who want to blame local corruption, rather than the normal process of American development, of which they are themselves a part, for the troubled circumstances of New Jersey's largest city.

Moreover, even when honest, Newark's municipal leaders too often sacrificed long-term interests for short-term advantages. For example, Jean Anyon has recently shown that contrary to popular belief, public education in Newark was of poor quality long before African Americans came to power in the 1970s. Instead, most of the schools in Newark were declining by the mid-1930s, even as those in nearby New York City were famed for excellence.[36]

Racial Unrest

A devastating race riot in July 1967 gave Newark a black eye that took decades to heal. The tragedy began on a hot summer evening, when white policemen allegedly abused a black driver for a minor offense. Within hours, thousands of angry demonstrators were shouting and throwing rocks at the precinct headquarters, demanding an end to business as usual and overwhelming the ability of the police department to control the situation. The disturbances lasted for days, and images of Newark in flames were flashed to television screens across the nation by the three major networks. Ultimately, after twenty-seven people had been killed, after thousands of state police and National Guardsmen had been ordered to the city, and after dozens of fires had caused tens of millions of dollars in property damage and leveled blocks of stores, quiet returned to the community. Springfield Avenue and many lesser streets were devastated. More important, middle-class whites decided that Newark was a place to avoid and escape. Some had already held that view, but the riots and the racial wounds they exposed deepened the psychological gulf between the city and the suburbs. The once grand movie palaces of Newark went out of business, and the downtown department stores, including even Bamberger's, closed. By 1998 the city had barely half the population it had fifty years earlier.[37]

Providing for the Poor and Minorities

Finally, Newark's problems became more severe *because* the city attempted to help poor and minority citizens and *because* it was a leader in civil rights, at least in comparison with the suburbs. To be sure, the Newark power elite generally ran the city in their own interests, and from their citadels in the exclusive Essex and Downtown Clubs, they erected formidable walls to keep out the Irish, Italians, Jews, and Portuguese. African Americans experienced the worst prejudice and suffered from the most limited residential and employment options. Such discrimination should have had no place in a nation that had recently fought a world war against racism run amok. But comparatively speaking, Newark was a haven for blacks, if only because nearby suburbs followed the lead of privileged communities elsewhere in closing their hearts, their wallets, and their subdivisions to the dispossessed.

Comparatively speaking, Newark was exceptional in terms of the economic opportunity, decent schools, and affordable housing it offered to minorities. James Baxter, for example, was one of the foremost black educators in the nation when he came to Newark from Philadelphia in 1864 to run what was then called the city's "Negro School." He retired in 1909, after serving for forty-five years as a principal in the Newark City Schools, and he died within six months of first receiving his monthly pension of $60. Moved by his example, the Newark Board of Education resolved on July 28, 1909 that "there shall be no more segregation of colored children by massing them in one school. The committee voted to recommend the abandonment of the Commerce Street Colored School and the placing of its pupils in the schools of the districts in which they reside." It was a small step, and it did not end school segregation in Newark, but it was a step that few other American communities were taking at the time.[38]

Similarly, during the 1930s, Newark became a national leader in building housing for the poor. In 1931, for example, the Prudential Life Insurance Company developed group housing in the Third Ward for families with annual incomes below $1,000. The object was to provide "modern facilities" for black families able to pay only eight to twelve dollars per room per month.

Later in the decade, Newark became one of the first cities in the United States to apply for public housing, and it ultimately built more units per capita than any other place in the nation. As elsewhere, these dwellings were racially segregated, beginning on June 14, 1941, when the James B. Baxter Homes opened for all-black occupancy, Four other housing projects admitted only white families. But Newark was still ahead of the suburbs in building anything at all for African Americans.

White Plains

The first inhabitants of what is now central Westchester County were Siwanoy Indians, a peaceful people who lived in houses built of poles covered with bark; for centuries they inhabited the land between Long Island Sound and the Bronx River. Their premodern world came to an end in 1683, when they sold the area they knew as Quarropas to a group of men from Rye. They had little concept of permanent land ownership, however, and were apparently unaware that the sale meant that they were not supposed to trespass on the property or sell it again.[39]

During the seventeenth century, White Plains was merely a cluster of houses along what is now Broadway. Roads were built, and churches and stores were established in the decades leading up to the American Revolution, when White Plains played a crucial role. On July 9, 1776, the Declaration of Independence was adopted by the New York Provisional Congress sitting in the courthouse on Broadway. Three months later, the Battle of White Plains proved to be a pivotal event in the military conflict.

For half a century after the American Revolution, however, White Plains returned to relative insignificance. It was simply a crossroads village whose storekeepers, millers, mechanics, and keepers were dependent upon the farming economy of central Westchester County. Largely because small-scale industries were usually located along waterways, and White Plains was not on water, the town did not match the early development pace of nearby Hudson River communities like Ossining and Yonkers, let alone booming Newark. The Red Bird Stage Line did make daily trips to New York City from Purdy's Store on Main Street, and scheduled connections were available to Manhattan, Boston, and Hartford. But White Plains remained isolated and quiet. Population growth was slow: the 505 inhabitants of 1790 had increased to only 689 by 1830.

The next thirty years witnessed increased economic development, however, and by 1860 the town had almost 2,000 inhabitants. An event that proved critical in the history of White Plains was celebrated on June 1, 1844, when the New York and Harlem Railroad made the village its new northern terminus. No longer isolated, the cornfields of White Plains were suddenly brought within an hour of Manhattan's bustling streets. By 1846 the *Journal of Commerce* announced that the yearly commutation charge to the city would be $90, or about fifteen cents each way. Even so, few persons could afford that much before the Civil War, and in any event, it was unnecessary to move all the way to White Plains in order to enjoy country living.

It took another half century for the intervening towns to begin to fill and for White Plains to become part of the metropolitan orbit of the metropolis at the mouth of the Hudson River. By the 1880s, however, wealthy citizens of New York City were beginning to discover central Westchester County as a place to build comfortable homes convenient to the rail line. Not surprisingly, between 1880 and 1910, the population of White Plains doubled every decade, and it doubled again between 1910 and 1930, when the population stood at about 36,000 persons.

In the first three decades of the twentieth century, White Plains became a kind of harbinger of what the rest of the nation would later become. Suburban, middle-class, prosperous, and increasingly automobile oriented, it represented success and status. Its small immigrant Italian population and respected black community were not allowed to detract from the image of a commuter's and businessman's paradise. Business opportunities expanded in turn, and the city soon had thousands of new jobs as New York City grew to the north.

As White Plains assumed its modern configuration before 1975, six public policy decisions shaped its development.

Zoning

First, unlike Darien and New Canaan, White Plains did not adopt exclusionary zoning for most of its area. Instead, it permitted a wide variety of housing types, and its zoning ordinance would have allowed 123,000 persons to live within its zoning envelope. In fact, White Plains never grew beyond 50,000 inhabitants. Thus it was never an exclusively wealthy town. Moreover, unlike Newark, it essentially zoned out industry in the 1920s even though it had been an early center of automobile manufacture, with more than one hundred vehicles being produced early in the century.

Becoming a Transit Hub

White Plains officials continuously lobbied to retain the town's early transportation advantages and to convince railroad and highway officials to make the community the transit hub of Westchester County. Ultimately, White Plains became the only suburb on the entire Harlem Division of Metro North where every local or express train routinely stopped. Similarly, when Interstate 287 (known as the Cross Westchester Expressway) was begun in the late 1950s, it cut directly across the northern edge of White Plains. When the controlled-access road opened in 1961, it redirected Westchester County's business and commercial traffic away from Yonkers, New Rochelle, and Mount Vernon and toward White Plains, because Interstate 287 was easily the best east-west route available for a dozen miles in either direction. Meanwhile, the White Plains airport expanded its commercial offerings and became the nation's busiest corporate airfield.

Recruiting Business

White Plains officials aggressively recruited both retailing operations and corporate offices. It was no accident that B. Altman's Department Store opened its first suburban branch in White Plains in 1930, or that Macy's and Alexander's soon followed, or that Sears Roebuck and Company built its largest store east of the Mississippi River in White Plains. By 1965 White Plains had the third-highest level of retail sales per capita in the United States (trailing only Beverly Hills, California, and Paramus, New Jersey), and by the 1990s, White Plains boasted two of the most successful megamalls in the nation. In New York State, it then ranked ahead of downtown Brooklyn, as well as Buffalo, Rochester, Syracuse, Albany, and Yonkers in retail sales.

White Plains was especially successful in attracting corporate headquarters. In 1954 the General Foods Corporation moved from its home office in midtown Manhattan to a spacious, low-slung campus in White Plains surrounded by acres of trees and free parking, initiating a corporate exodus from downtown America that would continue for the next half century. White Plains was one of the prime beneficiaries of the shift, and the Cross Westchester Expressway became so dotted with office parks that it was nicknamed the "Platinum Mile."

Civil Rights and Integration

White Plains followed a moderate course in civil rights issues and became a national leader in school integration. African Americans had played a prominent role in White Plains for more than two centuries: in 1790 blacks made up 11 percent of the town's population; by 1930 White Plains had a proportionately larger African American population than did Darien, New Canaan, or Newark.

The city's progressive racial course became clear in the late 1950s, when its school system became one of the first in the nation—along with those of Sausalito, California, and Teaneck, New Jersey—to integrate without major controversy. Faced with the need for a second high school, the White Plains Board of Education correctly determined that two high schools would inevitably lead to segregation, no matter where they were built. Consequently, in 1960 a new, modern, comprehensive high school, large enough for the entire city, opened on Bryant Avenue, and its handsome former building was converted to a junior high school. The elementary schools also were integrated. Led by Superintendent Carrol Frye Johnson and supported by the Board of Education and fifteen local clergymen, White Plains closed the perfectly good Rochambeau School, which was virtually all black, and initiated a controversial busing plan to ensure that no school would be more than 30 percent nor less than 10 percent black. The proposal survived litigation, a tough election fight, and the popular charge that the name of the city be changed to Black Plains.

Accepting Public Housing

Unlike Darien and New Canaan, White Plains embraced public housing, and unlike Newark, it was successful. After an investigation by the Mayor's Committee on Housing in 1941, a majority report recommended the building of a publicly assisted housing project. The White Plains Common Council officially approved the document on April 14, 1941. World War II put almost all housing construction on hold, but what finally emerged in 1948 was a project of five nine-story buildings containing 450 apartments. The Winbrook complex included two playgrounds, four social and recreation rooms, and a demonstration kitchen, and it increased the number of persons living in the area from 500 to about 2,000. Initially integrated, it gradually became a segregated island in the middle of White Plains. In 1968, for example, it was 90 percent African American. But compared to the residential options for poor people in surrounding suburbs such as Scarsdale, Bronxville, Armonk, and Larchmont, White Plains was exemplary, and its building of low-income units was a positive response to a demonstrated need.

Downtown Redevelopment

White Plains became the site of one of the largest downtown redevelopment programs in the United States. In 1949 Congress passed the Urban Renewal Act (subsequently expanded in 1954) that allowed municipal governments to condemn slum areas, clear the land, and then resell the acreage for new commercial or residential purposes. In White Plains the program involved 130 acres between the old courthouse and the railroad station, and it resulted in the razing of 580 buildings; the uprooting or destruction of 500 businesses in a densely settled, mixed-use area; and the displacement of almost 6,000 persons, most of them black or Italian. The destroyed buildings were typically decrepit, and a few, like the Senator Hotel, were infamous. But most housed successful businesses and law-abiding, ambitious families, and their owners and residents charged that the redevelopment project was simply an official way to displace black and Italian families and replace them with glittering commercial buildings. In the end, 1,271 families were evicted, and 917 units of low-rent or middle-income housing ultimately went up in their place. By that time, most of the persons who had lost their homes had long since left White Plains.

Breaching the Walls

"We gonna win. My God, we gonna win," exclaimed an elderly man listening to the election returns in the Georgian Room of Newark's Robert Treat Hotel. "Black power," charged a younger group, their fists raised. "Beep, beep, make way." And they did win. In the spring of 1970, thirty-seven-year-old Kenneth Gibson became the first black mayor of Newark and indeed the first African American chief executive of any major eastern city.[40]

Unfortunately, the blacks of Newark did not win much, because as more than one person noted, the city was an empty shell, containing few jobs, little money, and deteriorated housing. A community that once boasted the world's busiest intersection (at Broad and Market Streets) was already open only eight hours a day, and the central business district was a ghost town after 6 p.m.

This result was not foreordained by God, nor was it unrelated to what was happening in bucolic suburbs at the same time. The cities discussed here are part of a continuum: Darien and New Canaan are at one extreme of the nation's municipal experience, Newark is at the opposite end, and White Plains is somewhere in the middle. How did they come to be so different?

Certainly, geography and nature have been important. Each city has a particular and unique location. They were not and are not interchangeable. In 1900 Newark was already an industrial and working-class community on the major road and rail corridor in the Northeast. By contrast, White Plains was more distant from industry and instead was directly in the path of the suburban flow. Similarly, Darien and New Canaan were almost rural until 1945, and they were accessible only after a long and expensive commute. Even if their decisions had been different, Newark would not likely have been a bucolic preserve for the wealthy, nor is it probable that White Plains, Darien, or New Canaan could have become symbols of the Rust Belt.

Yet these patterns are not simply the result of geography or natural phenomena, nor are they inevitable. Instead, they result from a process that is as perverse as it is clear. Darien and New Canaan achieved status by becoming progressively more expensive and more exclusionary. They zoned out industry, raised minimum lot requirements for new houses, refused public housing, restricted their schools and even their beaches to the wealthy and the comfortable, and discriminated against minorities. For those self-centered decisions Darien and New Canaan have been rewarded by the American system—and they are not unique. As former secretary of labor Robert Reich has warned, "America's elite is retreating into a private utopia."

Newark, by contrast, encouraged industry, welcomed minorities, provided for entry-level housing, integrated its schools, and constructed public housing. For its pains it became one of America's poorest and least attractive cities. Newark has experienced some signs of life in recent years, most notably the glittering New Jersey Performing Arts Center, a new minor-league baseball stadium, and a proposed two-mile esplanade along the Passaic River. It also offers cost-effective office and industrial opportunities. Yet Newark has not recovered from decades of decline and decay, and perhaps it never will.

White Plains would seem to be the solution to the urban dilemma, lacking the excesses of snooty suburbs and depressed inner cities. A successful and pleasant community, it has high property values, an economically and racially diverse population, numerous corporate offices, and a thriving central business district replete with clean, modern, and efficient Bauhaus skyscrapers.

But White Plains is not America's solution. It is itself scorned by residents of surrounding towns precisely because it has opened its doors to the poor and integrated its schools. More important, every community cannot be a combination government center, corporate center, and retailing center or have more jobs than residents. What has worked with reasonable success in White Plains cannot be a blueprint for most towns and cities.

What then is the possible solution to municipal inequality and governmental balkanization in urban America? The major conclusion of this analysis is that no one city or suburb can alone do much about poverty and discrimination. If communities jointly support the needs of the poor, this can be an effective solution to metropolitan ills and disparities. In short, the histories and the futures of Darien, New Canaan, Newark, and White Plains are linked. Affluence and despair, in the modern American context, are as intertwined as day and night, as the wind and the rain. The New York metropolitan area, the largest and most complex in the United States, is really an interconnected job and housing market. If Wall Street investment banks lay off thousands of employees, Darien, New Canaan, Newark, and White Plains all feel the repercussions. Any solution to America's urban ills must begin with the recognition that residents of metropolitan regions share common challenges. Few people benefit when inner city schools are dysfunctional, when public housing projects become armed camps, or when minority jobless rates are double those of the middle class. Similarly, city dwellers should recognize that on balance, it is a benefit to them if the region includes a variety of residential and educational options, including many in the suburbs.

The "gentleman's agreement" of the United States is the shared willingness to ignore or to attribute to natural causes the maldistribution of poverty and wealth among local governmental jurisdictions. The problem will not be solved unless the local, state, and national

governments, encouraged probably by the court system, develop policies that can earn the contingent consent of most people. This is to
say that successful solutions and conditions must earn the willing and
active approval of the electorate, who must believe that other citizens
are doing their share. Several approaches are possible:

Annexation

Reduce balkanization by extending the boundaries of cities so
that, as was the general case in nineteenth-century America, most of
the people in a given metropolitan area would live within the same
municipal jurisdiction. Thus Philadelphia quadrupled its population
and expanded its area from 2 to 130 square miles in 1854. Chicago's
largest annexation took place in 1889, when 133 square miles and
most of what is now the far south side were added. Boston added
about fifteen square miles by joining with Roxbury in 1868 and
Dorchester in 1870, while New Orleans absorbed Carrolton in 1876 to
give the Crescent City most of the area it occupies today. Baltimore
more than doubled its size in 1888. If Newark were to expand to
include all of Essex County, for example, the city would grow from 23
to more than 120 square miles and broaden its tax base by incorporating a dozen middle-class suburbs. Even so, the city of Greater Newark
would be smaller by far than Houston, San Diego, Oklahoma City,
Memphis, or Jacksonville.

But the lesson of the past is that suburbs, especially in the Northeast, have been rejecting annexation to larger cities for more than a
century, and it is unlikely that such circumstances will soon change.
White Plains might have a better chance of absorbing Westchester
County, but that community is not in dire financial straits, and neighboring suburbs could be expected to vigorously oppose any such
notion. Darien and New Canaan, prospering in their isolation, would
not likely see advantage in greater size.

Regionalizing Governmental Functions

Move the fire, police, and educational functions of government to
state or regional levels, which would have the effect of broadening the
tax base without adding to city boundaries. This is essentially the
approach of Germany, Australia, Japan, France, and Great Britain, all
of which have many municipal subdivisions, and all of which vest

much greater power and financial responsibility in national or regional governments than is the case in the United States. Unfortunately, the American system delegates much power to local governments. Indeed, in recent decades the tendency has been to push responsibilities lower, not higher, on the governmental food chain.

Fair-Share Agreements

The third potential solution is to require regional planning and to encourage the development of a regional consciousness, especially as regards a fair-share distribution of the poor. Thus far, the most important example of this approach comes from New Jersey. In that state so-called "snob-zoning" litigation led to a Supreme Court ruling in 1975 affecting Mount Laurel Township that provides a model for other states. In effect, the court ruled that New Jersey was constitutionally obligated to provide realistic opportunities for constructing in each community a "fair share" of the regional need for affordable housing. While the results of the Garden State experiment are not yet clear, and while various New Jersey legislative compromises have watered down the original intent of the decision, the idea remains salutary. It suggests that every municipality in a given area set aside a certain percentage of its total housing stock for the needy. Within those basic parameters, each city, town, or village could move in different directions: high-density versus low-density development; exclusively residential versus mixed use; emphasis on excellent public schools versus emphasis on better parks or livelier entertainment districts.[41]

In the absence of such fair-share agreements, some jurisdictions—such as Darien and New Canaan—will remain privileged, while others—such as Newark—will have to deal with the full range of urban ills. Indeed, as Anthony Downs has noted, American urban development occurs in a systematic, predictable manner. It leads to results that are manifestly unjust and that contribute to crime, abandonment, and every other form of urban pathology. Affluence and despair are structurally linked in that there is a correlation between the development of large urban centers (together with manufacturing districts and immigrant neighborhoods), the construction of efficient and fast transportation technologies, and the desire of affluent families to escape from responsibility. Some separation is inevitable in a free and competitive society. But walling off central cities like Newark and walling in exclusive suburbs like Darien and New Canaan means that low-income housing is most needed in those jurisdictions where it is least wanted, and that most municipal jurisdictions have no incentive to improve the condition of the poor. When one type of community has much more than its share of economic resources and less than its share of the poor, some other place must bear a disproportionate burden.[42]

In 1957, soon after the Montgomery bus boycott in Alabama, the Reverend Martin Luther King, Jr. said, "Men hate each other because they fear each other. They fear each other because they don't know each other. They don't know each other because they can't communicate with each other. They can't communicate with each other because they are separated from each other."

Tearing down the very visible racial walls built by Jim Crow was King's dream for his people and his country. Tearing down the equally restrictive racial and economic walls built by public policy decisions in exclusive suburbs like Darien and New Canaan would mean redirecting public investment in infrastructure, housing, and schools away from exclusion and toward collaboration. Achieving the American dream of a single-family house on a separate parcel of land in a safe and supportive environment does not require the exclusion of less-affluent persons from particular communities. As Robert Frost wrote and as Martin Luther King implied, there should be something in all of us that doesn't love a wall, that wants it down.

Notes

1. Robert Frost, "Mending Walls," in Edward Connery Lathem, ed., *North of Boston: Poems* (Dodd, Mead and Co., 1977), p. 6.

2. On gated communities, see Evan McKenzie, *Privatopia: Homeowner Associations and the Rise of Residential Private Government* (Yale University Press, 1994).

3. The boundaries between cities and suburbs have had important political ramifications, a topic explored by Thomas Byrne Edsall, *Chain Reaction: The Impact of Race, Rights, and Taxes on American Politics* (W. W. Norton and Company, 1991).

4. The literature on homelessness in the United States is vast. See especially Eric H. Monkkonen, ed., *Walking to Work: Tramps in America* (University of Nebraska Press, 1984); John C. Schneider, "Skid Row as Urban Neighborhood, 1880–1960," *Urbanism Past and Present*, vol. 9 (Winter-Spring 1984), pp. 10–20; Kenneth T. Jackson, "The Bowery: From Residential Street to Skid Row," in Rick Beard, ed., *On Being Homeless: Historical Perspectives* (Museum of the City of New York, 1987), pp. 68–79; and Brendan O'Flaherty, *Making Room: The Economics of Homelessness* (Harvard University Press, 1996).

5. See Robert E. Park, E. W. Burgess, and R. D. McKenzie, *The City* (Univer-

sity of Chicago Press, 1925); Louis Wirth, "Urbanism as a Way of Life," *American Journal of Sociology*, vol. 44 (July 1938), pp. 1–24.

6. For a fine summary of the link between location and opportunity, see Douglas S. Massey and Nancy A. Denton, *American Apartheid: Segregation and the Making of the Underclass* (Harvard University Press, 1993). See also Michael N. Danielson, *The Politics of Exclusion* (Columbia University Press, 1976).

7. Robert C. Wood, *1,400 Governments: The Political Economy of the New York Metropolitan Region* (Harvard University Press, 1961). An excellent brief history of municipal annexation is provided by Jon C. Teaford, *City and Suburb: The Political Fragmentation of Metropolitan America, 1850–1970* (Johns Hopkins University Press, 1979).

8. Sidney Plotkin, *Keep Out: The Struggle for Land Use Control* (University of California Press, 1987).

9. For a comprehensive overview of the phenomenon, see Kenneth T. Jackson, *Crabgrass Frontier: The Suburbanization of the United States* (Oxford University Press, 1985).

10. On the trend toward "McMansions" in New Canaan, see *New York Times*, September 27, 1998.

11. Laura Z. Hobson, *Gentleman's Agreement* (Simon and Schuster, 1947).

12. There have been dozens of thoughtful newspaper articles on contemporary Newark in the past three decades but no sustained analysis. A 1970 snapshot, somewhat flawed, is provided by Ron Parambo, *No Cause for Indictment: An Autopsy of Newark* (Holt, Rinehart and Winston, 1971).

13. A kind of nadir was reached on February 20, 1992, when the official car of the Essex County prosecutor was stolen while he was speaking at a Newark church on the problem of automobile theft. *New York Times*, February 22, 1992.

14. As might be expected, there are few studies of New Canaan or Darien. Sources used for this section are Mary Louise King, *Portrait of New Canaan: The History of a Connecticut Town* (New Canaan Historical Society, 1981); J. Benjamin Corbin, *A Historical Account of Events in the Order of Time Which Have Taken Place Between 1641 and the Present in Darien* (Darien Historical Society, 1948); Charlotte Chase Fairley, "History of Canaan Parish From Founding to 1801," in *Readings in New Canaan History* (New Canaan Historical Society, 1949), pp. 123–56; and Charlotte Chase Fairley, "A History of New Canaan, 1801–1900," in *Readings in New Canaan History*, pp. 157–281.

15. Jackson, *Crabgrass Frontier*, pp. 241–43.

16. For the best studies of federal housing programs, see Mark I. Gelfand, *A Nation of Cities: The Federal Government and Urban America, 1933–1965* (Oxford University Press, 1975); Calvin Bradford, "Financing Home Ownership: The Federal Role in Neighborhood Decline," *Urban Affairs Quarterly*, vol. 14 (March 1979), pp. 313–35; and Henry Aaron, *Shelter and Subsidies: Who Benefits from Federal Housing Policies* (Brookings, 1972).

17. Neither Darien nor New Canaan continues to be overtly anti-Semitic, but both continue to have a decidedly Waspish reputation and few Jewish residents. Because the Census Bureau does not inquire about religion, precise statistics are not available.

18. Housing Files, Franklin D. Roosevelt Library, Hyde Park, N.Y.

19. *Annual Report of the United States Housing Authority for the Fiscal Year 1938* (1939), pp. vii, 38.

20. On occasion the federal government has threatened to withhold federal grants from communities that refuse to accept public housing, but such efforts have almost always been overridden by local congressional representatives. Some suburbs, such as Greenwich, Connecticut, manage to maintain an exclusive image despite the presence of public housing, but this is the exception and not the rule. See Jackson, *Crabgrass Frontier*, pp. 219–30.

21. This analysis draws upon James O. Drummond, "Transportation and the Shaping of the Physical Environment in an Urban Place: Newark, 1820–1900," Ph.D. dissertation, New York University, 1979. The only general history of Newark in print is a booster volume aimed at a secondary school market. It does, however, provide a readable overview of the city's development. See John T. Cunningham, *Newark* (Newark: New Jersey Historical Society, 1966). Other studies of the city used as sources for this section are William Shaw, *History of Essex and Hudson Counties* (Philadelphia: Everts and Peck, 1884); Joseph Atkinson, *The History of Newark, NJ* (Newark: William B. Guild, 1878); David Lawrence Pierson, *Narratives of Newark From the Days of Its Founding, 1666–1916* (Newark: Pierson Publishing Company, 1917); and Joseph Fulford Folsom, ed., *The Municipalities of Essex County, 1666—1924,* 4 vols. (Newark, 1924). The many excellent monographs on specialized topics include Susan E. Hirsch, *The Roots of the American Working Class: The Industrialization of Crafts in Newark, 1800–1860* (University of Pennsylvania Press, 1978); and Samuel H. Popper, "Newark, N.J., 1870–1910: Chapters in the Evolution of an American Metropolis," Ph.D. dissertation, New York University, 1952.

22. Barbara J. Kukla, *Swing City: Newark Nightlife, 1925–1950* (Temple University Press, 1991); and Ronald A. Mayer, *The 1937 Newark Bears: A Baseball Legend* (Rutgers University Press, 1996).

23. James G. Smith, "Newark at the Crossroads: An Economic Survey of the City and Its Environs," *Journal of Industry and Finance* (November 1930), pp. 7–24. See also L. H. Wendrich, "Greater Newark: A Quarter Century Vision," *Journal of Industry and Finance,* vol. 29 (1940), pp. 654–69.

24. Quoted in George W. Groh, *The Black Migration: The Journey to Urban America* (Weybright and Talley, 1972), p. 248. On recent Newark politics, see also Wilbur C. Rich, *Black Mayors and School Politics: The Failure of Reform in Detroit, Gary, and Newark* (Garland Publishing, 1996), pp. 91–127; and Katherine Yatrakis, "Electoral Demands and Political Benefits: A Case of Two Mayoral Elections in Newark, N.J.," Ph.D. dissertation, Columbia University, 1981.

25. Another kind of personal reminiscence, beautifully accompanied by photographs of the ghetto, is found in Helen M. Stummer, *No Easy Walk: Newark, 1980–1993* (Temple University Press, 1994).

26. Paul A. Stellhorn, "Depression and Decline: Newark, N.J.: 1929–1941," Ph.D. dissertation, Rutgers University, 1983, passim.

27. Frank Kingdon, "Newark a Hundred Years Hence," *Newarker,* vol. 1 (June 15, 1936), pp. 72–73.

28. The basic source on this topic is Stuart Galishoff, "Public Health in Newark, 1832–1918," Ph.D. dissertation, New York University, 1969, p. 62.

29. *Newark Daily Journal*, August 2, 1883.

30. *Newark Evening News*, June 10, 1884.

31. *Newark Evening News*, October 11, 1000,

32. *New York Times*, August 5, 1998.

33. Jackson, *Crabgrass Frontier*, pp. 190–218.

34. These records are available in the HOLC City Survey Files (Record Group 195) in the National Archives.

35. For a somewhat more favorable account of Danzig, and of urban renewal generally, see Harold Kaplan, *Urban Renewal Politics: Slum Clearance in Newark* (Columbia University Press, 1963).

36. Jean Anyon, *Ghetto Schooling: A Political Economy of Urban Educational Reform* (Teachers College Press, 1997). Still useful is Marion Thompson Wright, *The Education of Negroes in New Jersey* (Teachers College Press, 1941).

37. On the 1967 riots in Newark, see Joe Feagin and Harlan Hahn, *Ghetto Revolts* (Macmillan, 1973); and Tom Hayden, *Rebellion in Newark: Official Violence and Ghetto Response* (Vintage Books, 1967). On their impact, see Stanley B. Winters, ed., *From Riot to Recovery: Newark After Ten Years* (Lanham, Md.: University Press of America, 1979). Another riot broke out at a Puerto Rican Labor Day festival in Branch Brook Park in 1974 after mounted police broke up a dice game. In two days of rioting, punctuated by rumors that a young girl had been trampled to death, two people were killed and sniper fire was aimed at police from rooftops. *Star-Ledger*, November 5, 1998.

38. The Newark Board of Education never granted Baxter a salary equal to his position and responsibilities. In 1884 white elementary principals were paid $1,800, while Baxter was paid $1,200. Similarly, *The Forty-Fourth Annual Report of the Newark Board of Education, 1900* (p. 21) indicated that while white elementary principals were paid $2,000, the black principal made only $1,500. See Ralph K. Turp, "Public Schools in the City of Newark, 1850–1965," Ph.D. dissertation, Rutgers University, 1967, p. 83. See also John R. Anderson, "Negro Education in the Public Schools of Newark, New Jersey During the Nineteenth Century," Ed.D. dissertation, Rutgers University, 1972.

39. The published work on White Plains is not strong. The leading expert who has produced several small books aimed at a local audience is Renoda Hoffman, *Yesterday in White Plains: A Picture History of a Vanished Era* (Tuckahoe, N.Y.: Little Art Graphics, 1981). See also Edith Phillips, "The Development of White Plains," *Westchester County Historical Bulletin* (1948), pp. 104–18; and Ernest Freeland Griffin, *Westchester County and Its People*, vol. 1 (New York: Lewis Historical Publishing Company, 1946), p. 235.

40. *New York Post*, February 10, 1970.

41. The best account of the Mount Laurel decision is found in David L. Kirp, John P. Dwyer, and Larry A. Rosenthal, *Our Town: Race, Housing, and the Soul of Suburbia* (Rutgers University Press, 1995).

42. Anthony Downs has written often and effectively on this point. See especially Anthony Downs, *Opening Up the Suburbs: An Urban Strategy for America* (Yale University Press, 1973).

CHAPTER EIGHT

Addressing Regional Dilemmas for Minority Communities

john a. powell

I recently met with a high-ranking administrator in a large, predominantly African American city that faces a number of problems, including a failing school system, depopulation, business and job loss to the suburbs, and a housing crisis marked by boarded-up buildings and vacant lots. This city, like many American cities, has attempted numerous unsuccessful revitalization strategies, including enterprise zones, empowerment zones, a new downtown sports center, and other give-aways to entice businesses to remain in or return to the central city.

As the administrator, whom I will call Dr. Jones, and I discussed the problems he and the city face, we agreed that the city is in a major crisis, and that part of the solution is to build and attract businesses and a middle-class tax base. I suggested that one of the problems facing central cities and older, inner-ring suburbs is the constant pulling of resources away from the region's core toward the outer edges of the metropolitan area. I stated that this process, succinctly referred to as sprawl, not only eats up space and farmland but is a major contributor to the depopulation of central cities and older suburbs. Dr. Jones agreed and added that sprawl can only be fully understood in racial terms: the developing outer ring is always upper middle class and white.

I thank Colleen Walbron for her research and assistance with this chapter.

We agreed that while white flight has been the primary out-migration from American cities since the 1940s, more recently minorities in general, and middle class blacks in particular, have also moved outward.

It is not just the population exodus from the urban core that makes this problem so difficult to remedy; it is the removal of resources from the core and the subsequent refusal of the suburbs to share, or fairly distribute, the benefits. This walling-off of the more affluent developing suburbs from the central cities creates fragmentation. The dynamic of sprawl and fragmentation, with its strong racial component, leaves the central cities and older suburbs with growing social needs and shrinking resources. Dr. Jones added that he had witnessed this phenomenon firsthand. He had observed how sprawl and fragmentation destroy central cities and inner-ring older suburbs, transforming today's winners into tomorrow's losers. He related that many upscale suburbs, which saw themselves as better than the core cities, are now facing many of the same problems because resources continue to move farther and farther out. Dr. Jones and I were on the same page: we had quickly arrived at a consensus and comfort level based on our respective studies and living experiences.

As I had anticipated, our consensus faltered when our discussion turned to solutions. I asserted that the city and older suburbs must find a way to coordinate and develop a regional strategy to benefit from the resources that are spread disproportionately throughout the entire region, reverse the trend of fragmentation, and halt the continual pull of resources into new, undeveloped land. Dr. Jones disagreed: "White people in the suburbs are hostile to the city largely because the city is black. They will only work with the city if they think they can take it over. They are racist, I don't trust them, and I won't work with them." While Dr. Jones believes that the problems facing the central cities and older suburbs are regional in nature, he is unwilling to entertain a regional solution, because he fears a suburban power grab. He cited a number of supporting examples. He also mentioned a number of people who share his concern and suggest a solution that depends less on cooperation with the suburbs and more on building and relying upon a competitive advantage.[1] Dr. Jones made it clear that he would not embrace a strategy that required he trust or cooperate with the suburbs.

I knew that my time with Dr. Jones was running out. His concern was one that I have heard many times from black officials and community leaders in the central city. I tried to assure Dr. Jones that what I had suggested was not based on naive trust, and that I, too, was aware that regionalism had often been used to the detriment of the people of color living in the central cities. And while this issue must be addressed, a nonregional solution for the problems facing the urban core is not a solution at all. Dr. Jones was abruptly called away to deal with an emergency. We shook hands, both knowing that much had not been said, and we agreed to discuss the matter further at another time.

This chapter is written, in spirit, as a continuation of this discussion. Recognizing that the critical problems associated with the hollowing out of the urban core cannot be addressed without a regional approach, it focuses on how to move toward solutions that respond to the concerns raised by Dr. Jones and other like-minded individuals. In particular, the solution offered here is a form of regional policymaking best defined as federated regionalism: a type of regionalism that gives cities or communities a way to maintain appropriate control of their political and cultural institutions while sharing in regional resources and balancing participants' concerns.[2] The local municipality and the region interact in much the same way that states and the federal government do. Most issues have both regional and local aspects. Issues that are regional in scope and require regional solutions (for example, transportation systems) are addressed accordingly, whereas those matters that are mostly local in character (such as siting bus shelters in a neighborhood) are dealt with at the local level. Examples of regions that employ these strategies are explored in this chapter, and suggestions are made for further development of federated regionalism.

Metropolitan regions have become increasingly important over the last several decades. Many scholars suggest that metropolitan regions, and not nations or cities, are the key economic units in today's global economy. While this claim may be debatable, it is clear that in the United States power has decreased in the central cities and shifted to metropolitan regions at the same time that the federal government has shifted power to the states.[3]

Race and racism are central to understanding this shift in power, inscribed into our land by sprawl and political fragmentation. Although within a metropolitan region cities and suburbs are interdependent, the policies of suburban, state, and federal governments tend to isolate communities of color in the central cities and inner-ring suburbs and communities of privilege in the predominantly white suburbs. Indeed, there is often great tension between the inner cites and older suburbs on the one hand, and the newer developing suburbs in the region on the other. Most central cities in the United States continue to lose population and resources, while the suburbs continue to grow. Increasingly, the cities are the repository of poor racial minorities, while the newer suburbs receive the greater number of jobs, infrastructure funds, wealthy individuals, and whites.

Whether one looks at the distribution of housing, schools, tax bases, or transportation, a pattern emerges in which cities and older suburbs are increasingly resource starved, while developing suburbs are increasingly resource rich. Overlapping concentrations of people of color and poverty are increasingly found in central-city neighborhoods and schools. The problem is compounded by the declining availability of adequate resources to meet the increasing social needs within cities and older suburbs.

The isolation of poor minorities in the inner cities is primarily caused by white (and increasingly middle-class minority) flight and the resultant unchecked sprawl.[4] This process is facilitated by fragmentation of political structures within our metropolitan regions, which divides the regional whole into parts and allows each part to operate relatively independently. This impedes policymaking on a regional level and benefits the perceived self-interest of wealthy communities that enact insular and exclusive laws. Gregory Weiher notes this phenomenon in *The Fractured Metropolis* when he writes: "Local government formation in the United States. . .is usually undertaken in the pursuit of parochial interests. . .[where the] intent is to protect parochial interests from interference by overarching units of government."[5] Weiher defines these parochial interests as "narrow social and socioeconomic groups."[6] Raymond Vernon stated that land-use planning could more aptly be described as land-use warfare.[7]

The fragmentation of metropolitan areas into multiple, competing local governments creates segregation and a superfluous number of entities that control key regional powers, such as planning and zoning, that exercise these powers to the detriment of the region as a whole.[8] Consequently, political geography promotes racially separate and unequal distributions of political influence and economic resources.[9]

In theory, localized political structures are designed to address local problems, and it is clear that there are many matters best suited to local decisions incorporating local beliefs and needs.[10] In reality, the proliferation of municipalities in metropolitan areas facilitates race and wealth differences through territorial segregation and fiscal separation. To an extent, the localized model for governance also has

become an anachronism as the development of our society and technological advances in information and transportation have broadened the individual's spheres of activity and influence and connected
communities that at one time would have been considered distant.

Those of us who advocate regionalism are troubled by the resistance to it, not only from the developing suburban communities, but
from communities of color as well. While the suburban resistance may
be shortsighted, the reluctance to embrace something that will have a
short-term negative economic consequence appears to make sense.
What is more surprising, at least initially, is resistance from minority
communities at the urban core. This resistance is often based on non-
economic concerns: the loss of political control and cultural control
or identity. Supporters of regionalism often discount these concerns,
suggesting that minorities do not have meaningful political control or
cultural identity to begin with, and that the price paid for this minimal control is too high.[11] But to ignore these claims from the minority
community is a serious mistake, because it underestimates the value of
identity and makes regionalism feel like another solution imposed on
people of color by whites who "know better." On a more practical
level, proponents of regionalism will undermine the success of their
efforts if they do not engage minority communities. The possibility of
success for a policy that faces strong opposition from the inner-city
core and the developing suburbs is minimal at best.[12]

Federated regionalism has the potential to balance this need for
an integrated regional approach with the need to preserve local control on some issues. Its success depends upon recognizing that a number of important inner-city problems are caused by regional forces
and that the failure to confront central-city problems adversely affects
the entire region. There are a number of examples of federated
regionalism in practice, in which metropolitan governments of limited power or regional policies of limited effect coexist with a municipal government. Tax-base sharing, as practiced in the Twin Cities,
exemplifies this type of federated regionalism: local governments
retain control over most traditional functions, while a portion of their
commercial tax revenue is placed in a regional pool and redistributed
to municipalities in an equitable manner. (See subsequent discussion
under "Twin Cities.")

Regionalism properly conceived is an important strategy for
addressing some of the most serious problems facing minorities living
at the urban core. The increase in concentrated poverty is possibly the

most important issue facing cities and older suburbs in the United States. Sprawl and jurisdictional fragmentation implemented in a racially discriminatory way are the primary causes of this concentrated poverty. To effectively address concentrated poverty, regionalism is necessary though not sufficient. And regionalism should be viewed as a strategy to combat concentrated poverty, not as an end in and of itself.

One may question the focus on concentrated poverty, which may appear to be just another way of discussing economic concerns and not political or cultural dilution issues. But when one looks at the impact of concentrated poverty, it becomes clear that it destabilizes a community not only economically but also culturally and politically. Indeed, what is often referred to as a culture of poverty may more accurately be described as the culture produced by concentrated poverty. This chapter then is as much about concentrated poverty as it is about regionalism.

The following discussion attempts to examine how law and public policy, along with private discrimination, have created and maintained patterns of concentrated poverty and racial segregation in metropolitan areas. The theory behind a regional approach to these problems is outlined and accompanied by a review of some of the efforts undertaken and frustrations experienced in implementing such regional policies. Minority community resistance to regionalism is analyzed and addressed by articulating an approach that responds to the needs of minority communities in areas of concentrated poverty without compromising their political identity.

Segregation and Concentrated Poverty

"Neighborhood poverty is not primarily the product of 'the people' who live there or a 'ghetto culture' that discourages upward mobility, but the predictable result of the economic status of minority communities and the degree to which minorities are residentially segregated from whites and from each other by income."[13] In his book *Poverty and Place: Ghettos, Barrios, and the American City*, Paul Jargowsky explains the negative relationship between inner cities, older suburbs, and newer suburbs in the United States. He states that the segregation and concentrated poverty found within metropolitan areas is not self-induced but is the predictable result of a concerted effort to isolate poor minorities. That such segregation and concentrated poverty exist and are worsening, despite the healthy national economy, cannot be denied.

By definition, concentrated poverty occurs where 40 percent or more of a neighborhood's residents live at or below the poverty line. As of 1990, approximately 2,800 census tracts (among the nation's 45,000) experienced poverty rates of greater than 40 percent. Only 1,200 such tracts were recorded in 1970.[14] More than 8.2 million people live in areas of concentrated poverty—more than double the number of people who did in 1970. Furthermore, this concentration of poverty has disproportionately affected people of color, particularly blacks. Of those living in concentrated poverty, more than half are black (despite the fact that blacks make up only 12 percent of the national population), and one-fourth are Hispanic.[15] In fact, between 1970 and 1990, there was a 69.7 percent increase in the number of blacks living in neighborhoods of concentrated poverty, despite the fact that the 1990 national poverty rate for African Americans was the lowest ever.[16]

Such segregation and concentrated poverty are not self-induced, despite the nation's desire to describe itself as "color blind" and its tendency to look for behavioral causes of poverty. Nor did these problems arise by accident: they were generated by and perpetuated through governmental policies, institutional practices, and private behaviors.[17]

For decades federal, state, and local governments, the banking industry, and white homeowners directed their efforts at maintaining white dominance and separation through a number of policies and practices. For example, in 1933 the federal government established the Home Owners' Loan Corporation, which systematically undervalued racially diverse central-city neighborhoods, deeming them too risky for investment. Instead, the loan corporation channeled mortgage funds to white, outlying neighborhoods.[18]

Redlining was further institutionalized through Federal Housing Administration (FHA) policies that, from their inception in 1934, rendered FHA-guaranteed loans for minority homeownership practically unattainable while ensuring that home ownership for whites became more feasible than ever.[19] The racially discriminatory policies of the FHA were not merely de facto; the underwriting manual explicitly reflected its policy of refusing loans to homebuyers in minority or racially integrated neighborhoods: "Areas surrounding a location are [to be] investigated to determine whether incompatible racial and social groups are present, for the purpose of making a prediction regarding the probability of the location being invaded by such groups. If a neighborhood is to retain stability, it is necessary that properties shall continue to be occupied by the same social and racial classes."[20]

The FHA also preferred new construction to the purchase of existing units, thereby writing the prescription for sprawl as well as residential racial segregation. These programs paid whites to leave the central cities and confined blacks to these areas, which were then divested by the federal government and private capital. By some estimates, this subsidy of white out-migration cost nearly $1 trillion.

In the late 1950s, the federal government exacerbated the effects of these housing programs by embarking on a national highway campaign, for the ostensible purpose of national defense. The campaign facilitated the exodus from the central cities and destabilized many urban neighborhoods.

At the same time, public housing projects were administered in a segregative fashion, and "urban renewal" destroyed stable black neighborhoods to make room for elite institutions such as hospitals, businesses, and universities.[21] Local governments also contributed to the problems of segregation and concentrated poverty through the ongoing practice of exclusionary zoning, which made it nearly impossible for poor families to find suitable housing in white suburban communities. The banking industry contributed to this polarization through continued discriminatory policies, as evidenced by the rejection of minority loan applications at a rate nearly triple that of white applications.[22] Realtors, too, discriminated through practices such as racial steering[23] and blockbusting,[24] and private homeowners fashioned restrictive covenants to keep minorities out of their neighborhoods.[25]

Until the late 1960s, the flight from the central cities was composed of business, capital, and an overwhelmingly white population. The passage of the Fair Housing Act in 1968 began to change the racial composition of this migration. A crack emerged in the nation's housing caste system, and the growing black middle class began to leave the central cities in pursuit of opportunity. Accommodation of this flight from the central cities meant claiming more agricultural land and open space for suburban development, expanding suburban sprawl and fragmentation. Sprawl, as it developed in the United States, was not simply a spatial phenomenon without political, social, and racial motivations; it was spurred by the desire to flee the core, to be away and separated from the racial other. Until the 1960s, suburbs were nearly all white. Even as middle-class blacks moved out of the central city, they still found themselves in racially segregated neighborhoods as whites continued to flee farther out, avoiding both low-income as well as middle-class blacks. This racialized sorting process was carved into our metropolitan landscape with the support of powerful public and private institutional players, thus setting the stage for racialized concentrated poverty at the core and sprawling white suburbs at the edge.

Racialized concentrated poverty affects not only individuals but also entire neighborhoods, and all residents' life chances are compromised. High levels of crime, drug use, and other social pathologies emerge and become self-perpetuating. In addition to this poor quality of life, residents experience severely limited social and economic opportunities. The quality of schools, housing, and municipal services as well as the availability of transportation and employment are all undermined.[26] This in turn means that entire regions—not just the inner cities and older suburbs—have a real interest in reversing the policies that have concentrated poverty at the urban core, as well as contributed to the lesser, but nonetheless serious evils of traffic congestion, destruction of precious land, and pollution.

Fragmentation of urban areas and sprawl lead to extreme racial and economic segregation and the creation of persistent poverty and hopelessness. The more fragmented a metropolitan area is, the more segregation and concentrated poverty it will experience.[27] Federated regionalism is a solution to the failed "model" of metropolitan fragmentation.

The Contemporary Framework of Regionalism

If "the desperate struggle for exclusivity in the affluent suburbs is part and parcel of an effort by the upper class to reduce its responsibilities to society,"[28] then regional or metropolitan equity offers policymakers a way to reconceptualize metropolitan areas for the common good of all residents, affluent or not. Instead of calling upon each locality to take responsibility only for itself, regionalism recognizes the entire area as a system of interdependent parts. The whole will prosper only if all parts are able to function. Allowing richer parts of the region to externalize their social responsibility creates resource-starved, poorly functioning communities at the core. When one part becomes dysfunctional, the entire system is compromised. This is what is happening with the inner cities and their older suburbs—their difficulties are negatively affecting entire regions. Among other things, a poor and racially segregated urban core harms the reputation of the metropolitan region as a whole and makes it less inviting to international, national, and local businesses, as well as to families looking for homes. While the negative impact on poorer parts of the region is sometimes acknowledged, there is a failure to recognize this growing neighborhood poverty as a consequence of the creation of rich suburban enclaves.

Despite this reality, white suburbanites have traditionally resisted regional policies and denied any connection with the fate of the central city. The justifications offered have changed over time. The current one is expressed as the fear that the "culture of poverty" found in the inner cities will infiltrate their protected enclaves—a justification that is simply a new name for the long-standing racial hostility and aversion directed toward blacks and other people of color. White suburbanites attribute the lot of minorities to behavioral patterns and absolve themselves of any responsibility for institutional racism or white privilege. (Those white suburbs that do address some of the problems associated with fragmentation are usually working-class white suburbs, which are also subject to the negative consequences of the same process.) Proponents of regionalism challenge this line of thinking partly by redirecting the focus away from the issues of nonwhite poverty and toward the interaction between core cities and their suburbs.

Beyond the fear that regionalism would defeat the carefully constructed containment of poor minorities in the central cities, an economic rationale has historically served as a justification for whites' policymaking—a rationale tethered to the drive for political dominance. Douglas Massey and Nancy Denton described this historical resistance of whites to resource sharing with blacks in *American Apartheid*:

> Resources allocated to black neighborhoods detracted from the benefits going to white ethnic groups; and because patronage was the glue that held white political coalitions together, resources allocated to the ghetto automatically undermined the stability of the pluralist machine. As long as whites controlled city politics, their political interests lay in providing as few resources as possible to African Americans

and as many as possible to white ethnic groups. Although blacks occasionally formed alliances with white reformers, the latter acted more from moral conviction than self-interest. Because altruism is notoriously unreliable as a basis for political cooperation, interracial coalitions were unstable and of limited effectiveness in representing the black interest."[29]

The surest way to avoid or reverse patterns of racial and economic segregation is to create effective metropolitan governments or ensure that all local governments are pursuing common policies that will foster fiscal integration that is rationally related to collective needs. Because fiscal and other resources are more sensitive to jurisdictional boundaries than neighborhood boundaries, the priority must be to challenge jurisdictional as opposed to neighborhood fragmentation. Orfield calls this process of achieving regionalism "metropolitics."[30] One of the questions invariably asked is, if whites benefit economically and otherwise from opposing a more integrated regional structure, why should they support regional government? Orfield argues that most whites do not economically benefit from a fragmented, sprawling region; only about one-quarter—the favored quarter—of a region's population benefit from this arrangement. To state this differently, most whites living in the suburbs also are hurt economically by the lack of an effective regional structure. This analysis also suggests that the problems of sprawl and fragmented governance are not simply a city-versus-suburb issue; more accurately, they pit the city and developed suburbs against the growing new suburbs.

While there may be increasing support for these ideas, today only 3 percent of all people live in areas with regional governments. Orfield's approach may treat a number of white concerns about regionalism, but does it address black concerns about political and cultural dilution? To better answer this question, one must first understand the minority community's resistance to regionalism.

Minority Resistance to Regionalism

The concern about regionalism reflects a deep sentiment in the minority community and is not based solely on economic fears. Indeed, one of the primary attractions of a regional approach is the possible economic benefit to communities of color. Yet given the history of urban renewal, and racism in general, there is a strong concern that regionalism, if successful, would deal with concentrated poverty by dispersing the inner-city minority community.[31] Although this is not required by a regional strategy, the dispersal and dilution approach has been used, often without regard for whether people were moved closer to or farther away from opportunities.

Regionalism as a response to the problems of racial segregation and concentrated poverty is often associated with "mobility" strategies rather than "in-place" strategies, and the former is closely associated with dispersal. What distinguishes a mobility strategy from a dispersal strategy is its intent; while mobility strategies do disperse population, they do so with the aim of moving people toward opportunities that lie elsewhere in metropolitan areas. In a sense, mobility strategies can be seen as a positive subset of dispersal strategies, because they attempt to break down geographic barriers to housing, education, employment, and wealth creation for communities of color. Advocates of mobility strategies believe that if people who are segregated and isolated by race and poverty can move into neighborhoods with adequate community resources, they will gain access to the means and mechanisms of progress.[32]

In-place strategies, such as urban community development, attempt to move resources and opportunities to low-income, central-city residents and try to generate improvements in urban neighborhoods of color. Many of these neighborhood-level initiatives have had positive effects in the form of home renovation and mortgage loans, new affordable housing, new business development, and commercial revitalization. However, when they are not linked to a regional framework, in-place strategies are not able to redress concentrated poverty, the hollowing out of the urban core, and other issues associated with these phenomena.[33] The need to choose between a mobility strategy or an in-place strategy is a false choice; the effort should be people based and include a mix of both mechanisms.

White segregationism manifests itself as resistance to regionalism and support of in-place strategies, because these keep minorities "immobile" and out of their suburban neighborhoods. In-place strategies frequently receive support from minorities as well, though for a different reason: this approach allows people of color to remain in the urban core and preserve their cultural identity and political power.[34] The mobility strategies of regionalism are thus viewed as a threat to these interests. Reluctance to move to a suburb where jobs and other opportunities exist also arises because of perceived and actual racial hostility and the lack of people of color.

As Charles Smith, manager of the Access and Equity Centre of Metro Toronto argues, communities are more than just economic units; they also have social and cultural significance.[35] It follows, then, that integration through regional mobility programs can fragment a minority community and tear apart its "soul." Many argue that what is called integration is really assimilation. Cornel West, for example, argues that the dispersion of black professionals and entrepreneurs into predominantly white communities does little to change the culture and values of the white opportunity structure.[36] Instead, deconcentration of minorities is said to assimilate those who are pocketed in more affluent areas and diminish minority culture in predominantly black areas by removing valuable human resources.

To avoid the negative effects of cultural dilution, Smith and others, like Dr. Jones, argue for in-place strategies rather than integrationist urban planning: "For integration to be more than a ticket 'out of the ghetto' to a stress-filled life as an integration pioneer or neighborhood buster, governments must increase access to services and resources and work to improve the economic base within these communities. . . . Such strategies could recreate poor neighborhoods and make them vibrant cultural, social, and economic centers capable of supporting an opportunity structure that may attract and satisfy well-to-do racial minorities as well as white people."[37]

Minorities also resist regionalism out of a desire to preserve political power. Orfield notes that regionalism is often perceived as a threat to the power base of officials elected by poor, segregated constituents.[38] It is feared that control over the political process would be lost if the base of minority communities was diminished or if the minority population was dispersed throughout the region. Frequently, minorities would rather retain this control, even if opportunity structures are lacking in their communities. As Lani Guinier acknowledges, despite its capacity to marginalize, the recognition of race can be "empowering, affirming, and energizing."[39]

Geographic districting by race, however, has its limitations. First of all, it does not always work—that is, minority candidates are not always elected by this approach. Indeed, in places like Oakland and Los Angeles in California and Gary, Indiana, minority voters are not satisfied with minority elected officials who cannot improve economic conditions because they are isolated in the region and from the state legislature. In addition, as Guinier points out, the assumption that minorities, wherever they reside, are politically cohesive is unfounded.[40] Also, because the Supreme Court has severely limited majority-minority districting,[41] the number of minority electoral opportunities under this traditional approach has been reduced significantly.[42]

These limitations have led some to attack the viability of majority-minority districting and to support a mobility strategy that would create influence districts for minorities that are not dependent upon their geographic concentration and isolation. The assumption is that minorities, particularly blacks, living in communities with whites are able to influence the political agenda of their district through the "swing" value of their votes. While they may not be able to elect a representative in such districts, their elected officials would not be able to ignore their issues and concerns in the way that white elected officials from virtually all-white districts can. The indifference or even hostility of white, suburb-dominated legislatures to minority concerns—as embodied in the interests of central cities—appears to lend credence to this assessment.

While the city-suburb split in political interests is often real, the theory of influence voting does not accurately describe the political voice that minorities gain by living in majority-white districts. One limitation to their retention of political power is the backlash of the white electorate when the number of black voters within their district increases beyond a very small share. The premise that the mere presence of minorities in an electoral district will "influence" voting, and thereby ensure representation responsive to their needs, is true only when the size of the black population is not threatening to the white population. Pamela S. Karlan states, "As the possibility that blacks might be a dominant component of a biracial coalition grows, white backlash increases as well."[43] Thus the political influence of minorities does not increase proportionally with an increase in the minority voting population. According to Karlan, "Black influence grows as blacks increase to roughly 30 percent of the electorate; black voters face increasing resistance when they constitute between 30 percent and 50 percent of the electorate; and beyond 50 percent, the relationship between presence and influence is again positive."[44] In a metropolitan area with a small minority population, the percentage of minorities mobilized would only result in a small increase in their voting share in a suburb, and that population would most likely face little resistance or "white punishment" and could function as a sort of swing vote. However, in metropolitan areas with larger populations of color,

mobilization could cause a substantial increase in the minority population of a voting district—enough to trigger white backlash.

Edward A. Zelinsky, professor of law at Columbia Law School,
echoes minority concerns over the political implications of regional
approaches. He fears that metropolitan governments would be less
responsive than more local governments and "less likely to encourage
citizen participation and civic life."[45] Moreover, he believes that these
governments will not achieve increased racial and ethnic integration.
Zelinsky argues that instead of focusing on the structures of urban
governance, those concerned with segregation and concentrated
poverty should spend more time on schooling and employment
issues, where more practical results can be achieved.[46] But it is the
very fragmented nature of sprawl and the racial segregation it engen-
ders that Professor Zelinsky is trying to address: if he were successful
in making regional educational and employment resources available
to communities that are currently isolated, he would be moving
toward a federated regional structure.

Alternatively, Orfield suggests that proponents of regionalism
must carefully communicate to minorities the hopelessness of the
present course of action and the patterns of polarization it produces.[47]
However, regionwide approaches should not be proposed as alternatives to existing programs or as competition for resources and power.
Instead, they should be presented as complementary efforts that
reduce problems in the center cities to a manageable size and provide
more resources for development through such programs as tax-rev-
enue sharing. While Orfield's approach also seems to favor a federated structure, it is not explicit about protecting minority influence.

Each solution only addresses part of the problem, proposing
either political and cultural control in economically resource-starved
and isolated areas or access to resources at the cost of a silenced political voice and cultural assimilation or marginalization. These approaches must be rejected, because they fail to meet minority needs
for both resources and political and cultural empowerment. These
are the goals of federated regionalism.

Federated Regionalism as a Response to Minority Resistance

Federated regionalism requires entities within a metropolitan region
to cooperate on some levels and leaves them relatively autonomous

on others. It is based on two premises: first, many important problems within the inner cities and older suburbs can only be dealt with adequately at a regional level; and second, some issues, or some aspects of issues, are of a local nature and thus are more effectively handled by a local government. Federated regionalism also acknowledges the racial issues that underlie political polarization. Just as the choice between in-place and mobility strategies presents a false dichotomy,[48] so, too, does a rigid choice between regional and local approaches to solving the problems of segregation and concentrated poverty. Federated regionalism advances both approaches by striving to be sensitive to the concerns of communities of color and integrating regional and local policymaking. While there will often be conflicting interests and proposals from the white, black, and other communities of color, federated regionalism would balance them without allowing the parties to opt out of regional problem solving or to completely ignore the concerns of the other communities. It is not voluntary regionalism nor is it totally dependent on consensus. It is not mobility focused or in-place focused; it is people focused.

One way to describe the ability of federated regionalism to reconcile local and regional political interests is to analogize it to cumulative voting. Direct democracy and individual access to the ballot are inadequate primarily because they are based on certain pluralistic assumptions: the winner should take all, winners will vary and not be determined along racial and ethnic lines, and the majority can adequately represent the interests of the whole.[49] As Guinier argues, however, direct democracy reduces democracy into "its most crude. . . form, . . . simply an arithmetic exercise [which] allows little room for interactive democratic conversation."[50] If democracy is to be a broad-based public collaboration, continues Guinier, then "we should ensure representation for racial groups. . . particularly disadvantaged racial groups who have been denied historical access to this collaboration."[51]

Cumulative voting creates large electoral districts with multiple representatives and allows each voter to have as many votes as there are seats to be filled. Voters are not limited to casting only one vote for the candidate of their choice; they can "plump" or cast all of their votes to one candidate if such an intense preference for that candidate exists. This allows minority groups greater opportunity to win representation in elections beyond the municipal level—even without being geographically districted together.[52] Instead, voters "district" themselves by the way they cast their votes,[53] facilitating racial-group representation without race-conscious districting.[54] Cumulative voting in a metropolitan region would protect the political interests of people of color even when a mobility policy results in their geographic deconcentration. Thus people of color could pursue the benefits and opportunities of living in areas that are not poor and segregated while retaining the political voice that traditionally comes from geographic segregation.

Cumulative voting provides an "exit opportunity" for individuals.[55] In particular, it allows minorities a chance to vote as a community without staying in a geographic, racial cul-de-sac. Similarly, federated regionalism gives minorities the choice to stay in their communities and strive for more equitable regional plans that will improve their neighborhoods (as well as the entire region) or to move from their communities and retain their political power through a pooling of interests. In-place and mobility strategies become more a matter of personal choice, because no matter where minorities live, they can remain politically cohesive.[56] In addition, where minorities were once alienated by their lack of agency within the political process, they may become more politically active.[57]

However, cumulative voting must still be characterized as a long shot in the realm of political reform; it has been adopted in only a few areas and is frequently met with resistance from traditional majoritarians who fear that cumulative voting will empower "fringe dwellers" and will "create mosaic governments paralyzed by factionalism."[58] Sixth District Congressman James Clyburn, a cosponsor of the Voter's Choice Act, which would repeal the 1967 federal statute requiring states to draw single-member congressional districts and permit the adoption of methods like cumulative voting on a larger scale, warned in a March 1998 editorial that "the likelihood of this bill passing any time soon is at best negligible."[59] A more modest and familiar voting arrangement that moves toward a balance between large regions and local concerns is the way we elect members of the House of Representatives and the Senate: it allows local concerns and the voice of the community, as reflected in the House, to be balanced with larger regional and statewide concerns, more accurately reflected in the Senate, where small states have a voice numerically equal to large states. The fact that both bodies have to agree on bills to become law is a clear example of managing the tension between regional and local concerns. Without advocating for the particular form of federalism that we have adopted at the national level, this is an important example for study, and it underscores the familiarity of the concept of federalism in the United States.

Federated regionalism is like cumulative voting or the more familiar House and Senate arrangement in that it allows communities to maintain influence within a regional context. Federated regionalism rejects the Hobson's choice often posed to minorities regarding regionalism or voting: it does not lock minority members into isolated "districts," in the context of voting, or into segregated neighborhoods, isolated in the context of acquiring regional power and resources. Instead, it allows more dynamic decisionmaking processes to be used for metropolitan planning.[60]

A federated or cumulative voting structure coupled with regional districting is one of several initiatives that could constitute a form of federated regionalism. Other initiatives include tax-base sharing (as practiced in the Twin Cities),[61] metropolitan-wide school districting (as practiced in Charlotte-Mecklenburg County, Louisville-Jefferson County, and Raleigh-Durham),[62] and joint powers boards. Joint powers boards have been formed in metropolitan and rural areas throughout the United States to achieve specific short- and long-term goals, lobby for the solution of regional problems in state legislatures, and reduce bureaucracy. An example is the joint powers board established to combine planning strategies for both the city of Santa Fe and Santa Fe County. Recognizing that the city and county had collaborated successfully in a couple of areas—waste management and land use in the belt of land surrounding the city—the two governing bodies decided to expand their cooperation. The city and county agreed to form a joint powers board that would oversee urban boundary, water, housing, economic development, transportation, and growth issues; each entity is represented equally on the board.[63]

An examination of the evolution and results of regional strategies enacted within the last several decades demonstrates that regional improvement can be achieved when a sensitive balance is struck between local and regional matters. In particular, the forms of regionalism adopted by the Twin Cities and Portland have shown that the more multifunctional and politically balanced among the cooperating governments a regional approach is, the greater is its likelihood of success. That success is measured by the degree to which the strategy remedies the problems of racial segregation and concentrated poverty.

Conversely, Indianapolis exemplifies a regional government that failed because it was unbalanced and not federated to protect minor-

ity interests as identified in this chapter. As a result, it was nonrespon-
sive to the concerns of communities of color. The following is a more
detailed description of Indianapolis's regional government and the
more successful forms of regionalism at work in the Twin Cities and
Portland.

Indianapolis

The history of Indianapolis and its regional "Uni-Gov" illustrates
how a regional government of selectively limited authority can exacer-
bate the problems of racial segregation, concentrated poverty, and the
political disenfranchisement of people of color. Created in the 1970s
to retain federal funding, which would have been lost due to depopulation, Uni-Gov combined many of the fragments of the Indianapolis
metropolitan area. However, proponents of regionalism in Indianapolis were also motivated in part by a desire to defeat the expansion of
political power of communities of color in the central city and to
maintain Republican power over the increasingly Democratic urban
core. Significantly, certain functions of local government were not
united under Uni-Gov: school districts remained under local control,
as did police and fire departments. In fact, the decision to leave school
districts alone was largely political. Politicians were well aware that
consolidation of school districts would spark racial tension among
whites who had fled to all-white enclaves in Marion County. Without
their support, the legislation creating Uni-Gov would not have passed.

However, the decision to leave schools under local control ran
counter to the opinions voiced by members of communities of color
because it effectively perpetuated racial segregation and benefited
only the residents of suburban Indianapolis. This decision was later
corrected as the result of a racial discrimination lawsuit.[64]

The suburban municipalities and townships of Marion County
were not consolidated. Although townships have fewer functions than
the county, they still create another layer of local government that
contributes to fragmentation. Indiana is unique in that individual
townships are partially responsible for their welfare costs—"poor
relief"—and some rudimentary municipal-type services.[65] This places
a heavy burden on those townships with a disproportionate share of
poor people, particularly Center Township (Indianapolis). Instead of
pooling Marion County's tax resources for poor relief, individual
townships are expected to support their "own."

Uni-Gov today is both divided and inequitable. Because so many of the region's poor live in Indianapolis, it has to tax its residents and business for poor relief at rates ten times that of any other township in the region. Because Indianapolis houses a disproportionate amount of tax-free governmental, educational and cultural facilities—which benefit the entire region—the burden of property tax is assumed by only two-thirds of the township.

Marion County houses the overwhelming majority of the state's poor and minority populations, and its residents pay the highest taxes for the least adequate public services. While the creation of Uni-Gov has helped secure federal funds that aided in revitalizing downtown Indianapolis, it is a highly fragmented form of regional government with an insufficient power base to significantly affect regional issues. Equalizing mechanisms, such as tax-base sharing, are beyond the scope of Uni-Gov's powers, and as long as the metropolitan tax base remains fragmented, residents of Center Township will pay dearly for substandard public services.

The Twin Cities

A better balance has been struck between local and regional concerns in the Twin Cities, where the strategy involves regional policymaking and tax-base sharing. The Metropolitan Council ("Met Council") was formed by the Minnesota Legislature in 1967 as a policy-setting and planning agency whose members were appointed by the governor.[66] The Met Council had a duty to review "all proposed matters of metropolitan significance,"[67] including land development, and to adopt a development guide that addressed the present and future needs of the metropolitan area.[68] The council also had a duty to review all applications made by local government units for federal and state aid to ensure that project proposals were consistent with its goals for metropolitan development.[69]

The Met Council had direct control over funding for key metropolitan services such as regional transit, waste disposal, and airports. With these powers the Met Council was able to institute in the 1970s one of the most progressive suburban affordable-housing programs in the United States. It did so by conditioning infrastructure funding for individual municipalities upon their compliance with regional growth plans and affordable-housing goals.[70]

In the early 1980s, political changes led to the abandonment of these progressive policies, and the Met Council's broad powers to regulate growth and condition funding went unused.[71] This was due largely to the composition of the Met Council, whose members at that time had been appointed by Republican governor Arne Carlson.

In 1995 the Minnesota legislature passed the metropolitan Livable Communities Act (LCA), which focuses on community efforts to bolster economic vitality, job growth, and efficient use of existing public services. The LCA also supports metropolitan communities in their efforts to expand affordable-housing opportunities, recycle polluted sites, and restore neighborhoods. The act creates three funding accounts that make loans and grants available annually for

—affordable and life-cycle housing programs (the latter referring to transition period housing for college students, individuals, senior citizens, and divorcees, rather than to housing for low-income families) to meet the needs of people of all incomes and life stages,

—clean-up of polluted lands for business development and job growth,

—compact, creative, and transit-oriented development and redevelopment projects.[72]

Participation is voluntary for metropolitan municipalities, and to date more than half of the area's communities have signed on as partners under the LCA, including Minneapolis and St. Paul. To be eligible for these funds, participating communities must negotiate affordable and life-cycle housing goals with the Met Council. Ultimately, these negotiations must culminate in the municipality's submission of an action plan that states how it intends to establish affordable and life-cycle housing that will meet the needs projected by the council. Ideally, these goals should suit the council's long-term regional investment plans. They also must meet benchmarks in the following areas: percentage of affordable housing, both owned and rented; percentage of non-single-family detached units; owner-tenant split of housing stock; and density of residential development for both single-family and multifamily units.[73]

The framework of the Livable Communities Act legislation has several key weaknesses that prevent it from functioning effectively. One is that participation by municipalities is voluntary. Another is that the LCA does not even require the Met Council to critically review the plans once they are submitted, but only to serve as a depository. Nor does the LCA provide the council with any authority to reject the plans. Another weakness of the LCA is that it defines "affordable housing" very liberally. These generous definitions have enabled many municipalities to claim that they have satisfied their commitments under the LCA without actually building any integrative housing.[74]

The track record of the Livable Communities Act reveals its impotence in the face of municipal resistance. Because the act requires the Met Council to negotiate rather than impose integrative housing goals for suburban municipalities, exclusive municipalities have been able to attain key regional funding from the council with little or no commitment on their part. However, the newly appointed council has expressed a willingness to limit the delivery of essential benefits to municipalities unless commitments are made.

Minnesota also has a partial tax-base-sharing scheme under which each city in the region contributes 40 percent of its commercial-industrial tax revenues to a regional fund. This money is then redistributed so that those municipalities with lower commercial tax capacities receive more funds. The regional fund totals $367 million annually and accounts for 20 percent of the regional tax base.[75]

Because this tax-base sharing is only partial, there are still fiscal disparities between municipalities; the "effective net capacity" of households, after redistribution for the period 1980–1990, ranged from only $1,800 in the central cities to $2,749 in the suburbs to the south and west. However, the reduction in disparities is significant: without a system of tax-base sharing, the disparity between affluent suburbs and the cities would be 50:1, but the actual disparity ratio under the scheme is approximately 12:1. According to Orfield, this has resulted in marginal improvement, but actual disparity levels remain high. Nevertheless, this system has channeled significant funds to poorer districts that need them.[76]

Portland

Another example of an existing regional strategy that comes close to the ideal of federated regionalism is Portland's attempt to control growth and affect regional mandates. There is some degree of racial and economic polarization in Portland, and it is increasing over time. However, this polarization is less extreme than that found in older, larger metropolitan areas. One reason for this is the urban growth boundary (UGB), administered by Portland's regional governing body, Metro. Because there is limited space for new housing on the suburban fringe, the demand for housing from middle- and upper-income homebuyers is directed back toward the neighborhoods of Portland proper.[77] This same phenomenon holds true for business and commercial development that might otherwise move outward. There is evidence that the UGB, as a powerful regional land-use planning tool, has created a more balanced pattern of redevelopment and shared economic growth. Metro's growth management policy also includes investments in transit projects and downtown revitalization, which has increased the amenities available to Portland neighborhoods, thus contributing to their vitality and desirability.[78]

Portland's regional strategy for housing is federated in that, while the regional governing body sets the requirements for affordable housing, the municipalities themselves are ultimately responsible for zoning and how they choose to meet their share of the regional affordable-housing need. The measures taken are reviewed, but the exact steps to be taken are not mandated. For communities of color, this retention of local power may not be sufficient, given Portland's small (but increasing) minority population and the difficulty minorities have had in exerting political influence, even at the local jurisdictional level.[79]

While the UGB has helped restrict the allocation of monetary resources to a well-defined metropolitan area, there have been unintended side effects. Of particular concern are the clustering of affordable housing, loss of affordable housing as a result of escalating housing prices, the presence of new sprawl beyond the UGB, and the disproportionate impact these phenomena are having on minority populations. Portland has begun to explore ways of addressing these issues by a fair-share housing plan that includes protecting low-income communities from gentrification. The elected Metro Council is crucial to the success of this plan. This advance limits the fragmentation of housing planning in the region. Despite troubling side effects, Portland's efforts to contain sprawl and address fragmentation demonstrate the positive results of a well-planned federated regional strategy.

Neighborhood Control

A federated regional strategy could address fragmentation without specifically targeting sprawl, as David Rusk has discussed in *Cities without Suburbs.* Rusk asserts that without fragmentation there is less disparity between the core and the edges. His focus is on Albuquerque (and cities like it), which has been able to annex outlying areas, making it one large city rather than a hub surrounded by spokes. Rusk contends that the positiv ꞏ m w ꞏ ꞏ of this form of regionalism include less segregation in the school system, less concentrated poverty, and a unitary tax base. The issue that is not raised is that of cultural identity and dilution of political power for communities of color. It is clear that large, sprawling cities can be structured so that the influence and control of minorities is diluted—as occurred in Indianapolis after the adoption of Uni-Gov. On the other hand, cities could create neighborhood control of important institutions, which would afford minority communities greater autonomy. One example is the Neighborhood Revitalization Project in Minneapolis, which allows neighborhoods to have control over certain funds.[80] Similarly, charter schools and site-based management are other types of neighborhood control that would empower minorities where their numbers may be quite small, as in a place like Albuquerque.

Rusk's observations of Albuquerque and the above-mentioned ideas for recentralizing some power at the neighborhood level suggest that while sprawl is a serious problem in the production of concentrated poverty and residential segregation, fragmentation may be even more central. Massey and Denton suggest as much when they note that the new form of segregation based on municipal jurisdiction is much more pernicious than neighborhood segregation because it creates more fragmentation.[81] Federated regionalism, then, is an important response to the problem of fragmentation while being sensitive to the need of communities of color for political power and retention of cultural identity.

Conclusion

None of the examples discussed is the sort of federated regionalism that will fully redress concentrated poverty and residential segregation. However, some clearly demonstrate the potential of strategies presently at work and suggest approaches to be developed in the near future. Crucial to any current and future attempts at reform is establishing a balance between regional and local concerns—the *federated* component of federated regionalism. Portland's tactics with respect to housing demonstrate this balance: the metropolitan government sets affordable-housing goals for its member municipalities but allows those municipalities to choose the ways in which those housing goals will be met. In contrast, the regional government in Indianapolis exemplifies an imbalanced system, where regional concerns such as the schools were intentionally treated as local concerns until the courts intervened; the result was aggravation rather than reparation of the problems of concentrated poverty and racial segregation.

If federated regionalism is not balanced, it runs the risk of being too respectful of local autonomy or becoming too fragmented to function. This is demonstrated by the problems with the Livable Communities Act in the Twin Cities, which gives too much weight to local autonomy; therefore, it has inadequately implemented its housing goals and failed to protect the urban core. A lack of balance can also produce an overemphasis on regional concerns, resulting in a large political entity that can dilute the political power and cultural identity of minority communities. Uni-Gov in Indianapolis demonstrates the worst of both kinds of imbalance with respect to its schools and other regional issues. The ideal balance between local and regional control will hinge upon recognition of the concerns of communities of color, which require regional approaches to address concentrations of poverty and local approaches to address the need for political and cultural empowerment.

Representation of communities of color on a regional level is critical and could be implemented through neighborhood and interest groups or entities at the municipal and even federal level. The governance structure could also involve floors, ceilings, and the requirement of a supermajority. One example of a potential regional-federal engagement that could address concentrated poverty, sprawl, and local job growth is a scheme whereby the U.S. Department of Housing and Urban Development (HUD) could make its presently unconditioned federal funding contingent on municipalities' development of Housing Assistance Plans (HAP) that actually deal with these issues. HUD could spur local stakeholders to design a HAP application that demands that municipalities articulate solutions to problems of sprawl and poverty and draft implementation steps.

Minorities have cause to be wary of regional solutions to the problems of segregation and concentrated poverty. What little political power they wield seems at risk of dilution if the regional framework created ignores their interests. Federated regionalism, however, offers communities of color hope that their interests will not be compromised under a regional system, but rather will be balanced and augmented. The tension between local concerns and the needs of the whole metropolitan region can be healthy if properly managed. The challenge is to balance these functions in a way that leads to true democratic cooperation in metropolitan planning—a cooperation that transcends racial polarization. The suggestions discussed in this chapter are illustrative; while a particular suggestion may or may not work in a given region, it is clear that some structure must be put in place to address minority concerns and a myriad of others. As long as we continue to allow and support a racialized and fragmented jurisdictional structure, we will continue to limit the reach of civil rights, social justice, and environmental protection.[82] Federated regionalism can begin to meet these challenges.

Notes

1. See Michael E. Porter, "The Competitive Advantage of the Inner City," *Harvard Business Review,* vol. 73 (May–June 1995), p. 55. Porter calls on the cities not to mimic the suburbs but to build on their own competitive advantages. Given the fluidity of capital and people, as well as how regions are structured, I doubt that the concept of competitive advantage is sufficient to address the pressing needs of central cities without a more integrated and aggressive regional strategy involving some coordination and cooperation.

2. The idea of federated regionalism is both old and new. It is new in my explicit application to regional issues that affect minority communities. It is old in the sense that our government has always been based on a federated model that balances larger concerns with the need for local control.

3. See Neal R. Peirce, Curtis W. Johnson, and John Stuart Hall, *Citistates: How Urban America Can Prosper in a Competitive World* (Washington D.C.: Seven Locks Press, 1993).

4. Some would argue that federal public housing policy has played an equal, if not more important role. As Florence Wagman Roisman makes clear, however, "the presence of large public housing developments and poor neighborhoods stem from the same cause," namely racial animus that is empowered through local control of public housing policy and inadequate oversight of racist implementation. Florence Wagman Roisman, "Intentional Racial Discrimination and Segregation by the Federal Government as a Principal Cause of Concentrated Poverty: a Response to Schill and Wachter," *University of Pennsylvania Law Review,* vol. 143 (1995), pp. 1351, 1368.

5. Gregory Weiher, *The Fractured Metropolis* (State University of New York Press, 1991), p. 165.

6. Ibid., p. 188.

7. Raymond Vernon, "The Myth and Reality of Our Urban Problems," *City and Suburb: The Economics of Metropolitan Growth* (Englewood Cliffs, N.J.: Prentice-Hall, 993), p. 101.

8. David Rusk, *Cities without Suburbs* (Washington, D.C.: Woodrow Wilson Center Press, 1995).

9. Richard Thompson Ford, "The Boundaries of Race: Political Geography in Legal Analysis," *Harvard Law Review*, vol. 107 (1994), pp. 1841–1921.

10. Richard Briffault, "Our Localism: Part II–Localism and Legal Theory," *Columbia Law Review*, vol. 90 (1990), pp. 346–454.

11. In the context of political control, many proponents of influence districts in voting, instead of majority-minority districts, make this claim. See Lani Guinier, "More Democracy," *University of Chicago Legal Forum* (1995), pp. 1–22.

12. This does not mean that there needs to be complete consensus. Indeed, such a requirement is probably a recipe for inaction.

13. Paul Jargowsky, *Poverty and Place: Ghettos, Barrios, and the American City* (Russell Sage Foundation, 1997), p. 193.

14. Ibid., pp. 34–35.

15. Paul Jargowsky, "Ghetto Poverty among Blacks in the 1980s," *Journal of Policy Analysis and Management*, vol. 13 (1994), p. 288.

16. Institute on Race and Poverty, *Examining the Relationship between Housing, Education, and Persistent Segregation* (Minneapolis, 1998), p. 11.

17. Douglas S. Massey and Nancy A. Denton, *American Apartheid: Segregation and the Making of the Underclass* (Harvard University Press, 1993), p. 19.

18. Ibid., pp. 51–52.

19. Ibid., pp. 54–55.

20. Michael H. Schill and Susan M. Wachter, "The Spatial Bias of Federal Housing Law and Policy: Concentrated Poverty in Urban America," *University of Pennsylvania Law Review*, vol. 143, no. 5 (1995), pp. 1285–1342 (citing Dennis R. Judd, *The Politics of American Cities: Private Power and Public Policy* [Boston: Little Brown, 1979], p. 281, as the source for FHA underwriting material).

21. Massey and Denton, *American Apartheid*, p. 56.

22. "Boston Fed Issues Study Showing Connection Between Race and Credit," *Fair Lending News*, vol. 3 (1994).

23. In the practice of "steering," the prospective home buyer is taken only to neighborhoods whose demographics are consistent with his or her own race or ethnicity.

24. Blockbusting is the inducement of panic selling of homes by realtors who prey upon white fear of minority "invasion."

25. Massey and Denton, *American Apartheid*, p. 36.

26. Paul A. Jargowsky, "Metropolitan Restructuring and Urban Policy," *Stanford Law and Policy Review*, vol. 8, no. 2 (1997), pp. 47, 49. See also James E. Rosenbaum, "Changing the Geography of Opportunity by Expanding Residential Choice: Lessons from the Gautreaux Program," *Housing Policy Debate*, vol. 6 (1995), p. 231. The Gautreaux Mobility Program in Chicago showed that when low-income minorities are moved to less segregated areas, they fare substantially better in terms of graduation, teen pregnancy, employment, higher education, and salaries.

27. Rusk, *Cities without Suburbs*.

28. Myron Orfield, *Metropolitics: A Regional Agenda for Community and Stability* (Brookings, 1997), p. 38.

29. Massey and Denton, *American Apartheid*, p. 155.

30. Myron Orfield, *Metropolitics*.

31. Ibid., pp. 104–05

32. Kenneth T. Jackson, *Crabgrass Frontier: The Suburbanization of the United States* (Oxford University Press, 1985).

33. For a discussion of the limits of in-place strategies, see John Foster-Bey, "Bridging Communities: Making the Link Between Regional Economies and Local Community Economic Development," *Stanford Law and Policy Review*, vol. 8, no. 2 (1997), p. 25.

34. Advocacy of in-place strategies by members of communities of color as a means of preserving political power and cultural identity is undermined, to a degree, by the fact that many middle-class minorities are moving away from the central cities. There is a conflict between this act of moving away from the central cities and the need for a solidarity of culture and political power that is impervious to the assimilationist influences located outside of the central cities.

35. Charles Smith, "Racism and Community Planning: Building Equity or Waiting for Explosions," *Stanford Law and Policy Review*, vol. 8, no. 2 (1997), p. 64.

36. Cornel West, *Keeping Faith: Philosophy and Race in America* (Routledge, 1993), p. 282.

37. Smith, "Racism," p. 65.

38. Orfield, *Metropolitics*, p. 169.

39. Lani Guinier, "More Democracy," p. 6.

40. Lani Guinier, *The Tyranny of the Majority* (Free Press, 1994), p. 98.

41. See *Shaw v. Reno*, 509 U.S. 630 (1993) and its progeny: *Lawyer v. Department of Justice*, 117 Sup. Ct. 2186 (1997); *Abrams v. Johnson*, 117 Sup. Ct. 1925 (1997); *Bush v. Vera*, 116 Sup. Ct. 1941 (1996); *Shaw v. Hunt*, 116 Sup. Ct. 1894 (1996); and *Miller v. Johnson*, 115 Sup. Ct. 2475 (1995).

42. Richard L. Engstrom and Robert R. Brischetto, "Is Cumulative Voting Too Complex? Evidence from Exit Polls," *Stetson Law Review*, vol. 27 (1998), p. 813.

43. Pamela S. Karlan, "Loss and Redemption: Voting Rights at the Turn of the Century," *Vanderbilt Law Review*, vol. 50, no. 2 (1997), pp. 312–13.

44. Ibid.

45. Edward Zelinsky, "Metropolitanism, Progressivism, and Race," book review, *Columbia Law Review*, vol. 98, no. 3 (1998), p. 667.

46. Ibid., p. 668.

47. Orfield, *Metropolitics*, p. 169.

48. Scott A. Bollens, "Concentrated Poverty and Metropolitan Equity Strategies," *Stanford Law and Policy Review*, vol. 8, no. 2 (1997), p. 19.

49. Guinier, "More Democracy," pp. 11–12.

50. Ibid., p. 10.

51. Ibid., p. 11.

52. Engstrom and Brischetto, "Cumulative Voting," p. 815.

53. Guinier, "More Democracy," p. 15.

54. Guinier, *Tyranny*, p. 142.

55. Guinier, "More Democracy," p. 17.

56. Ibid., p. 18.

57. Guinier, *Tyranny*, p. 97.

58. David Van Biema, "One Person, Seven Votes," *Time*, April 25, 1994.

59. James E. Clyburn, "In Search of a Better Voting Method," *Capitol Column* (http://www.house.gov/clyburn/col1980313b.html [March 13, 1998]).

60. Guinier, *Tyranny*, p. 111.

61. Under Minnesota law, approximately 188 municipalities in the seven-county metropolitan area pool 40 percent of the increases in taxes from commercial-industrial property, which is then redistributed among all municipalities based on annual estimated population and how per capita market value of property compares with the metrowide value.

62. Gary Orfield, "Metropolitan School Desegregation: Impacts on Metropolitan Society," *Minnesota Law Review*, vol. 80, no. 4 (1996), pp. 827, 845.

63. Dale Lezon, "Forum Sets Stage for Cooperation," *Albuquerque Journal*, October 23, 1997.

64. *United States* v. *Board of School Commissioners of Indianapolis*, 332 F. Supp. 655 (S.D. Ind. 1971), affirmed, 474 F.2d 81 (7th Cir. 1973), petition for certiorari denied, 413 U.S. 920 (1973).

65. For example, volunteer fire and ambulance departments.

66. Orfield, *Metropolitics*, p. 182.

67. Minnesota Statutes, sec. 473.173.

68. Minnesota Statutes, sec. 473.145.

69. Minnesota Statutes, sec. 473.171. This duty is what enabled the council to advance desegregation in the 1970s by enabling it to condition approval of aid applications on a municipality's willingness to allow low-cost housing within its borders.

70. Orfield, *Metropolitics*, p. 183.

71. Ibid.

72. Ibid., p. 188.

73. Metropolitan Council, "Minority Population Distribution Trends in the Twin Cities Metropolitan Area." Pub. No. 620-93-085 (1996).

74. Orfield, *Metropolitics*.

75. Ibid., pp. 153–54.

76. Ibid., pp. 64–65, 87.

77. Ibid., p. 157.

78. Consolidated Plan, *Action Plan for City of Portland, City of Gresham, and Multnomah County* (May 12, 1997).

79. Orfield, *Metropolitics*, pp. 157–58.

80. Kevin Diaz, "For NRP, Survival Likely Has a Price," *Minneapolis-St. Paul Star-Tribune*, April 26, 1999.

81. Massey and Denton, *American Apartheid*.

82. john a. powell, "Race, Poverty, and Urban Sprawl: Access to Opportunities Through Regional Structures," *Forum for Social Economics*, vol. 28, no. 2 (1999), pp. 1–20.

PART FOUR

A CONTRARIAN METROPOLITAN VIEW

CHAPTER NINE

Empowering Families to Vote with Their Feet

PAUL R. DIMOND

The right to travel is embedded in the structure of the U.S. Constitution and the fabric of American life. It includes the basic protections owed by one state to persons visiting from another state and is closely related to the essential free flow of commerce among the several states. The right to travel also includes one of the most important individual rights—the right to move.

Families in America have always exercised this right to move by "voting with their feet" whenever they want to escape intolerable conditions or simply live in a better place. Examples include the restless drive west to new frontiers, the trek from hardscrabble day labor on the farm to better-paying factory jobs in the city, the step from renting an apartment to owning a home, the great migrations from North to South and back again, the move to a place with better jobs or schools, safer streets, a more hospitable climate, or the hope for a brighter future. Between March 1996 and March 1997, 42 million Americans— 16 percent of the population—moved to a new home. This movement was led by younger households, lower-income families, and renters. They were joined by an additional 1.3 million immigrants.[1]

Voting with their feet about where to live, learn, and work is how families most powerfully choose to build a better life for themselves and their children. Of course, not all families have been able to make this choice. The entrenched discrimination that contributed to racial segregation in schools and housing throughout much of metropolitan America primarily restricted the opportunities of black families to make their own choices.[2] The limits of majority rule and judicial review in our democracy, however, mean that the resulting racial ghettoization simply cannot be remedied by expecting any government or judicial decree to dictate a different school or housing outcome for all families.[3] Governments and courts contravene the fundamental right to move when they tell families where to live, work, or send their children to school. Instead, entrenched discrimination is better remedied by *extending* the right to vote with their feet to *all* families regardless of race, national origin, or income. This right to travel is the most enduring wellspring of the American dream.

By the same token, communities thrive when they attract new families, and communities decline when families choose to move elsewhere. Just as technological advances, business innovations, and the new skills and value added by workers change the means of production from one economic era to the next, individuals and families choosing where to live, learn, and work fuel dynamic market forces that shape communities over time. People in America vote with their feet; therefore, the primary public policy goal should be to expand this opportunity for all families.

Competing Myths

Myths persist about how urban America has grown and what goals should guide communities in planning for the future. Consider several of the competing myths now making the rounds.

Myth: Cities thrived during the industrial boom of the first post–World War II generation, but they are doomed to decline in the new information age.

One popular misconception is that central cities boomed during America's rapid industrial expansion from 1946 through 1972, declined during the waning of the industrial era over the next twenty years, and are now doomed in the new information age. In fact, major midwestern and northern industrial cities lost jobs throughout the first generation after World War II. In the old industrial cities, aging and inefficient factories closed by the thousands as more efficient long-line plants opened in greenfield sites in the surrounding areas and in more wide-open spaces in the South and West. At the same time, tens of millions of Americans chose to buy new single-family homes built on cheaper and more available land surrounding central cities. Built-up cities simply lacked the vacant land to accommodate long-line industrial plants as well as families seeking new homes with a yard and more space. Tens of millions of jobs and the bulk of new investment followed the new plants and new homeowners to suburban frontiers, thereby expanding the geographic scope of metropolitan areas throughout the country.[4]

From 1946 through 1972, suburbs increasingly became the preferred location for new jobs, homes, stores, investment, and consumption throughout America. During this period, however, entrenched discrimination denied most Americans of color the same right to move that was generally available to white Americans. From 1973 through 1992, stagnating median family incomes during the waning industrial era and continuing vestiges of entrenched discrimination compounded the decline of many neighborhoods in central cities and older suburbs.

In contrast, the new information age substantially levels the playing field for central cities, as well as older suburbs, expanding suburbs, exurbs, and rural areas. At the very least, cheap land for long-line industrial plants no longer confers comparative economic advantage in the information age. Instead, the new engines of growth are clusters of knowledge and higher education, research and innovation, customized services and goods, and convenient access to services (investment, financial, and technical), culture and entertainment, and large markets. Even with digital networks of communication and commerce girdling the globe and connecting those who live in the remotest rural areas to the World Wide Web, these denser clusters are likely to be the most dynamic places for generating economic growth in the new economy. At the same time, fair housing and lending laws and more affordable and accessible home mortgages make home ownership and choice of residential location more broadly available to all, regardless of race, color, or national origin.

Compared with other nations in the world, the United States is blessed with *many more* seedbeds of growth in cities, towns, universities, research centers, and metropolitan areas throughout this large and diverse country. There is, of course, no guarantee that any particular place—or type of geographic arrangement for living, work, or school—will thrive. Put differently, central cities—like all other places—will have to find their own niches of comparative advantage in the new economy in order to prosper.

Myth: Urban sprawl and lack of regional planning, transit, and financing increase congestion and commute times in the United States compared to other developed countries.

This belief also does not fit the facts. Despite greater governmental planning for locating businesses, homes, civic centers, and open space and more extensive mass transit in other developed countries, the average commute time of workers in the United States is one-third less than that of our counterparts in Western Europe and one-half that of the Japanese. In fact, despite the far greater increase in the number of households in the United States over the past twenty years, congestion has declined by more than 20 percent, while the average speed of car commutes has continued to increase.[5] How is this possible? The lower density of America's expanding urbanized areas and greater availability of affordable land nearby allow families and firms to vote more freely with their feet. Not surprisingly, over time they locate more conveniently to one another.

Nevertheless, many now tout schemes to limit the geographic expansion of metropolitan areas by establishing no-growth greenbelts, preserving farmland on the frontiers of urban areas through public purchase of private development rights, limiting construction of new housing and businesses to designated growth areas, and providing regional zoning and taxation to promote supposedly more convenient transit, housing, and work. Insofar as these proposals seek to limit the right of families to vote with their feet, it is unlikely that they will achieve their stated goals.

First, the number of homes in America will continue to grow at a substantially faster rate than the overall population, as household size continues to fall and more families choose to buy second homes. As a result, many schemes for preserving open space on the frontiers of urbanized areas will primarily *fuel* the geographic expansion of metropolitan areas and their exurban frontiers. Such "farm preservation" and "rural designation" schemes—like their earlier large-lot and multiple-acre zoning kin—will just chew up more land faster as the growth in households and firms continues. Instead of thinking in such exclusionary terms about *regional* land-use planning, it makes more sense to join the "new urbanists" in thinking in smaller terms: greater density and mix of uses in *local zoning* should be encouraged to expand the opportunity for families and firms to live and work in more convenient, diverse, and compact communities. Designed with nature to preserve wetlands, estuaries, and public open spaces essential to clean water and recreation, denser and more diverse development will also preserve an important economic advantage for most metropolitan areas in the United States: the availability of affordable vacant land on the frontiers of urban areas. This will enable families and businesses to locate more conveniently to one another than any regional plan can arrange, no matter how comprehensively detailed and rigidly enforced.

Second, other growth management schemes seek to contain all new development within currently urbanized areas by providing targeted incentives, while seeking to exclude such development beyond a designated growth boundary. If successful, such expansive zoning and expensive taxpayer subsidies will just limit the supply of affordable land, drive up the costs for living and doing business throughout the local region, and substantially increase congestion for all. If unsuccessful, such costly strategies will just pay for consuming more land as development leapfrogs the designated growth boundaries. A more economic approach is simply to require all new development of greenfields and other vacant land to bear the full cost for new and improved roads, water and sewerage, and other infrastructure and utilities without *any* government subsidy (beyond the home mortgage deduction available to all homeowners wherever they choose to live). This straightforward approach to disciplining sprawl then can be complemented by thin—and relatively inexpensive—federal and state tax credits to enable new private owners to invest in cleaning up and developing the least contaminated and most valuable urban brownfields without fear of liability for prior owners' contamination. Such market-based approaches to growth and development also will restrain the real estate expenses for living and doing business throughout the local region by making affordable vacant land available for competing development.

Eliminating government subsidies for greenfield development also will mean that the federal government can stop subsidizing most new local and state roads, transit, sewers, and other infrastructure. Except when directly related to essential interstate and international travel and commerce, federal transportation subsidies are only tempting pork barrel treats that most states fight to consume in order to build and then repave short-lived roads on a slapdash basis every few years. Just imagine the savings if, for example, midwestern states offered a joint prize—a guaranteed purchase order of $20 billion—to the first three consortia of researchers, investors, and innovative highway construction firms that could rebuild roads to withstand fifty years of hard winters and more traffic. Coupled with charges for traffic congestion and vehicle axle-weight, such an approach to highway building, replacement, and repair would enable families to choose where to live, work, learn and shop much more conveniently at a much lower total cost to taxpayers.[6]

Third, far-reaching proposals for metropolitan government ignore a primary benefit of local jurisdictions for families and firms. Diverse local jurisdictions act as an important economic check to ensure that local public services, user fees, and taxes are limited to the real value they provide to families and firms. Some cities ignore this economic check and impose taxes higher than the value of the public services provided. Such high-tax strategies are counterproductive for cities, because families and firms are free to move to places nearby with a better local tax deal. As a result, high-tax cities must learn to increase the productivity and customer responsiveness of a more limited range of services, remove burdensome bureaucracy and outmoded regulation, and lower their overall tax rates on families and firms if they are going to meet the economic competition from their neighboring jurisdictions. It is only when suburban governments with coercive tax power and zoning authority seek to exclude new entrants and impose costs on their neighboring central cities and older suburbs that such decentralization risks becoming state-supported fiscal balkanization.[7]

In our increasingly mobile society, some public services do provide benefits that extend well beyond any city, local district, or regional authority. Higher education, publicly supported schools, and highways and transit are good examples. Thus states across the country provide an increasing majority of the nonfederal tax dollars supporting such public services. However, it makes no economic sense to consider any form of regional government that seeks income or general service redistribution through regional taxation. In fact, local government, no matter how broad its geographic and service scope, is generally in no position to ask firms or families to subsidize one another. They are free to move elsewhere, and they are more likely to do so if the public services and public benefits they receive from any local government, including a regional authority, are of less value than the local taxes they pay.

The rub for cities and other local governments comes because the private markets for housing, jobs, finance, and innovation that drive metropolitan economies are at least regional in scope. Rather than prescribing any particular regional approach to local government, it makes more sense for civic entrepreneurs from all sectors to join in considering alternative ways and diverse means to enable all families and firms to better connect to these regional markets. When considering how to make these connections, it should be remembered that government at any level is not the sole or even primary resource. For-profit firms have an economic incentive to seek profitable new niches by serving unmet market demands in every corner of any local region. In addition, America's vibrant and rapidly growing nonprofit sector can fill in many gaps. Better information on unmet demands and underused sources of supply throughout the local region will help both for-profit and nonprofit enterprises connect families and firms, wherever located, to these vital areawide markets for housing, jobs, and investment. Given the ingenuity of American people and the diversity of metropolitan and regional landscapes around the country, a wide variety of creative responses will emerge, be explored, and tested.[8]

Myth: Urban sprawl in America threatens the environment.

Many environmentalists argue that sprawling development and Americans' long-standing love affair with the car pose a mortal threat to forest, farmland, water, and air. However, as detailed in Greg Easterbrook's analysis *A Moment on Earth: The Coming Age of Environmental Optimism,* the facts once again belie the myth. Adjusting for Alaska's entry into the Union, forest acreage in the United States has increased almost 25 percent since 1920. Farming has become increasingly productive, diverse, and environmentally friendly, even as substantially more of the least productive farmland is "lost" to nature than to man's expanding suburbs and exurbs. In fact, between 1980 and 1990, approximately 2.4 percent of the land area in the United States was removed from cultivation and handed back to nature, more than *all* of the land put to human urbanization in the United States since the first settlement by Native Americans.[9]

Just as important, the United States has responded remarkably to Rachel Carson's warnings of a *Silent Spring* in 1962.[10] Thanks to environmental regulation, technological advance, business innovation, and consumer demand, America's air, water, and soil are much cleaner today than thirty-five years ago—substantially cleaner than any other developed country in the world. Cars sold in the United States today produce 99 percent less carbon monoxide, nitrous oxide, sulfur dioxide, and lead than they did a generation ago. In environmental terms, the cleaner cars of the twenty-first century will bear even less resemblance to the carbon-fuel-burning gas guzzlers of the first generation after World War II. The worldwide abolition of chlorofluorocarbons in the early 1990s has already eliminated this man-made threat to depletion of the ozone layer.[11] Similarly, if Americans can agree on how much they want to limit their contribution to global warming, they will also invent new ways to produce and operate cars, homes, factories, utilities, businesses, and farms to meet whatever performance standards are set. It has been shown that Americans can clean up their old messes and prevent new ones once they have a mind to do so.

As the transition from the old industrial economy to the information age is completed, there will be even fewer environmental reasons to restrict the opportunity for Americans to continue to vote with their feet. Compared to the industrial era, the means of production and consumption in this new economy will reward thinking work, knowledge, and humans adding value to new networks of commerce and innovation over machines levering muscle power, consuming natural resources, and burning fossil fuel. Rather than debate the marginal impact of the geographic expansion of urban development on the environment, Americans should enact major tax reform to *speed* the transition to more environmentally friendly production and consumption in this new economic era by taxing employers' payrolls and workers' wages and salaries less and taxing pollution, waste, and contributions to global warming more. Such a new tax compact for the twenty-first century would employ the dynamic market force of families and firms voting with their feet, pocketbooks, innovation, production, and consumption to make the environment cleaner and the climate as habitable as the more powerful and changing forces of nature will permit.

Myth: Most poor people live in areas of concentrated high poverty.

Once again the myth misses the facts. Paul Jargowsky's detailed analysis, *Poverty and Place: Ghettos, Barrios and the American City,* shows that in 1990 "only one-sixth of the poor . . . live in high-poverty neighborhoods," where more than 40 percent of the residents are below the poverty line.[12] Of the white poor, who represent more than 56 percent of all poor persons, only 5.6 percent live in high-poverty neighborhoods. Despite their limited means, almost 95 percent of the white poor—compared with three-quarters of the black poor and four-fifths of the Hispanic poor—have voted with their feet to live in more mixed-income neighborhoods throughout metropolitan and nonurban America. In fact, more than two-thirds of the white poor live in low-poverty neighborhoods, where less than 20 percent of the residents are poor.[13]

High-poverty neighborhoods are no longer the teeming, overcrowded city slums depicted in bygone eras. In 1990 high-poverty census tracts contained only two-thirds the population of other census tracts in metropolitan America. As Jargowsky notes, many families—including black families with means—are voting with their feet to leave high-poverty neighborhoods: "The low and declining population density of high-poverty neighborhoods and the great expansion in their number [from 1,171 census tracts in 1970 to 2,726 in 1990] suggest that the recent increases in neighborhood poverty have been driven at least partly by migration out of inner-city areas, particularly of persons with incomes above the poverty line."[14] Overall, 8.4 million residents—only 4 percent of the United States population—lived in high-poverty neighborhoods in 1990.

Although racial segregation by residence is on the decline, the vestiges of entrenched discrimination—racial ghettoization and neighborhood succession—are still apparent. In the older, more established cities of the eastern Midwest and the Mid-Atlantic states, more than 40 percent of the black poor live in high-poverty neighborhoods, and the number of high-poverty census tracts more than tripled from 1970 to 1990. In contrast, there is reason to hope that the surge in high-poverty Hispanic census tracts due to immigration and higher birth rates during this period will abate as succeeding generations join with past ethnic migrations in moving wherever they choose throughout metropolitan and nonurban America.

Perhaps Jargowsky's most revealing finding, however, is that regardless of race, the sources of support for high-poverty neighborhoods are similar to those for all other neighborhoods: residents earn more than 70 percent of their income from work. Apart from social security, they receive only a small fraction of their support from public assistance. The primary source of poverty also transcends neighborhood type: in all metropolitan neighborhoods, 60.9 percent of female-headed households live in poverty, ranging from 55 percent in low-poverty neighborhoods to 73 percent in high-poverty neighborhoods. The difference is that a far greater proportion of female-headed households are clustered in higher-poverty neighborhoods.[15]

Finally, Jargowsky concludes that the extent of and changes in neighborhood poverty within a metropolitan area are largely determined by metropolitan-wide factors. The most important is the overall health of the metropolitan economy, as measured by the median income of all its residents.[16] In sum, thriving metropolitan economies driven by private markets that generate increasing median family incomes will do more than targeted government services to alleviate neighborhood concentrations of family poverty. The best antipoverty solution—for neighborhoods and families—is a job. We should remember that the great increase in family incomes and even greater reduction in family poverty among all races and income groups in the first generation after World War II was driven not by government redistribution or transfer programs, but by more workers earning more from more jobs.

Myth: Comprehensive government services and place-based subsidies are essential to help poor families thrive in high-poverty neighborhoods.

Any local government that seeks to provide additional income support or extra social services to high-poverty neighborhoods by redistributing taxes from other neighborhoods will have a tough time retaining and attracting families and firms that are free to locate elsewhere. That always has been the rationale for asking the federal or state government to redistribute income and social services from those who are better off to those who are poor. Over the past generation, however, a new political consensus emerged in the states and throughout the nation: while in 1973 average federal and state welfare payments provided 50 percent of national median income and ensured that families on welfare would live above the poverty line, by 1993 average welfare payments had fallen to 25 percent of national median income and ensured that a family would live in poverty as long as it stayed on welfare. At the same time, majority support has solidly backed increasing the minimum wage and the earned income tax credit so that every full-time worker can earn a living wage after taxes to support a family above poverty.

As a result, the sure way out of poverty for every family is to earn income from work, defer childbearing until after high school graduation and marriage, and continue to learn new skills on the job and off. Both parents—including unwed, divorced, and otherwise absent fathers—must bear primary responsibility for supporting their own children. The 1995 Welfare Reform Act did no more than ratify this growing national consensus. As these norms for new family formation and parental responsibility are understood and accepted, births to unwed mothers generally and to unwed teenagers in particular will decline; and both parents (including those who might previously have joined the ranks of deadbeat dads) will work to support their children. Early evidence on births by teens is encouraging: the rate of new births by teenagers in 1996 was 54.7 per 1,000, down more than 4 percent from 1995 and down 12 percent from the rate of 62.1 births per 1,000 teens in1991.[17]

Evidence is even clearer that any level of government that seeks to concentrate poor persons in particular neighborhoods to provide comprehensive social services offers a fool's bargain for taxpayers and poor families. Isolating poor persons in inner-city ghettos and barrios does not help them connect to the rising demand for more workers throughout the local regional labor markets or take personal responsibility for learning skills that will earn them higher wages at new jobs. Thus federal, state, and local governments act irresponsibly and waste taxpayer dollars whenever they limit housing and job-training subsidies to particular projects or places—public or private—rather than putting such subsidies directly in the hands of poor families so they can choose for themselves where best to live and learn in order to find new and better jobs.

Fortunately, the House and Senate have finally joined with the president in enacting legislation that will convert all federal job-training funding for dislocated and lower-income workers into individual training accounts. This will provide a fitting capstone to a historic national achievement: the expanded federal support for student aid which now ensures that every family or individual, regardless of color or income, has the purchasing power to invest in the postsecondary education and training they choose. Unfortunately, despite congressional funding for more portable vouchers for the first time in years, most federal low-income housing subsidies go to support particular projects that just continue to add to racial isolation, high concentrations of poverty, and ongoing deterioration of many inner-city neighborhoods.

In considering *any* place-based initiative, it is important to remember that distressed inner-city and rural communities must, like all other places, find their own competitive niches within their local regional economies if they are ever going to prosper. Place-based government subsidies will not gild the ghetto any better today than the Great Society programs did more than a generation ago. High-poverty neighborhoods can only be transformed into thriving communities by

— working families with their own incomes and homes,

— businesses that effectively supply unmet demands locally and throughout their region,

— convenient access to private capital and investment,

— concerted civic action.

Thus the first two criteria for judging the merits of any place-based initiative to aid high-poverty neighborhoods should be the extent to which private, regional capital will invest in expanding enterprise in these communities, and the extent to which regional employer demand for additional workers will connect to the labor supply in the targeted communities.

In addition, many high-poverty neighborhoods are filling with abandoned homes and buildings as families and firms move to places with more opportunity and less crime. States must revise their tax reversion laws to swiftly return such buildings to private ownership for rehabilitation before they are ruined. Waiting several years for titles to clear on such abandoned buildings while delinquent taxpayers refuse to pay back taxes is a losing proposition: the structures fall into disrepair and threaten surrounding homes, businesses, and blocks. Once such abandoned properties are beyond cost-effective repair, cities must also act rapidly to demolish them and provide affordable vacant land for immediate redevelopment by private owners or for safe, open, green space for recreation. Any city that maintains a large and increasing inventory of dilapidated, abandoned buildings just invites further neighborhood decline and disinvestment.

There is, of course, one public service without which no family, business, neighborhood, or metropolitan area can hope to prosper: safety and security of person and property. This was the focus of the nation's first civil rights law enacted in 1866—to ensure that the freedmen could make their way the same as whites, free of violence, crime, or other unlawful intimidation. No local government will succeed in attracting families or firms to any neighborhood if it fails to work with the community to ensure this first civil right. More cities are turning to community policing with the full support and assistance of the vast majority of law-abiding citizens, who will no longer tolerate broken windows, litter, or other invitations to crime, drugs, or violent intimidation in their neighborhoods. Growing respect for this first civil right and declining crime rates can reduce the fear of living, learning, and doing business in every neighborhood, no matter how poor.[18]

Myth: Most local regions lack the private resources and market incentives to connect high-poverty neighborhoods and the families who live there to the areawide markets for jobs, capital and financial services, and retail goods and services.

Our thriving national economy is the sum of local regional economies and their trade with other regions in the United States and throughout the world. Sustained job growth of almost 2.5 million net new jobs annually from 1993 through 1999 and the continued decline in the unemployment rate to 4.2 percent in 1999 result from strong job creation and prolonged economic growth at the local level throughout the country. The labor demands of an expanding economy increase incentives to tap the pool of available labor in high-poverty neighborhoods.

In addition, most of these new jobs have been created by new businesses and the expansion of small and midsized firms. This, in turn, is fueled by the more efficient financial services made available by the increasingly global capital markets as they find more good investment opportunities and a hospitable investment climate in regions throughout the United States. There is no lack of private resources to invest in new ventures and expanding business in high-poverty neighborhoods so long as there is a market demand—in the community or throughout the region—for the goods and services produced and distributed. What is missing is sufficient information, innovation, and will among firms, large and small, to put the labor, financial, retail, and business formation markets to work in high-poverty neighborhoods. To fill this gap, new intermediaries and better networks of information are forming.

LOCAL LABOR MARKETS. Jeremy Nowak describes how a community development corporation in northwest Philadelphia has joined with a consortia of community colleges, engineering schools, and employers throughout the region to create an innovative "work-force intermediary" to connect residents of high-poverty neighborhoods to the rising demand for workers by employers throughout the region. In six cities the Annie E. Casey Foundation is providing support for such work-force intermediaries to link targeted inner-city residents with regional job opportunities.[19] The Welfare-to-Work Partnership, with 5,000 participating firms, is also demonstrating how employers seeking new workers can act alone and in consortia to connect unemployed parents to jobs so that they can support their children.

More retail and fast-food chains are now hiring inner-city workers with little previous job experience or training. These firms provide transportation and work experience with on-the-job training in information systems, responsive customer service, just-in-time inventory and distribution, teamwork, and problem solving. These firms can then assist these newly skilled workers to move to new and better jobs for which they qualify through personal recommendations and informal referral networks, cooperative consortia with other employers seeking trained workers, and referrals to job-placement agencies serving employers throughout the region.

In Milwaukee a private job-placement firm has located an office in the inner city to meet the substantial hiring demands of employers throughout the metropolitan area. This for-profit firm actively searches for potential workers in churches, other volunteer community organizations, hospitals, schools, and neighborhoods through advertising, word of mouth, and direct contact. Regardless of race, every person who can read is being successfully placed in a job, at no expense to any taxpayer or jobseeker; the new employer pays the job-search firm for every new hire. Such job-placement firms have a strong and increasing market incentive to expand into every inner city to find the supply of labor they need to meet the growing demands of employers for workers.

Burgeoning on-line job banks and counseling from an array of job placement intermediaries, community colleges, and technical schools are also providing more job seekers, including those in high-poverty neighborhoods, with access to the growing demand for new workers. For example, the Department of Labor started America's "Job Bank," an Internet listing of available jobs. Increasing numbers of employers post available jobs on-line, and both prospective employees and search firms can access this rapidly growing database. Local newspapers are supplementing their traditional "help wanted" ads with their own on-line listings. Similar on-line postings by job seekers of their résumés and career interests in "talent banks" also help job-search intermediaries and prospective employers to tap into the labor supply. A number of on-line job search firms are adding value to this growing labor market information network to help employers and workers find suitable work.

In sum, the continuing low unemployment rates and strong hiring demand in most local regions present a historic opportunity to end, once and for all, the underemployment in many high-poverty neighborhoods.[20] Contrary to the concerns of many, the transition to higher-value-added work in the new economy also can help all regions seize this opportunity. Most new workers are learning and applying new skills on the job, including much-maligned, entry-level construction, retail, hospital, and other service-oriented jobs. These new workers are learning every day at work how to add value to the goods and services they produce, distribute, or sell. As the persons employed in these lower-skill jobs earn a living wage after taxes, learn new skills on and off the job, and move on to better-paying jobs for which they qualify, new jobs will in turn open for more entry-level workers. The tighter the labor market, the more incentive there is for employers and placement networks to better match prospective workers, wherever located, to jobs throughout the region. Such market-driven responses can connect the strong employer demand for workers to the sources of labor in each region, including inner cities.

LOCAL REGIONAL MARKETS FOR FINANCIAL SERVICES AND BUSINESS FORMATION. In Detroit, for example, Mayor Archer used the Empowerment Zone application process to challenge major corporate and financial firms throughout southeastern Michigan to invest in the inner city. Corporations responded and have already invested more than $2 billion in new plants and in plant expansion, just-in-time suppliers, distributors, and other new businesses. Major financial institutions added another $1 billion for investing in businesses and homes in the designated high-poverty areas.

Similarly, Michael Porter, the Harvard Business School competitiveness guru, has joined with business schools, corporations, and community leaders in five cities. They are demonstrating that comparative advantages of each inner city within its local economy can be identified and that profitable retail and service businesses can be built there to better serve both neighborhood and regional markets.[21] The Kaufman Foundation is working with successful entrepreneurs and venture capitalists to train a new generation of seed capitalists to build new enterprises, including those in high-poverty areas.

The Alliance for Families and Children, the McKnight Foundation, and the Bank of America have joined to make affordable loans for inexpensive used cars and vans more available to low-income workers in inner cities. This enables them to connect to available jobs throughout the local regional labor market by convenient point-to-point commutes that no mass transit or fixed-route bus system has yet offered.

The response of the housing finance industry to the flow of information under the Home Mortgage Disclosure Act is even more impressive. From 1993 through 1996, home mortgage lending to African Americans was up 67 percent; to Hispanics, up 50 percent; and in low- and moderate-income neighborhoods, up 37 percent. Between 1994 and 1998, an additional 805,000 African American households and 867,000 Hispanic households became homeowners, with a net increase in home ownership rates to 46 percent and 44 percent of each group, respectively.[22] Minority households are the key to even greater growth in the home mortgage business in the future: with rising median incomes, these families can increase their home ownership rates by almost half over the next generation to achieve the current national rate of 67 percent. Fannie Mae will ensure that an additional $1 *trillion* in mortgage lending funds are available to finance home ownership for minority families and in low- and moderate-income communities.

Similarly, powerful information on investments in business in lower-income neighborhoods is now being made available to banks and thrifts pursuant to new regulations under the Community Reinvestment Act (CRA). The new CRA regulations call on the country's banks and thrifts to make creditworthy loans and sound investments to businesses and families in low- and moderate-income communities in urban and rural America. Banks and thrifts over the past five years have increased their lending and investment commitments in such communities more than sixtyfold to $180 billion annually—compared to only $2.6 billion annually in the first fifteen years after the enactment of CRA in 1977. These loans and investments are not charitable contributions, nor are they government-directed allocations of capital to doubtful enterprises or bad credit risks. Instead, these commitments represent loans and investments by profit-motivated banks and thrifts to creditworthy borrowers, businesses, and homeowners in lower-income communities.[23]

With the megamergers sweeping through the financial services industry, major banks are now in a position to teach their new insurance, securities, and credit partners how to make money by providing the full range of financial services to meet the demand in low- and moderate-income neighborhoods. After all, most lower-income neighborhoods in the United States have much more purchasing power, consumer demand, human capital, and convenient access to even larger markets nearby (and to a sound dollar) than any emerging economy around the globe! That is why America's leading financial firms also can risk a small amount of capital to finance innovative entrepreneurs and promising new businesses in distressed communities right here at home.

Our national and local regional economies will grow in the decades ahead, whatever the short-term ups and downs in the business cycle. And as the supply of labor remains tight due to lower birth rates and retirement of the baby boomers, the employer demand for workers, wherever they are located, will continue to grow apace. After-tax earnings will continue to rise as the skills and learning opportunities of all workers and students increase, on the job and off. Financial services will continue to extend their reach into every profitable niche in every corner of America's diverse regions. The nation's fair-housing and fair-lending laws will become more embedded in custom and practice throughout the country.

The combination of these factors offers the prospect of realizing Jargowsky's primary hope and conclusion: thriving metropolitan economies, reflected in rising median family incomes, will lead over time to a substantial reduction in unemployment rates and the number of poor families and high-poverty neighborhoods.[24] Preliminary evidence indicates that just such a virtuous cycle may already be occurring: central-city unemployment fell nationwide from 8.5 percent in March of 1992 to 5.1 percent in 1998, while the rate of poverty in central cities fell from more than 21.5 percent in 1992 to about 19 percent in 1998.[25]

Myth: Local school districts provide an efficient and equitable way for families to choose among "tuition-free" public schools.

This myth does more damage to open and honest debate about K–12 education and improving public schooling in America than any other. For several generations now *most* families, except those restricted by their race, color, national origin, or income, have selected the public school they wanted their children to attend by their choice of residence. However, as the state share of nonfederal financing of public schools continues to outpace local support all across the country, continued reliance on the price of the parents' home as the cost of their child's tuition for admission to supposedly free public schooling becomes ever more inequitable and undemocratic. In addition, the size of the monthly mortgage or rent payment is a very indirect and inefficient way for families to choose among what are supposed to be competing, tuition-free public schools. Unfortunately, too many well-intentioned defenders of public schools continue to argue that there should be *no* other form of public school choice and competition.

Because of this refusal by states and local public school monopolies to permit greater competition and family choice, inner-city parents increasingly object to being assigned by any government to inadequate schools, and they demand the opportunity to choose the publicly supported school that will be best for their own children. That is one of the reasons why business leaders, parent groups, governors from both parties, and Presidents Bush and Clinton have consistently argued for credible and reliable information on school and student performance—so that parents can make more informed choices. Even parents who are very satisfied with their public schools join others in strongly supporting the right of all parents to choose the publicly supported school that will do best for their children. There also is support for the formation of charter schools to expand educational choice, regardless of where people reside.

It is time to recognize that the cost of their parents' monthly housing payments (which determines where they live) is no longer acceptable as the price of students' admission to a decent publicly supported school. *No* tuition should be required from any family, whether in the form of a monthly house payment or a school fee, for admission to *any* publicly supported school. Instead, provide parents with reliable information on the performance of all publicly supported schools and on the progress of their own children so that they can choose the school that will best educate their child. Let the tax dollars for each child's education follow each family's choice of school, whether chartered or otherwise approved by the state, local school districts, colleges and universities, state school boards, or other designated accrediting agency. Then, let the people and government at all levels debate the merits of appropriate performance conditions and time limits for charters for *all* publicly supported schools and what types of locally elected school boards, colleges and universities, and nonprofit and for-profit organizations should be eligible to be chartered to compete for students supported by tax dollars.

Different states and communities may make different judgments about how best to implement such a market-driven but equitable system of genuinely tuition-free public schooling. Many will determine that pursuant to their own state constitutions and laws, parochial schools are not eligible to compete for such public support. Also, different types of schools will make their own judgments about whether and how to compete: many parochial and nonsectarian private schools may decide not to accept any students supported by tax dollars because of the nature and scope of conditions attached to any charter granted by the designated public authorities. To the extent such charter conditions go beyond school and student performance, states that seek to make parochial schools eligible will become entangled in substantial federal constitutional questions concerning state establishment of, or interference with, religion.

It is also time to stop bashing teachers as the defenders of the status quo. Too often maligned for not being good enough, America's teachers have joined with the nation's governors, business leaders, and parents to propose high professional standards for knowledge and ability to improve student learning. They have developed rigorous, year-long assessments, based on actual performance in the classroom, to identify accomplished teachers. Increasing numbers of teachers are welcoming the opportunity to earn higher pay if they succeed in demonstrating such proficiency.

Together, these two reforms will create dynamic markets for continuous innovation and constant improvement in student learning and teaching. Such a genuinely tuition-free system of public schooling also will enable families to move to neighborhoods more convenient to their work—and to the worship, service, recreation, entertainment, and community-building they seek. It also will substantially level the playing field for many inner cities and older suburbs: instead of having to choose where to live based on the perceived quality of the school provided by geographically isolating, state-mandated local school monopolies, parents will be empowered to choose the community in which they wish to plant roots because they will retain the right to choose the publicly supported school, wherever located, that will best serve their children.

Toward a New Regional Policy

In thinking about urban policy today, we should stop wringing our hands over the decline of many older cities and stagnating incomes in the old industrial economy. We can not reverse—and should not mourn—the waning of the industrial era. Nor should we brace for the next, inevitable downturn in the business cycle. Instead, we should focus on how to enable families and communities to share in and contribute to rising prosperity over the long haul in the new economy of information, innovation, and enterprise. A summary of proposals follows:

— First and foremost, empower all families—regardless of race, national origin, and especially economic status—to choose where to live, work, and go to school. Place the resources and the responsibility for these important choices directly in the hands of individuals and families who have the greatest personal stake in the outcome.

— Second, impose the full costs of developing greenfields on the developers; permit much greater density and mix of uses throughout the local region; and end wasteful federal subsidies for building new highways, roads, sewers, and other infrastructure to serve such new developments. Allow market forces to discipline urban sprawl and the cost of living and doing business throughout each local region, including on its frontiers.

— Third, shift from regressive payroll taxes to taxes on environmental pollution and emission of gases that contribute to global warming. Allow this economic incentive to work with technological advances, business innovation, consumer demand, and new capital investment to better the environment and the climate as much as nature permits.

— Fourth, rely on responsive local political leadership, creative civic entrepreneurs, the commitment of ordinary Americans to voluntary service and charitable support, the innovation of free enterprise, and the market forces of expanding family choice and business competition to explore and exploit innovative ways of empowering all families and neighborhoods to connect to regional job, housing, learning, and capital markets.

— Finally, challenge high-tax cities to make hard choices about cutting taxes and increasing the productivity and responsiveness of a more limited range of public services at lower cost, eliminating burdensome bureaucracy and outmoded regulation, and swiftly returning abandoned buildings and vacant land to private ownership for redevelopment. Ensure that police join with the vast majority of law-abiding residents in local communities to honor the first civil right for all, safety and security of person and property; this is a precondition for enabling every neighborhood, worker, student, and business to thrive wherever families choose to live, learn, work, spend, and invest.

There is no guarantee that any specific locale or type of community—city, new or old suburb, exurb, town, village, rural area, or high-poverty neighborhood—will thrive more than any other in the generation ahead. But that should not trouble us. Whether we realize Thomas Jefferson's original ideal of pastoral rural bliss, Jane Jacobs's ideal of a vital city, or the new urbanists' vision of more convenient mixed-use towns and villages cannot be predicted. Nor should there be any illusion that central cities will capture the majority of new households, business expansion or net new jobs in the generation ahead, or that most high-poverty neighborhoods will witness increasing population without a substantial influx of new immigrants. In 1997, for example, central cities lost a net total of 2.38 million persons, while suburbs gained 3.36 million new residents.[26]

One of the many surprises of this new age of information, innovation, and enterprise is that we cannot plan certain outcomes for particular places. In fact, niches and nodes of growing commerce and home ownership will spring up in many places that we least expect today, as the supply of vibrant communities grows apace to meet the diverse demands of families voting with their feet to earn their own shares of rising prosperity.

In considering regionalism today, we should remember the most enduring lesson of our nation's history: families vote with their feet. Communities will work smarter and harder to thrive if we expand the opportunity for *all* families to choose where to live, work, learn, spend, and invest.

Notes

1. Bureau of the Census, "Geographical Mobility of People 1 Year Old and Older, by Sex, between March 1996 and March 1997" (http://www.bls.census. gov/cps/pub/1997/mobility.htm [October 1, 1999]).

2. See, generally, Paul R. Dimond, *Beyond Busing* (University of Michigan Press, 1985).

3. See, generally, Paul R. Dimond, *The Supreme Court and Judicial Choice*

(University of Michigan Press, 1989); Paul R. Dimond, "A Tribute to Justice Marshall," *Fordham Law Review*, vol. 61, no. 1 (1992), pp. 63, 65–67; Dimond, *Beyond Busing*, note 2 at p. 399.

4. For the story of the development of the Detroit metropolitan area, see Thomas J. Sugrue, *The Origins of the Urban Crisis* (Princeton University Press, 1996).

5. Peter Gordon, "Prove It: The Costs and Benefits of Sprawl," *Brookings Review*, vol. 16, no. 4 (1998), p. 23.

6. See Kenneth A. Small and Cliff Winston, *Road Work* (Brookings, 1989).

7. See Paul R. Dimond, *A Dilemma of Local Government* (Lexington, Mass.: Lexington Books, 1978).

8. See Rosabeth M. Kanter, *World Class: Thriving Locally in the Global Economy* (Simon and Schuster, 1995); AnnaLee Saxenian, *Regional Advantage* (Harvard University Press, 1994).

9. See Greg Easterbrook, *A Moment on Earth: The Coming Age of Environmental Optimism* (Penguin Books, 1995), pp. 8–14, 398–400. Easterbrook's analysis is based on the U.S. Geological Survey, which was last updated in 1992. While this article was in page proofs, the U.S. Department of Agriculture published its National Resources Inventory (NRI) to update its own sampling of land use for the period 1992–97. The NRI confirms that between 1982 and 1992 nearly three times as much "cropland" was returned to less intensive use (for example, as "forest land," "rural land," or "CRP [Conservation Reserve Program] land") than was transformed into "developed land." From 1992–97, however, the rate of net gain in "developed land" doubled over the prior ten years, as more than 15 million acres were added to this category. This rapid rate of increase in "developed land" explains the growing interest in many metropolitan regions across the country in containing urban sprawl. To place this real concern in context, however, remember that 15 million acres accounts for less than eight-tenths of one percent of the United States and is only one-third of the land mass returned to uses less intensive than "cropland" over the prior ten years. Meanwhile, during the period from 1992 to 1997, the amount of net new land going to uses less intensive than "cropland" plummeted relative to prior years, primarily because the federal government added almost no net land to its Conservation Reserve Program, having added more than 30 million acres from 1982 to 1992. (www.nhq.ncrs.usda.gov/NRI/summary_report)

10. Rachel Carson, *Silent Spring* (Boston: Houghton-Mifflin, 1962).

11. Easterbrook, *A Moment on Earth*, pp. 186–93, 528–30.

12. Paul Jargowsky, *Poverty and Place: Ghettos, Barrios and the American City* (Russell Sage, 1997), p. 60.

13. Ibid., pp. 69–73.

14. Ibid., p. 36.

15. Ibid., pp. 100–03, 108–10.

16. Ibid., p. 144.

17. National Center for Health Statistics, "Teenage Births in the United States: National and State Trends, 1990–96" (http://www.cdc.gov/nccdphp/drh/pdf/teenbrth.pdf [October 1, 1999]). See also Belle Sawhill, "Welfare Reform and Family Structure" (forthcoming).

18. See George Kelling and Catherine Coles, *Fixing Broken Windows* (Free Press, 1996); Andrew Cuomo, *The State of the Cities* (Department of Housing and Urban Development, 1998).

19. Jeremy Nowak, "Neighborhood Initiative and the Regional Economy," *Economic Development Quarterly*, vol. 11, no. 3 (1997).

20. Compare Richard Freeman, "Employment and Earnings of Disadvantaged Young Men in a Labor Shortage Economy," in Christopher Jencks and George Peterson, eds., *The Urban Underclass* (Brookings, 1991), with William J. Wilson, *The Truly Disadvantaged* (University of Chicago Press, 1987). The challenge now is to enable the competing, market-driven information and job-search networks to better connect all sources of labor supply and employer demand throughout each local region.

21. Michael Porter, "The Competitive Advantage of the Inner-City," *Harvard Business Review* (1995). See also Robert Weissbourd and Christopher Berry, *The Market Potential of Inner City Neighborhoods* (Brookings, March 1999).

22. See Robert Rubin, remarks to the National Community Reinvestment Coalition, Washington, D.C., March 19, 1998. The rate of increase of African American and Hispanic mortgages slowed in 1996, while the rate of rejection among minority applicants increased. Home Mortgage Disclosure Act data provide a useful starting point to enable lenders, enforcement officials, and community activists to search harder for ways to serve all creditworthy market niches and root out any lending discrimination.

23. Rubin, remarks; National Community Reinvestment Coalition, "CRA Commitments, 1977–1998," Washington, D.C., 1998.

24. Jargowsky, *Poverty and Place*, p. 144.

25. Andrew Cuomo, *The State of the Cities* (Department of Housing and Urban Development, 1999), pp. vii, 7.

26. Bureau of the Census, "Inmigration, Outmigration, and Net Migration for Metropolitan Areas: 1985–1997" (http://www.census.gov/population/socdemo/migration/tab-a-3.txt [October 1, 1999]).

Contributors

Paul R. Dimond
Miller, Canfield, Paddock and Stone

Robert Fishman
Rutgers University

Kenneth T. Jackson
Columbia University

Rosabeth Moss Kanter
Harvard Business School

Bruce Katz
Brookings Institution

john a. powell
University of Minnesota

Henry R. Richmond
*National Growth Management
Leadership Project*

David Rusk
*Former mayor and housing
administrator*

Margaret Weir
University of California, Berkeley

Robert D. Yaro
*Regional Plan Association of
New York*

Index

Breinigsville, PA USA
01 October 2009
225053BV00001B/11/A